WHAT REALLY WORKS

WHAT REALLY WORKS

THE 4+2 FORMULA FOR SUSTAINED BUSINESS SUCCESS

WILLIAM JOYCE,
NITIN NOHRIA,
AND BRUCE ROBERSON

COLLINS BUSINESS

An Imprint of HarperCollinsPublishers

HarperCollins books may be purchased for educational, business, or sales promotional use. For information please write: Special Markets Department, HarperCollins Publishers, Inc., 10 East 53rd Street, New York, NY 10022.

First HarperBusiness paperback edition published 2004.

Designed by Ellen Cipriano

The Library of Congress has catalogued the hardcover as follows:
Joyce, William F.
  What really works: the 4 + 2 formula for sustained business success / William Joyce, Nitin Nohria, and Bruce Roberson.—1st ed.
    p. cm.
  Includes index.
  ISBN 0-06-051278-4
  1. Success in business. 2. Strategic planning. 3. Executive ability. 4. Organizational effectiveness. 5. Corporate culture. 6. Leadership. 7. Management. I. Nohria, Nitin. II. Roberson, Bruce. III. Title.

HF5386.J79 2003
658.4'09–dc21

                                                                    2003041665

ISBN 0-06-051300-4 (pbk.)

13 14 15 ❖/RRD 10 9 8 7 6 5 4

WILLIAM JOYCE:

For Linda, with love

NITIN NOHRIA:

For my daughters, Reva and Ambika

BRUCE ROBERSON:

To my parents, who provided me with the values
and the opportunities that made
this book possible

CONTENTS

❋

Part 3

The 2 in 4+2: Secondary Practices

ACKNOWLEDGMENTS

I would like to acknowledge the support of my team of coders at Brigham Young University, who performed the formidable job of designing and creating the databases for the sequence comparison analyses. Jared Hansen was particularly helpful in this regard, and the research owes much to his able contributions.

—William Joyce

I would like to thank Mark Maletz for introducing me to Bruce Roberson in 1996. That fateful introduction and Mark's continued support have been vital to this project. I have always believed that collaborations, when they work, can produce fabulous results, better than any of the collaborators could have produced individually.

This book is the result of an extraordinary collaborative effort, and I am grateful not only to my coauthors, but to many other academics and consultants who worked with us on this project. Participating academicians include:

- Dr. Lisa Ellram, Arizona State University
- Dr. Henry Eyring, Brigham Young University
- Dr. Sydney Finkelstein, Amos Tuck School of Business
- Dr. Brian Hall, Harvard Business School
- Dr. Don Hambrick, Columbia Business School
- Dr. Rakesh Khurana, Massachusetts Institute of Technology
- Dr. John Kotter, Harvard Business School
- Dr. Stan Liebowitz, University of Texas at Dallas
- Dr. Victor McGee, Amos Tuck School of Business
- Dr. Ben Powell, Wharton School of Business
- Dr. Phanish Puranam, Wharton School of Business
- Dr. Tim Reufli, University of Texas at Austin
- Dr. Harbir Singh, Wharton School of Business
- Dr. Harvey Wagner, University of North Carolina

Among the participants from McKinsey:

- Tom Ball
- Diana Batiz
- Daniel Chavez
- Dr. Patricia Clifford
- Dick Foster
- Diane Gutheil
- Miriam Herman
- Ben Hertzog
- Jim Humrichouse
- Bill Huyett

- Larry Kanarek
- David Laycock
- Kent Lietzau
- Mark Maletz
- Scott Nyquist
- Jay Odell
- Cindy Perrin
- P. O. Pettersson
- Daniel Pullin
- Rick van Nostrand
- Lance Wiggs

In addition, I wish to acknowledge the untiring research assistance I received from Misiek Piskorski during the initial stages of the project and from David Foster and Bridget Gurtler during the final push to get this book completed. The Division of Research at Harvard Business School has always generously supported my research, for which I am grateful.

Helen Rees, our literary agent, has been a true believer in this book from the first day she heard about it.

Dave Conti, our editor at HarperCollins, has the two virtues any good editor must possess—patience and persistence. He patiently gave us extra time when we needed it and persisted in proposing changes that made the book better. We would like to thank the many other supporters of this book at HarperCollins: Carie Freimuth, Lisa Berkowitz, and Knox Huston.

Last, but most important, I am grateful to Donna Sammons

Carpenter and Maurice Coyle and the other talented professionals at Wordworks, Inc.—Larry Martz, Toni Porcelli, Cindy Sammons, Robert Shnayerson, and Robert W. Stock—who transformed our ideas and inchoate writing into a beautifully written book.

—Nitin Nohria

This book is the culmination of a very long intellectual journey. All mistakes, errors, omissions, and shallowness are solely attributable to me and my fellow authors. Along the journey several folks made particularly important contributions that I'd like to thank them for.

David Murphy, who helped me in far too many instances to even begin to mention, first framed the issues and took a run at resolving them. David was, and remains, one of the sharpest, most inquisitive, and most tireless colleagues I've ever worked with. Dick Foster, Bill Huyett, Scott Nyquist, and Larry Kanarek all provided insight, inspiration, and resources. Dick, Bill, Scott, and Larry were terrific colleagues, both professionally and personally. I am particularly thankful for their passion for the truth and their willingness to speak their minds, even when the truth meant starting over with a fresh lens on what the questions ought to be. Bob Hallagan made many valued contributions. Bob's energy and enthusiasm were infectious. Dr. Harvey Wagner supported me over many years. Harvey has truly got the gift of "practical analytics," and more than a few of those practical analytics fundamentally redirected my points of view. Finally, a handful of folks did most of the heavy lifting along the journey: Daniel Chavez, David Laycock, Jay Odell, Cindy Perrin, P. O. Pettersson, Patrick

Porter, Rick van Nostrand, and last but certainly not least Lance Wiggs (who inspired the journey metaphor). You are as talented and as dedicated a group of professionals as I have had ever had the pleasure of working with, and I owe a debt to each of you.

—Bruce Roberson

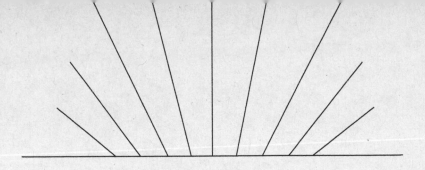

PART 1

Why 4+2?

4+2 Equals Business Success

Business is full of mysteries, but none greater than this: What really works?

The grand illusion of the 1990s was that nothing from the Old Economy really mattered, provided you were blessed with a sexy IPO, cold nerve, and the magic carpet of momentum trading. If you looked and talked like a dot.com tycoon, reporters fawned, headwaiters beamed, your Porsche gleamed. The so-called New Economy was a dream world ruled by the arrogance of youth, the naivety of new money, the ignorance of alleged visionaries. Blind as bats at high noon, amateur robber barons declared the business cycle obsolete.

We know better now. Infinitely and painfully better. In the aftermath of a burst bubble, its hot air now frigid, we know anew that business is, was, and always will be hard, risky, insecure, and unpredictable. Optimism drives every entrepreneur, but dreams of success are more often a reality of failure. Businesspeople spend their best years in daily combat, fighting competitors, flattering customers, mollifying shareholders, cajoling employees, importuning bankers, and fending off landlords, tax collectors, and government regulators.

In short, today's sobered managers realize all too painfully that many, many things matter in achieving business success. But the galling fact is that few if any of the most successful managers can tell you much more than what worked for them.

For decades, one of the great puzzles of business life has been why a few companies thrive in the worst of times, contradicting all the bad numbers that afflict their industry peers. In the downturn of the early 1990s, for example, certain enterprises seemed immune to misfortune—Campbell Soup in the food and snack industry, Conseco in life and health insurance, Gap in specialty retail, Duke Energy in electric utilities, Nucor in steel, Sony in consumer electronics, Walgreen in the pharmacy business. Yet, it won't escape your notice that today's version of this list would not include all these names—a sign that even the best managers may not fully know what they are doing right in good times, much less how to keep their companies booming in bad times.

Surely this can't be true, you say. Winners must know something that losers don't. And so, given our abiding faith in experts and how-to books, managers savor every word of wisdom from legendary chief executives like GE's Jack Welch, AlliedSignal's Larry Bossidy, and IBM's Lou Gerstner, whose writings rivet businesspeople everywhere. These eminences offer actual answers: Gerstner, for example, largely attributed IBM's resurrection as an industry leader to his overhaul of its ingrained, feudal corporate culture.

But such answers don't translate well. They derive from local conditions and unique situations. They aren't universal. Gerstner's work makes a great story, but your own company is unlikely to resemble the IBM he inherited, much less the one he reinvented. The same goes for silver-bullet cures prescribed by many management thinkers. The ultimate answer, they tell us, is to focus single-mindedly on some newly coined management buzzword or principle. Consider just a partial roster of these formulations: learning organizations, matrix management, management by objectives, peak performance, team-based management, total quality management.

These ideas are sometimes brilliant and often useful, but they have about as much staying power as the length of hemlines. For one thing, they become passing fads because managers are too busy to absorb or apply them as effectively as their inventors hope. Cynicism ensues, followed by irritation when the idea flops. Soon it is abandoned. Nothing is less enduring than yesterday's half-nibbled panacea.

So the great question remains, unanswered and not even well asked: What really works?

The truth is that managers have spent more than a century guessing at what really matters in business—and guessing wrong. Managers have embraced fad after fad, all to their detriment. Like other stubborn mysteries, the puzzle of why some companies win and most lose has been reduced to blind faith or luck rather than hard investigation and solid proof. It is time for the first book identifying the fundamental practices that create business success—the ones that do indeed really matter.

This is that book—the world's most systematic, large-scale study of the practices that create business winners. Instead of anecdotal evidence or personal intuition, it is based on a massive research project conducted with scientific rigor and verified by measured fact.

The Evergreen Project

The Evergreen Project, as we called it, was the first statistically rigorous search for the key to "evergreen" business success. Evergreen mobilized more than fifty leading academics and consultants, who used well-accepted research tools and procedures to identify, collate, and analyze the experience of dozens of companies over a ten-year period (1986 to 1996). From that examination emerged the 4+2 formula that is at the heart of this book.

Essentially, we found eight management practices—four primary and four secondary—that directly correlated with superior corporate performance as measured by total return to shareholders (TRS). And we discovered that winning companies achieved excellence in all four of the primary practices, plus two of the secondary practices—hence our 4+2 formula. Losing companies failed to do so.

For managers, the formula represents a proven guide to what really matters—the crucial practices that achieve lasting business success. In addition, the Evergreen Project revealed that each of the eight practices evokes certain behaviors typical of winning companies. These behaviors—we call them mandates—give managers practical benchmarks to help reinforce the practices.

What Doesn't Work

Before getting into the details of our formula and how it was derived, let's consider some of the 200 management practices that didn't make the cut, highly touted practices that turned out to have no cause-and-effect connection to sustainable, superior returns.

Superb information technology, for example, is widely considered a sine qua non of business success. Our research found no correlation between a company's investment in technology and its total return to shareholders over the decade of our study.

The same absence of correlation marked corporate change programs. Despite their popularity, they were not the determining factors in achieving superior TRS. Neither were purchase and supply-chain management practices. They may, in the short run, increase profit margins and customer responsiveness, but they have no sustainable cause-and-effect relationship with TRS.

Another striking finding involved corporate governance. It is widely accepted that companies should attract high-quality outside directors. Indeed, winning companies in our study did better than losers in that respect. But there was no evidence that attracting better outside directors specifically improved TRS or sustainable business performance. The causality may actually run in reverse: perhaps being a winner helped a company upgrade its board.

One caveat: the lack of a significant relationship between a given practice and superior returns doesn't indicate that the practice is irrelevant or can be ignored. It simply means that these practices are unlikely to yield sustainable superior returns, and they deserve less attention than the practices our study highlighted.

The 4+2 formula casts a new light on the manager's role, making it clear why winning is so hard to sustain. Winning managers tend to be master jugglers, keeping six balls in the air at the same time. Sporadic victories, however spectacular, aren't enough. A consistently successful company never stops pursuing success. More tortoise than hare, it keeps working at all the small wins that ensure repeated big wins.

All companies, successful or not, have days when the stock market hates them; equally, winners are no more likely than losers to have days when their stock moves up sharply. Winners simply have more days when their stock inches upward. As in football, winning is the difference between averaging three yards per carry and four yards per carry. And to do that, you must consistently outdo your competition on all the fundamentals—blocking and tackling, giving the passer extra protection, holding down turnovers, converting on third down. The 4+2 formula is a lesson in life.

How Do We Know What Really Works?

Why is our formula valid? Because the methodology we used in developing it was appropriate, honest, and effective—in short, as reliable as many good minds could make it. Let's now examine our procedures here in some detail.

We began by selecting hundreds of enterprises that varied in terms of their total return to shareholders. We chose TRS as our standard even though many managers are uncomfortable with its use as a primary metric of managerial performance. They prefer to be judged by their operating results, and they view TRS as an "irrational" measure, driven by the vagaries of the markets.

This makes good sense if you view investors as lemmings swayed by momentum buying and panic selling. Our hunch, though, was that the markets as a whole reflect astute analysis of corporate performance. If it is true that some bad companies were oversold in the roaring 1990s, it is also true that good companies ultimately prevail and command high share prices accordingly.

To test our hypothesis, we asked Dr. Harvey Wagner, a professor at the University of North Carolina, Chapel Hill, to conduct a rigorous analysis of the financial statements of all the companies in our study. He found that the winning organizations as measured by their TRS were also winners by almost every other meaningful measure of operating performance.

In all cases, the Evergreen Project compared a company's TRS results to those of its peers within the same industry. We understood, from our years of academic research, and from our common sense, that an individual organization's TRS sometimes reflects not its own performance so much as the state of its industry.

From the initial list of companies, we selected 160 for detailed study and divided them into groups, each comprising four enterprises representing one of forty narrowly defined industries. To keep the playing field level, we made sure that as of 1986, the start of our ten-year study period, the four companies in each industry group were reasonably equivalent—meaning similar to each other in scale, scope, financial numbers, TRS, and future prospects. We left out failing enterprises as well as big conglomerates with diverse businesses that could not be meaningfully compared with each other.

The vast majority of corporations in our study had market capitalizations between $100 million and $6 billion. And though they began the Evergreen decade as peer enterprises in their own industries, they didn't remain that way. They parted company during the decade's two five-year periods (see Exhibit 1.1), just as people do in responding to career challenges.

As the companies evolved differently over the decade, we classified the four in each industry to represent four archetypes: Winners, Climbers, Tumblers, and Losers. Winners outperformed their peers in TRS during both the first and second five-year periods. Climbers lagged behind their peers in the first period, but moved up in the second. Tumblers outdid their peers during the first period, and faltered in the second. Losers were bested by their peers through both five-year periods.

The decision to choose four matched companies (we called them "quads") whose performance trajectories differed over time distinguished our study from all others. It also ensured results that would have greater validity than previous efforts to identify winning management practices.

Some studies, such as *In Search of Excellence*, identify best

1.1 Total Return to Shareholders*

for Winners, Losers, Climbers, and Tumblers

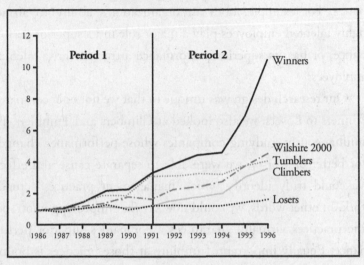

* Median cumulative return to shareholder (year 0=$1).
  Sources: Compustat, Evergreen team analysis.

practices by studying a sample of successful organizations. But using winning companies alone limits your analysis. You can't tell whether or not losers are pursuing similar practices. And when successful businesses falter, as they often do, you can't be sure why. Did they falter because they stopped doing things that once made them successful, or did they go on doing those things and falter nonetheless?

Other studies, such as *Built to Last*, identify best practices by comparing winning companies' behavior with a control group of average performers or with losing organizations. This approach is better than studying successful organizations alone, but it leaves out distinctions between cause and effect. You can't tell whether a winner's practice is actually a key reason for its superior performance. For example, does an organization's ability to attract highly talented employees play a major role in its superior performance, or has its superior performance attracted those talented employees?

Our research design was unique in that we not only compared Winners to Losers; we also looked at Climbers and Tumblers. By simultaneously studying companies whose performance changed (for better or worse), we were able to separate cause and effect. We could truly identify which management practices actually work. In other words, we could now say that improving upon specific practices virtually guarantees a company's superior performance. Equally important, fumbling at those practices is bound to worsen performance.

Our study was also special in its use of three distinct methodologies to determine management practices that truly influence company performance:

1. We began with a survey methodology. Using broadly accepted industry guidelines and our own research, we identified more than 200 management practices that were thought to influence business success, ranging from broad areas such as strategy, innovation, and business processes, to specific practices, including 360-degree performance reviews, supply-chain management, and the use of intranets. All publicly available information on the 160 companies was collected and read by coders trained to score each organization on all

200 practices on a scale of 1 (poor relative to peers) to 5 (excellent relative to peers). We verified the reliability of the survey by obtaining additional information from dozens of people familiar with each company, among them knowledgeable outsiders, senior executives, and former executives who had been present during the study period. Their perspectives helped us cross-check the coders' analyses.

2. We also pursued in-depth studies of a number of the management practices that we had concluded were potentially major factors in company performance. This second set of studies, many of which were done at our request by academic experts, allowed us to verify and extend the larger survey findings. In each case, though, the experts had to test their ideas on the same 160 companies that comprised our study. These in-depth analyses of different types of management practices within a single integrated research program enabled us to see connections among management practices more easily than had ever been possible in the past.

3. In the next phase of our study, we collected and analyzed hundreds of documents concerning these companies— newspaper and magazine articles, business-school case studies, government filings, and analysts' reports. Each enterprise accumulated a stack of paper three inches deep, adding up to sixty thousand documents filling fifty storage boxes. Under the supervision of Bill Joyce, fifteen graduate students at Brigham Young University's business school coded the documents. The

material was so voluminous that we had to develop new statistical procedures to analyze the data.

This third data collection enabled the biggest such content analysis ever undertaken. It involved market-shaping information, such as the opinions of analysts and journalists. This sort of buzz or conversation has a huge impact on investor perceptions and thus on every public company's stock price. In our view, the data from the coding process further verified the results of the first two sets of analyses.

We believe that, taken together, these three sets of analyses comprise the most inclusive study of company performance ever attempted.

The 4+2 Formula for Business Success

The results of the Evergreen Study were startling. Most of the 200 practices we started with turned out to be chaff—their success or failure was irrelevant to TRS. But we found a clear and compelling correlation between TRS and eight general areas of management practice: four primary and four secondary.

In shorthand, the four primary areas were strategy, execution, culture, and structure. The four secondary areas were talent, leadership, innovation, and mergers and partnerships.

The companies with high scores in all four primary areas and any two of the four secondary areas—hence 4+2—consistently outperformed their competitors and delivered shareholder value.

1.2 Winners Outperformed Losers on Every Financial Measure

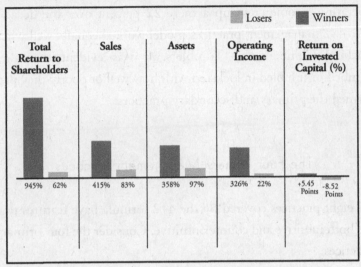

		Losers		Winners

Total Return to Shareholders	Sales	Assets	Operating Income	Return on Invested Capital (%)
945% 62%	415% 83%	358% 97%	326% 22%	+5.45 Points -8.52 Points

Source: Compustat.

In fact, the link between 4+2 practices and business success was astonishing. A company consistently following the formula had a better than 90 percent chance of being a Winner.

We don't maintain that our formula for predicting, achieving, and sustaining superior performance is the only way to go. We do say that it stacks the odds heavily in favor of success.

Just consider the actual record (see Exhibit 1.2) of Evergreen Winners and Losers over the ten years of our study. Investors in the average Winner saw their money multiply nearly tenfold, with total returns to shareholders of 945 percent. For average Winners, sales rose 415 percent, assets 358 percent, and operating income 326 percent. By contrast, the average Loser produced only 62 percent in total returns to shareholders over the entire ten years. Loser sales rose only 83 percent and assets 97 percent. Loser operating income crept up a mere 22 percent over the decade. The 4+2 management practices model worked equally well when tracking Climbers and Tumblers. It was evident that they climbed or tumbled in lockstep with how well or poorly they performed the primary and secondary practices.

The Four Primary Management Practices

All eight practices covered by the 4+2 formula have features that are both intuitive and counterintuitive. Consider the four primary practices:

1. *Strategy:* Devise and Maintain a Clearly Stated, Focused Strategy

Whatever your strategy, whether it is low prices or innovative products, it will work if it is sharply defined, clearly communicated, and well understood by employees, customers, partners, and investors. One of the key mandates that winning companies followed was a focus on growth. Your strategy should enable you to double your existing core business every five years, while simultaneously building a closely related new business to about half the size of your existing business. It doesn't matter how you achieve this growth. You can do it by organic expansion, mergers and acquisitions, or a combination of both. What matters is that you hit these ambitious growth targets while avoiding the temptation to enter unrelated areas that may appear to be more promising. Winners like Target and Flowers Industries stay focused and find ways to grow their core business.

2. *Execution:* Develop and Maintain Flawless Operational Execution

You might not always delight your customers, but make sure that you never disappoint them. Winners consistently meet the expectations of their customers by delivering on their value proposition. Bad quality will surely hurt. You can never afford to be in the bottom half of the perceived quality rankings in your industry, but you will be safe as long as you remain in the top third.

To be a steady Winner, you must constantly slash operational costs while increasing productivity by 6 to 7 percent every year. Technology investments must always be judged by this standard. Will they significantly lower your costs and improve your productivity? If not, don't expect hot new technology to boost performance any more than steroids necessarily turn good athletes into gold medalists.

3. *Culture:* Develop and Maintain a Performance-Oriented Culture

Corporate culture advocates sometimes argue that if you can make the work fun, all else will follow. Our results suggest that fun, useful as it may be, is secondary to performance. Winners like Campbell Soup and Home Depot embraced corporate cultures that supported high performance standards, which employees universally accepted.

One of the best indicators of being performance-oriented is the way you deal with your own poor performers. It is easy to reward good performers. What matters is whether you have the courage to get rid of poor performers, especially those who don't abide by the values of your organization. If you can't bring yourself to fire such people, just remember that they are quite likely to corrode your culture and weaken the performance of those around them.

4. *Structure:* Build and Maintain a Fast, Flexible, Flat Organization

Managers spend hours agonizing over how to structure their organizations (by product, by geography, by customer, etc.). Companies like Nucor and Valspar show that what really counts is whether structure reduces bureaucracy and simplifies work. Simpler and faster—such are the best goals for all reorganizations.

Exhibit 1.3 shows the stark difference between Winners and Losers in carrying out the four primary management practices. Ranked on their strategy performance, for example, 82 percent of the Winners were highly positive and 77 percent of the Losers were highly negative.

1.3 Primary Practices: Winners *versus* Losers

	Losers	Winners
Percent of companies		
	Highly negative	**Highly positive**
Strategy: Devise and maintain a clearly stated, focused strategy.	77 / 7	9 / 82
Execution: Develop and maintain flawless operational execution.	56 / 4	14 / 81
Culture: Develop and maintain a performance-oriented culture.	47 / 3	17 / 78
Structure: Build and maintain a fast, flexible, flat organization.	50 / 3	14 / 78

Sources: Evergreen team analysis, Dr. Harvey Wagner, UNC, Chapel Hill.

The Four Secondary Management Practices

Now, let's consider the four secondary management practices. Oddly, it doesn't matter which of these practices you choose to pursue: any combination of two will suffice. But they have their surprises.

1. *Talent:* Hold on to Talented Employees and Find More

The most important indicator of the depth and quality of talent in your organization is whether you can grow your own stars from within—not whether you can buy talented outsiders in a crisis.

The latter may provide brilliance but not for long, since they typically move on to greener pastures. The best sign we could find that a company had great talent was the ease with which any executives it lost to competitors could be replaced from the company's backup staffers and understudies. Like General Electric, Procter & Gamble, and Citigroup, Winners in our study are masters of the deep bench.

2. *Leadership:* Keep Leaders and Directors Committed to the Business

Choosing great chief executives can raise performance significantly. Our research shows that chief executives, on average, influence 15 percent of the variance in corporate performance, for better or for worse. At Seagate Technology and Schering-Plough, it was for the better.

Good chief executives are likely to be chosen by good boards. Our results suggest that of all the characteristics that make for a good board, only two really matter: Do the board members truly understand the business and are they passionately committed to its success?

3. *Innovation:* Make Innovations That Are Industry Transforming

Needless to say, an agile company is one that keeps turning out innovative products and services. But it is equally important to anticipate rather than react to disruptive events in an industry.

Winners like Avery Dennison tend to foresee such disruptions about 80 percent of the time, whereas Losers tend to be much more reactive.

4. *Mergers and Partnerships:* Make Growth Happen with Mergers and Partnerships

Internally generated growth is essential, but companies that can also master mergers and partnerships are more likely to be Winners. Moreover, our research indicates that companies that do relatively small deals (less than 20 percent of their existing size) on a consistent basis (about two or three every year) are likely to be more successful than organizations that do large, occasional deals. Some of the companies that excelled in this practice were Walgreen, Cardinal, and Valspar.

Exhibit 1.4 shows the percentages of Winners and Losers within the 40 industry "quads" that ranked highly positive or highly negative on the four secondary management practices. Notice that Winners, in this case, were only half as likely to score highly on any of these secondary practices than on the primary practices. That is because you only need to excel on any two of these practices to be a Winner. The 4+2 formula holds that Winners excelled on just two of the secondary practices.

1.4 Secondary Practices: Winners *versus* Losers

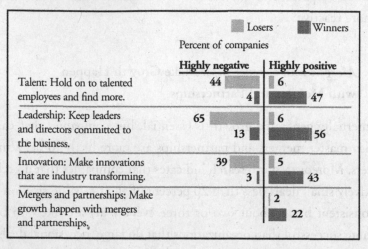

	Highly negative		Highly positive	
Talent: Hold on to talented employees and find more.	44 (Losers)		6 (Losers)	
		4 (Winners)		47 (Winners)
Leadership: Keep leaders and directors committed to the business.	65 (Losers)		6 (Losers)	
		13 (Winners)		56 (Winners)
Innovation: Make innovations that are industry transforming.	39 (Losers)		5 (Losers)	
		3 (Winners)		43 (Winners)
Mergers and partnerships: Make growth happen with mergers and partnerships.			2 (Losers)	
			22 (Winners)	

Losers ■ Winners ■
Percent of companies

Note: There are no negative results in the fourth secondary practice; companies either merge or form partnerships with other organizations or they don't.

Sources: Evergreen team analysis, Dr. Harvey Wagner, UNC, Chapel Hill.

The 4+2 Formula: Dangerously Simple, Because It Is Hard to Do

What do the Evergreen results mean for managers? At bottom, they show why success is so elusive, and why so few companies achieve it in the long term. On the one hand, a company that succeeds in all four primary practices and any two secondary areas has a 90 percent chance of becoming a Winner. On the other, a company that fails in any primary area or more than two secondary practices is in serious danger of becoming a Loser. In short, a business has to run full speed on six tracks at once in order to win, and a single misstep on any of them can be fatal. That is why it is so difficult to be a long-term, consistent Winner.

That reality can be seen in the changed fortunes of a number of our companies since 1996, the last year covered by our research. Some Winners are now Tumblers; some Losers are now Climbers. Former star performers stumbled into that one bad misstep; former Losers saw the light. Even though we were unable to replicate our entire study for the five-year period from 1997 to 2002, we were gratified to find in the forty-plus cases we did evaluate that the fortunes of these companies during this period were entirely consistent with the predictions of our formula.

In the hurly-burly of business competition, no less than in the fog of war, managers yearn for clarity and certainty and solid directions for success. Until now, they had only gut instinct, guesstimates, and celebrity tycoons to suggest which maze might or might not lead to victory, let alone consistent victory. Now that they have the results of the Evergreen Project, the long era of trial and error is over. The 4+2 formula is not a myth, not a theory, not a mere notion of how to get from here to there. It is the first proven set of approaches that tell managers precisely where to focus their efforts and where not to. It is a True North compass that works in any business weather. Now let's take a detailed look at how it can work for you.

2

Meet a Winner

How does the 4+2 formula work in the turmoil and stress of the real business world? Part of the answer can be found in the case studies that make up this chapter and the next. The companies, both retailers, have been chosen from among the dozens studied in order to illustrate two of our four prototypes—a Winner and a Loser.

No real business, of course, ever perfectly fits a theoretical profile. The Winner, for instance, found one of the secondary practices—growth by mergers and partnerships—to be irrelevant. By the same token, virtually no company is going to be able to maintain its winning ways indefinitely. It is so much easier to tumble out of the top of the heap than it is to climb back up, all of which makes the record of our prototype Winner all the more remarkable.

Dollar General

In this day and age, can a retailer thrive:

- by deliberately targeting customers whose household income is less than $20,000 a year?
- by putting its stores in small towns and low-income urban areas?
- by selling half of its items for just $1 each, and offering nothing that costs more than $35?
- by catering to customers who spend, on average, less than $8 on any given visit to its stores?

Not likely, but the Dollar General Corporation has done precisely that. This *Fortune* 500 company has 5,000 stores, $5 billion in annual sales, and an earnings growth that has averaged a remarkable 31.8 percent a year from 1990 to 2000.

"The success comes from doing more for our customer than nearly anybody else in the business," chairman Cal Turner, Jr., noted not long ago. "The customer gets a whole lot of stuff for the money spent at a Dollar General store. It's amazing—when you lower your price, they will come."

Dollar General is a Winner because it exemplifies the 4+2 formula: across-the-board pursuit of all four primary practices (a clear, focused strategy; flawless execution; a performance-oriented culture; and a fast, flat organizational structure), while also carrying through on two of the secondary factors (maintaining a talented workforce and developing a top management team and board of directors that demonstrate a true understanding of and a deep commitment to the long-term success of the business).

Dollar General—which we analyzed for the two five-year periods of the Evergreen study (1986 through 1996) and again in an update of some of our research for this book (1997 through 2001)—was started in the 1930s by J. L. Turner, a Tennessee merchant with a talent for buying up and liquidating failing dry-goods stores. His son, Hurley Calister Turner, known as Cal, was still in grade school when he began helping with the business, and in 1939 the two opened a wholesale dry-goods store, J.L. Turner & Son, in Scottsville, Kentucky. They started the first Dollar General store in nearby Springfield in 1955 with a brilliantly simple business proposition: price every item in the store at one dollar.

J. L.'s grandson, Cal Jr., joined the business in 1965, and 3 years later, with more than 400 stores and $40 million in sales, Dollar General went public. By 2001, the company owned more than 5,000 stores and was opening two new branches every business day; sales passed the $5 billion mark. With inflation, prices crept up, but no item in any Dollar General store costs more than $35; and each store still offers as many $1 items as did the original branch in 1955.

How did this unpretentious and quite unfashionable retail chain achieve its remarkable success? Consider Dollar General's commitment to the four primary practices.

PRIMARY PRACTICE 1:

MAKE YOUR STRATEGY CLEAR AND FOCUSED

Dollar General maintains a clear and intense focus on its chosen market of low-income customers. Having started out in business in the Great Depression and sharing its customers' roots, the Turner family has always understood and respected its clientele. J. L. Turner dropped out of school at the age of 11 to help support his family after his father died. Cal Jr., the CEO from 1977 to 2002, was so intent on helping the poor that his father thought he might become a minister.

The company's strategic purpose is to help its customers improve their standard of living by selling them high-quality goods at the lowest possible price. "It's a store full of bargains," Cal Sr. said. "We have a lot of items that we sell below value. The idea is for the consumers to get more than their money's worth."

Dollar General's customers are pursued by many companies, but few, if any, focus on them exclusively. Most businesses consider this segment incidental, and seek more affluent clients to provide fatter profit margins. Dollar General sees its 9.7 million low-income customers differently. "Our customers are the salt of the earth," Cal Jr. has often said. "They are economically smarter because they have to be, and they appreciate a fair price and good quality."

They also comprise a sizable market slice: 37 percent of all U.S. households have incomes of $25,000 or less, and they represent one of the fastest-growing segments of the population as people live longer and retire on fixed incomes. The typical Dollar

General customer is a forty-nine-year-old woman, whose household is occupied by three or four people; the annual income of the household is $17,231. As it has in the overall population, the median age of the chain's customers has risen.

To differentiate itself from other "big-box" retailers, such as Wal-Mart, Dollar General keeps its stores small (6,800 square feet, on average). Most of them are in communities of less than 25,000 people or in low-income urban neighborhoods, but a growing number of Dollar General stores are located near the company's biggest competitors. "We love to be next to them," Cal Jr. recently remarked. "We are in a different niche. We're a convenience bargain store, and our prices are excellent, relative to theirs. They run their promotions . . . we inherit the traffic."

In fact, he says, convenience is one of Dollar General's key strategic advantages over its competitors: "The stores today are getting so big that they're a major hassle for a customer to negotiate, but a Dollar General store has personality. You can find what you want, get in, get out—and, by the way, spend less money than you would in the big-box store."

Pricing is a key part of the strategy. All Dollar General prices are set at one of twenty fixed points—even-dollar figures ranging from $1 to $20 for the core items and up to $35 for special attractions. The formula is flexible (for example, customers may get two greeting cards for $1 or five bars of soap for $2) but the fixed points never vary. The system "has set us apart," Cal Sr. once explained, because it is easy to understand, and it calls attention to the bargains.

PRIMARY PRACTICE 2:

EXECUTE FLAWLESSLY

As the Evergreen study demonstrated, even the most ingenious strategy cannot guarantee success unless it is flawlessly implemented, the sine qua non for maintaining the company's customer base. Dollar General is diligent on both counts.

The company consistently delivers on its promise to provide quality goods at everyday low prices. Flannel shirts and Fruit of the Loom sweatshirts sell for $5; blue jeans for $10; brooms and mops for $1 each; a radio-controlled toy car for $10; a twenty-two-ounce bottle of Dawn dish detergent for $1; a twenty-ounce bottle of Heinz ketchup, also for $1. The stores are replete with bargains designed to astonish customers.

Since its stock is basic consumer goods, Dollar General holds no special sales. Though Turner used to advertise his stores a dozen times a year, he gradually phased out all ads. Now, relying on word of mouth, he uses what he saves on advertising costs to cut prices even deeper.

Dollar General's buyers negotiate fiercely with suppliers who, for their part, are anxious to do business with Dollar because it guarantees their products both high volume and limited competition. For example, the makers of the six recognized brands of toothpaste that Dollar General sells in sixteen-ounce tubes for $1 each know that one brand they *won't* be competing against on Dollar's shelves is the nation's best-seller, Crest.

Another way of keeping prices low is a relentless squeeze on all excess costs. Across the company, overhead has been slashed from 25 percent of sales in 1992 to 19 percent in 1997, and on down to 15 percent in 2000. Sophisticated techniques of inventory management have cut costs in a distribution center by 50 percent over five years. Adopting high-tech checkout registers and scanners helped, not only in managing inventory, but in accelerating the checkout process. Each store now requires only two counters, down from three.

A Dollar General store carries, on average, 3,500 items, or stock-keeping units (SKUs). After an annual review of every SKU, to make sure that it is still delivering the best value at the lowest price, the company drops, on average, 150 to 200 items, which are replaced with better offerings.

In addition to its annual review, Dollar General periodically takes a close look at itself to see if it is still in touch with its customers' needs. In 1997, for instance, it added 700 items, mainly in nonperishable food lines, and cut back soft goods (apparel) to basic items, such as chinos. The result was a reduction in clothing from 50 percent of the SKUs to 33 percent, and that process has continued. At last count, apparel was down to 18 percent of the total items offered, with hard goods accounting for 82 percent. This, in turn, has forced changes in the distribution system, since the hard goods turn over faster. "We had to jump-start our distribution to support our emphasis on fast-turning goods," Turner said.

In the 1990s, he doubled the amount of space in his distribution centers, bringing the total to 7 million square feet. And he continues to add new centers each year to accommodate the increased traffic. The expansion delivers savings on each shipment, because the additional centers have reduced the distances the trucks have to travel.

As a result of another review in 2000, the stores were redesigned with new display systems, wider aisles, and an overall brighter, cleaner look.

Dollar General has been able to move more goods for each square foot of space by making more efficient use of its space and adding faster-turning items. All of these savings translate directly into lower-priced, higher-quality goods. By maintaining these practices, the company hopes to increase profit margins from 8.8 percent to 10 percent over the next five years without raising prices.

PRIMARY PRACTICE 3:

BUILD A PERFORMANCE-BASED CULTURE

Winners design their corporate cultures to support the highest possible levels of performance, fulfilling their strategies and satisfying the specific needs of their markets. Dollar is a case in point.

"Our mission is to help our customer," Cal Turner explained. "My dad said we don't want to make more money, we want to make more friends." Of course, that didn't rule out making a profit—far from it—but the Turners and Dollar General people do seem to have an unfeigned interest in improving the quality of their customers' lives. Many of the company's employees grew up in small towns, and their customers are friends and neighbors or people just like their friends and neighbors. Leigh Stelmach, a company executive during the years of the Evergreen study, said that the company values employees "who are focused on accomplishing something with their lives [and are] . . . digging deeper into themselves. . . . Dollar General is very accommodating to those with a spiritual position on life." The buyers, who share that commitment to customers, actually view themselves as "customer representatives" whose responsibility it is to make sure that the store's patrons are receiving the best goods available at the lowest possible cost.

Excellence in management, Turner noted, "has to do with the fundamental values. We believe in hard work, the dignity of work, the dignity of every person. And people respond to that. People want to be part of an organization that makes a difference and that values them." In 1999, when Dollar General opened its new corporate campus in Goodlettsville, Tennessee, no one snickered or even cocked an eyebrow when its first building was named Integrity Place.

Beyond its ethical stance, Dollar General's culture is based on performance. The "hard work" that Turner cites is also in the service of lifting earnings and total shareholder return. The corporate culture sets the highest standard of performance, and assumes that employees will meet it.

And that goes for everyone in the organization. Only once did Dollar General stray from its strategic focus on its core customers. In 1987, Cal Jr.'s brother Steve, who had become Cal's second-in-command following their father's retirement, purchased a chain of 206 pricier stores that he thought could be merged with Dollar General. Debt soared and the company floundered badly. Cal Jr. returned the company to its focus on low-income customers—and fired his brother.

Managers as well as employees are expected to identify with these core customers. At the same time they are given stock options to make sure they keep an eye on Dollar's share price. The business is run, Turner says, "for the true shareholder, not for Wall Street. And the true shareholder is the long-term investor."

The culture's devotion to performance finds expression in Dollar General's website, which tells visitors that the company consists of "good people committed to simplicity, courageous development, and tough expense control." It boasts of "team creativity and prompt decision-making close to the action," and proclaims: "We believe in emphasizing strengths in a positive and blame-free environment, where accountability for mistakes is processed in a personal and team developmental way."

Dollar General's commitment to the overall well-being of its customers goes well beyond providing affordable, quality goods. In its inner-city stores, where the company has invested heavily in community career development, it runs learning-center work programs, and, in cooperation with state coordinators, promotes programs that teach people to read, write, and earn a GED (equivalent to a high-school diploma). "We and our customers are pretty grassroots folks," Turner said recently. "We saw this as a cost-effective means of helping our customers."

PRIMARY PRACTICE 4:

MAKE YOUR ORGANIZATION FAST AND FLAT

The final primary characteristic that all Winners share is a flat, quick organization that responds rapidly to market changes without wasting time or incurring unnecessary costs. Dollar General's model corporate structure is what emerged from the same 1987 merger that temporarily led the company away from its core customer strategy. The crisis spurred Cal Turner, Jr., to transform what had been a traditional, family-run enterprise into a modern organization with professional management. "It was glaringly obvious," he said, "that the company's seat-of-the-pants management style could no longer be maintained with a chain of thirteen hundred stores."

Insisting that the new corporate structure, no matter how big it became, must always remain lean, trim, and responsive, Turner extolled "the genius of simplicity" and declared that productivity is a natural by-product of operations that are easy to run. The company has never developed layers of bureaucracy—what it calls "staff infection"—and it encourages, in Turner's words, the "entrepreneurial spirit and simplicity inherent in the small-town values upon which our company was founded."

Though Dollar General remains a conservative company, its executives are proud of its "lightness of foot," well demonstrated in 1997, when 2,700 stores converted to a new format in just five months. Another example of the importance accorded flexibility: movable walls and partitions were built into the company's corporate headquarters, allowing them to accommodate 200 additional employees whenever they are needed.

Dollar General is no longer a family company, according to Turner, and the next chief executive may have a different last name, but that hasn't changed the fact that the corporation "itself is family."

It is clear that Dollar General, like the other Winners, has excelled in all four of the primary management practices: strategy, execution, culture, and corporate structure. It has also met the standard of the 4+2 formula by shining in two of the four secondary practices, talent and leadership.

SECONDARY PRACTICE 1:

MAKE TALENT STICK AROUND AND DEVELOP MORE

Dollar General watches out for its employees. All levels of management are eligible for stock options, and all employees receive up to $600 a year in profit-sharing bonuses, depending on their store's profits. The aim is to make all the employees feel like owners, operators, and independent merchants—and, by all accounts, they do.

The company's concern extends beyond employees' financial needs. For instance, before the new, $50 million headquarters campus was built, employees were encouraged to make suggestions. As a result, the campus includes a daycare center staffed by professional child-care workers, equipped to care for seventy-five children. The campus has a training center, a fitness center, a career-development center, a cafeteria, ATMs, a dry cleaner, a travel agent, and a closed-circuit television channel that carries company news. There is parking for all 600 workers in three underground levels, leaving the wooded landscape intact.

In a typical display of consideration for its employees, the company announced its intention to build the new campus a full three years in advance, so that workers at widely scattered offices in disparate states had time to decide if they wanted to move to Goodlettsville. Dollar General relocated those who did, recruited replacements for those who didn't, and set up interim offices for the three-year transition.

Employees clearly appreciate the amenities, and Turner considers the investment well worth its cost. "We're even more of a family now," he said.

The new campus was intended to be a magnet for talent, but in the end, says Turner, it is Dollar General's strong corporate culture and values that attract and keep the most appropriate employees. This is crucial because "the right kind of employee can make even bad strategy sometimes work. The wrong employee can ensure that good strategy fails."

SECONDARY PRACTICE 2:

MAKE LEADERS COMMITTED TO THE SUCCESS OF YOUR BUSINESS

The dedication, intelligence, and personality of Cal Turner, Jr., have played a major role in making Dollar General a Winner. "Some CEOs are uncomfortable with the idea that good ideas would result from anything other than their own brilliance," a colleague once told a reporter. "Cal is a person who is very willing to give and share credit. He is a very secure human being who wants people to grow and take responsibility for themselves."

In fact, there have been three generations of strong and modest leaders at Dollar General. According to Cal Jr., his grandfather, J. L., was a genius who "felt he could learn from everybody."

His father, he has said, shared the same attitude: "My dad felt he never had an original idea in his life. He was always giving credit to others." People wanted to live up to Cal Sr.'s praise. When his father declared his son the smarter of the two men, Cal Jr. devoted himself to earning his father's trust and respect. All his life, Cal Sr. remained unpretentious, frugal, and appreciative of the struggling farmers who were his first customers.

Cal Sr.'s modesty did not hinder his strength as a leader. He had confidence in his judgment and his capacity to anticipate his customers' needs accurately. Once, he bought a huge shipment of men's corduroy trousers, which the manufacturer had inexplicably dyed pink. Turner got them so cheaply that he was able to sell them for $1 a pair and still make a profit. They sold in spite of the color, his son reported, because "our customers are practical," which of course Cal Sr. knew very well.

When Cal Jr. reinvented his company's organization practice in 1987, as discussed above, he also set a new leadership tone, replacing 200 of his top executives with seasoned professionals. No longer would key decisions be made casually over dinner. In fact, most of the Turner family board members left to make way for what he called a "go-to-hell board" of experienced outsiders who he knew were capable of telling him just that.

"A CEO needs any avenue to the truth he can get," Turner once observed. He wanted people to tell him what they thought was wrong. Turner's board meetings operate like a tennis match: the board members are on one side of the room, the managers reporting to them are on the other, and Turner stands at the net watching the volleys go back and forth.

SECONDARY PRACTICE 3:

MAKE INDUSTRY-TRANSFORMING INNOVATIONS

By any conventional yardstick, Dollar General is not a highly innovative organization. For example, Cal Turner doesn't feel that he must rush into industry-transforming technologies, his own or others'. He prefers to let others spend top-dollar on innovations and work out the bugs. He will buy only after prices drop, and the bugs are gone. Dollar General didn't exchange its old cash registers for electronic terminals until 1993. Even then, it began with a trial of the checkout scanners, which competitors, such as Kmart and Wal-Mart, had been using for years. "We've always been pretty far behind on new technology," Turner admitted. "And I want us to stay slightly behind."

On the other hand, once he is convinced that technology will deliver real value, he proceeds full throttle. In the late 1990s, he came to see technology not as complexity but actually as something that "keeps the business simple." Over a period of five years Turner made a clean sweep of all Dollar General's systems, replacing outdated technology in warehouse management, human resources, payables, and financial management. By turning to electronic data interchange (EDI) to deal with its 900 core vendors, the company replaced a cumbersome paper system with one that automatically replenishes inventories. In 1999, Dollar General again upgraded its checkout terminals with flatbed scanners that not only speeded up transactions and eliminated one counter per store, but also further automated the supply chain.

Despite Turner's wish to "stay slightly behind," Dollar General has been innovative in the design if not the technology of its stores. As part of the research for the 1997 makeover, Turner set up a mock store in one of the warehouses, where engineers experimented with various systems of lighting, merchandise display, price tags, labels, and traffic patterns. They developed a new system using cubicle bins, baskets, hanging displays, and bold signs to fit the goods into a smaller volume without sacrificing the display's appeal. The new system provided wider aisles, which made shopping more comfortable, and still allowed Dollar General to introduce 500 new items to its inventory.

The laboratory store worked so well that it was installed as a permanent feature at the new headquarters campus. Without doubt, Dollar General will continue its merchandising innovations, but its focus is its own operations, not the transformation of its industry.

SECONDARY PRACTICE 4:

MAKE GROWTH HAPPEN WITH MERGERS
AND PARTNERSHIPS

Dollar General attributes none of its growth to mergers or partnerships, and, in light of its 1987 fiasco, Turner feels no temptation to change that. And why should he? As we noted earlier, the company's internal growth has been spectacular.

The practice of growing through mergers and partnerships can help a company, but as Dollar General demonstrates, it is not a necessary ingredient of success. Indeed, this is why it is one of the secondary, rather than the primary, practices in our 4+2 formula.

Whither Dollar General?

Dollar General's low-income customers, its frugality, and its cautious approach to technology and mergers may lead some to view it as the epitome of an old-fashioned business, but it is also the model of a 4+2 Winner. To win, managers must master the four primary practices and excel in at least two of the four secondary ones.

As this chapter was written, Dollar General, along with most U.S. businesses, was confronting the challenge of a slumping economy, but Cal Turner seemed unfazed. "I can't claim that it's good for Dollar General," he said. "But our company, in bad times, doesn't have the downside that more upscale retailers have.

Our low-income, fixed-income customer is in a permanent reces-sion. So when an actual recession comes, our customer says, 'What's new?'"

Dollar General shows no sign of changing its basic strategy or jumping into unfamiliar new businesses. By way of contrast, the company whose history occupies most of the following chapter, Kmart, has tried both those tacks—which helps to explain why, after a most promising start, it has ended up a Loser.

3

Meet a Loser

The year is 1962. In Garden City, Michigan, Harry Cunningham, president of the five-and-dime pioneer Kresge's, opens the company's first discount department store and calls it Kmart. In Rogers, Arkansas, Sam Walton, another five-and-dime merchant, opens his version of a discount department store and calls it Wal-Mart. (When Cunningham later claims that Walton has copied his ideas, Walton readily agrees, adding: "I've probably been in more Kmarts than anybody else in the country.") Meanwhile, out in Roseville, Minnesota, John Geisse is cutting the ribbon on the Dayton Department Store's first discount operation, which he calls Target.

For four decades, these three trailblazers of the discount world have done battle, matching wits and products. Wal-Mart, of course, has gone from strength to strength to become the world's biggest retailer—in the terms of this book, a distinct Winner. Target, after a slow start, has, over the last fifteen years, taken off like a rocket, both in size and profitability. It is the compleat Climber.

And then there is Kmart. After many years of furious growth, during which it became one of the nation's foremost mercantile icons, the company began to stumble badly. In the 1990s, the period covered by the Evergreen Project, and ever since, Kmart struggled mightily to find some way out of its morass. One new leader after another tried one new strategy after another. Each seemed, for a moment, to have the answer—but in the end, nothing worked. Deep in debt, losses mounting, Kmart was forced to seek bankruptcy protection in 2002.

For all its size and history of past success, and despite the millions of people who remain loyal customers, Kmart, for the two five-year periods of the Evergreen study (1986 through 1996), must be considered a Loser, and it remained a Loser from 1997 through 2001 in an update of some of our research undertaken for this book. In the pages ahead, the company's troubles are analyzed according to the 4+2 formula. The conclusion?

Over the last dozen years, Kmart's leaders failed in their exercise of all four primary management practices and three of the secondary practices that the Evergreen Project identified as the hallmarks of corporate success.

PRIMARY PRACTICE 1:

MAKE YOUR STRATEGY CLEAR AND FOCUSED

A single set of numbers tells the story of Kmart's futile efforts to compete successfully with its major rivals. Between 1990 and 2000, the company's market share plunged from 30 percent to 17 percent. Meanwhile, Wal-Mart's share rose from 30 to 55 percent and Target's climbed from 10 to 13 percent.

During that time and thereafter, successive chief executives struggled to devise a strategy that would make Kmart more competitive. How could the company compete with Wal-Mart's everyday low prices? How could it compete with Target's superior products and merchandising panache?

Each chief executive had his own answer, but none of their strategies met the 4+2 mandate. They lacked clarity. They lacked consistency and focus.

Kmart's market strength had always been among low- and middle-income customers. Wal-Mart and Dollar General were nibbling away at the low end; and so, by 1990, Kmart had decided to move upscale in pursuit of a more affluent, fashion-conscious customer. This boiled down to two new strategies, couched by *Discount Store News* in these terms: "Kmart stores are bigger, easier to shop, better at meeting customer needs. Kmart creates dominant lifestyle departments to meet America's changing lifestyles." The company was going to offer the public a new value proposition, a store that was physically welcoming, staffed by friendly, helpful employees, and filled with stylish merchandise across a much wider range of price.

Over the next years, the company spent billions of dollars on its remodeling program to fulfill the first strategy. To pursue the second, it reinvented itself as a developer of products, not just a seller. Several in-house programs were added, including the Martha Stewart and Kathy Ireland celebrity lines, plus Basic Essentials, a private-label apparel line.

But some key elements of the value proposition were never fully realized, and the company's focus on these goals was constantly being undermined.

In a major detour away from its core business, Kmart had plunged into specialty retailing. At one time or another, its empire of retail chains included American Fare, a combination of supermarket and department store, along with Builders Square, Office-Max, Payless Drug Stores, The Sports Authority, the Borders Group, Waldenbooks, and Pace Membership Warehouse.

As of 1993, Kmart was running the largest specialty retailing group in the country. Some of the chains, like Sports Authority, were expanding and profitable; others, however, were struggling. Builders Square was rapidly losing ground to Home Depot, while earnings at Waldenbooks were negligible, a weak performance that Joseph E. Antonini, the CEO, blamed on the high price of the leases the firm held in upscale malls.

Pace was a disaster. Kmart's management insisted on invading territories where Wal-Mart's Sam's Clubs were firmly entrenched, refusing to acknowledge that membership clubs are different from discount stores—that card-carrying members are far less likely to switch to a new club than their discount-store counterparts.

The specialty group sapped the time and energy of Kmart's management, not to mention the drain on the company's finances. Eventually, they were all sold off on far less than generous terms—an embarrassed Antonini had to peddle Pace to archenemy Wal-Mart—but not before they had taken their toll on the company's ability to meet its strategic goals.

The upmarket strategy set forth by Kmart management at the start of the 1990s sounded clear and focused, but it suffered from an unstated addendum: the Wal-Mart obsession.

Time and again over the last dozen years, the urge to go head-to-head with Wal-Mart, particularly on price, has led Kmart to fudge the clarity and focus of the strategy it was then pursuing.

In the early 1990s, Kmart cut prices on thousands of items with the stated goal of matching Wal-Mart. The theory was that the bargains on low-profit items like household goods would attract more customers, who would also buy apparel, which delivers higher profit margins. As usual, Wal-Mart refused to be undersold, such that the surge of new customers never arrived and the price cuts did nothing but reduce earnings.

A decade later, Chuck Conaway took the company in the same direction. In April 2001, he announced the revival of an old Kmart tradition, the Blue Light Special. At arbitrary intervals, blue lights throughout the stores would blink on to announce special bargains. The program had been banished years earlier as out of keeping with the company's upscale thrust, but Conaway had a new and different strategy. Kmart would now focus on its key customers, whom he identified as "bargain-hunting moms." He hoped to wean customers away from the expensive Sunday newspaper inserts that had been the company's major promotional vehicle and turn them on to Blue Light Instead.

The flashing lights, however, had little resonance for younger shoppers, and in September Conaway expanded the program to include everyday low prices on an ever-growing number of goods. By month's end, 30,000 items had been discounted. Once again,

Kmart was at war with Wal-Mart, this time on a massive scale. Once again, the tactic failed.

The company also failed over the years to offer customers a coherent, consistent value proposition. Though most of the stores were remodeled at one time or another, as a group they never approached the style and shopping ease of Target's. Friendly, helpful employees were far from the norm, and customers were often disappointed by shortages of products that had been featured in promotions.

Conaway's declared strategy—to pursue bargain-seeking moms—had a familiar ring for Kmart watchers. When his predecessor, Floyd Hall, took over in 1995, he'd announced that his strategy would be to target low- and middle-income families with children. The need to reach those groups was clear. The average Kmart customer was more than fifty-five years old and had no children at home. The contrast with Wal-Mart was striking. The average Wal-Mart customer was under forty-four and did have children at home. (The disparity in terms of average income was even greater: $40,000 for Wal-Mart versus $20,000 for Kmart. Customers at upscale Targets averaged $50,000 annually.)

The solution, Hall said, was to "find our niche" between Wal-Mart and Target as a "promotional discounter." His company would offer "competitive" prices on a daily basis and true bargain prices in the stores' circulars in the Sunday papers. It would steal customers not from its discount competitors but from specialty and department stores. That seemed clear enough, and narrowly focused, but many observers insisted that the "niche" was too narrow to meet Kmart's needs. And in any case,

Hall (and Conaway, in turn) veered from the strategy to challenge Wal-Mart.

Hall received high marks for his operational changes, which included efforts to make Kmart employees more customer-oriented and to burnish the company's tarnished image. But all through his tenure, critics insisted that he had not actually found the strategic answer to Kmart's long-term health. The company's failure to create a focused strategy that was clearly and consistently communicated to all its constituencies sealed its fate as a Loser.

PRIMARY PRACTICE 2:

EXECUTE FLAWLESSLY

From the very start of the decade covered by the Evergreen Project, Kmart suffered from an inability to execute.

CEO Joe Antonini and his aides clearly recognized that this old, conservative company would have to change the way it delivered its products and services. Wal-Mart and Target had raised the bar, and customers were no longer willing to put up with small, crowded, dirty stores that were often out of the goods the customers had come for and were staffed by blasé employees. Antonini knew that Kmart would have to remodel its existing stores and build new ones that included attractive display areas and good shelving, along with spotless housekeeping and better checkout procedures. Relationships with suppliers would have to be improved as part of reinventing the distribution system. New technologies would have to be introduced to match those already installed by Kmart's competitors.

In January 2002, a dozen years later, the head of a home-decorations manufacturer and Kmart vendor had this to say about his customer Kmart: "As far as operations, logistics, and so forth, they really suck. As a company, they make commitments and can't stick to them. It's not because of lack of intent; they just can't execute."

The previous November, as part of a test of a new product line, the vendor had shipped items to 390 Kmart stores. More than two months later, they were on display in only 310. "Some of it got lost, even though we have notice it was received," he said. "Some store managers refused the goods. It's a nightmare doing business with these guys."

Another vendor, who made lighting fixtures, described his experience with Kmart this way: "The lighting department, as well as other departments, are often nearly unshoppable—merchandise scattered through many aisles, poor displays, merchandise over-stocked—and stacked everywhere—or out of stock."

As confused and changeable as Kmart's strategic management practices were, they were nothing compared to its flawed and hapless operational practices. And even as the company, through the 1990s, drastically overhauled most of its 2,200 stores—a monumental task—and installed vast quantities of state-of-the-art technology, execution remained uncertain and sporadic. It never rose high enough to erase the negative image of the past.

Kmart's product selection, for example, left much to be desired. At one point, the men's clothing department offered eighteen different private labels, many of which simply stayed on the racks. The appliance department carried thirteen different kinds of toasters (two of them producing 85 percent of sales). The sports department had forty different fishing reels.

Instead of discontinuing the items that were not selling, as Dollar General did in such a disciplined manner, Kmart held on to them, creating an inventory nightmare. Customers would find shelves loaded with products they did not want, while the better-selling goods they did want were often out of stock. Store clerks spent hours shuffling paperwork in the back room, while customers had trouble finding someone to point them in the right direction and impatiently waited in ever-longer checkout lines. When Chuck Conaway took over, he said he was amazed to discover that clerks were spending an average of just 22 percent of their workday interacting with customers.

The inventory problem wasn't simply a failure of information systems according to David Carlson, who resigned as Kmart's chief information officer in 1994. As he told *Crain's Detroit Business* years later, the technology to keep Kmart management abreast of its product sales was in place, but the information his department produced was frequently ignored. "If headquarters said you had to carry thirteen toasters, you carried thirteen toasters," he said. "Never mind the fact that the bottom five were each selling one or less a year."

During his years at Kmart, Carlson explained, the company operated two distribution networks, one for soft goods like clothing, another for all other products. The two networks relied on different computer programs, distribution centers, and ordering processes. Carlson proposed combining the two distribution systems, based upon data his department developed. He estimated that the change would produce a savings of $40 million a year. Management turned him down flat, unwilling even to spend $150,000 to study the idea.

The information technology to determine which products were moving and to rapidly replenish shelves with the fast-selling items had in fact been installed. By the end of 1990, all of Kmart's 2,300 stores had point-of-sale scanning and satellite technology, for example, capable of sharing merchandising information with buyers and vendors. And by the end of 1992, all of its apparel lines and more than two-thirds of the hard-lines items were processed through high-tech distribution centers. Yet a decade later, there was CEO Conaway reporting proudly that he had raised Kmart's in-stock level from 79 percent to 87 percent, still no match for Wal-Mart's longtime level of close to 100 percent.

In other words, Kmart's inventory and distribution problems never did go away. The company simply lacked the high-level operational practices and the managerial will to make the most of its technology. Kmart's failure to execute was a big reason for its losing performance.

PRIMARY PRACTICE 3:

BUILD A PERFORMANCE-BASED CULTURE

In 1997, Floyd Hall set forth Kmart's five strategic priorities for the following year. Last but not least among them was the following: "Create a high-performance culture." That same rallying cry had been sounded by his predecessors, and it would be repeated by his successors. All through the decade covered by the Evergreen study, Kmart managers decried the sorry state of employee morale and developed programs to improve it. Yet the problem never went away.

In any business, the attitude of employees toward their work is an important element; positive attitudes breed high performance. Nowhere is that equation so crucial as in the retail trade, where store employees are constantly in direct and immediate contact with customers. There, "performance" is defined not simply in terms of the quantity or quality of items produced but as a function of the customers' personal reaction to the employees.

In the decades after Kmart, Wal-Mart, and Target first appeared in 1962, Kmart was the Winner. While its competitors stuck to their regional bases—Wal-Mart in the South, Target in the Midwest—Kmart became the first important national discount chain. When the other two companies began their march toward a national presence, they focused on developing a culture that could maintain standards of behavior and performance all across the country. Kmart's culture never measured up to that goal.

The company tried a variety of approaches. At first, it sent so-called mystery shoppers into its stores. Unknown to managers or employees, these individuals would prowl the aisles and report back to headquarters the positives and negatives of each outlet. Half of every store manager's bonus would be determined by these random evaluations. This system proved inadequate, not to say arbitrary, and by 1995, managers' pay was directly linked to their performance as determined by their store's numbers.

With some exceptions, Kmart's culture-building emphasis has been less on the individual employee, *à la* Wal-Mart, and more on the store manager, on the assumption that he or she will build the culture needed to get the job done. That was in keeping with the traditional top-down culture of the company as a whole. Thus it is not surprising that, over the years, the same adjectives were repeatedly applied to Kmart: "stodgy," "hidebound," "cold," "bottom-line." Even when new executives sought to change the company's personality and culture, that old perception proved impossible to erase.

One who tried was Floyd Hall. By 1997, Kmart's skill at gauging shoppers' reactions to a store's employees and the level of customer service had become much more sophisticated. Like his predecessors, Hall was dissatisfied with his stores' scores. He was unhappy with the continuing low morale among store employees. He decided to tie managers' compensation in part to the company's customer-service ratings. He also pushed Kmart into a host of new programs intended to create a high-performance culture. "We have hundreds and hundreds of initiatives aimed at training people and motivating our associates," he said.

Hall's successor, Chuck Conaway, carried on the struggle. Store employees were urged to sign a customer-service pledge. Among other things, it called upon them to assist any customer within ten feet, to keep aisles clean—*and* to smile. A toll-free number was printed on the back of all Kmart receipts, inviting customers to rate the service they received during their visit, pro or con. Once a month, a customer who went to the trouble to provide such feedback would receive $10,000 from the company. The number of "excellent" ratings a store received would determine its so-called Super Service Index, and employees at those stores with a high or improved SSI score would receive quarterly cash bonuses. Conaway himself was the host each quarter at a celebration for the highest SSI store in each of Kmart's five divisions.

"This is our new culture—fact-based, analytically driven, driving customer service," Conaway said in May 2001.

Eight months later, Kmart went bankrupt, and *DSN Retailing Today* canvassed industry observers as to the chances the company would survive. Many of those interviewed said the company "has yet to transform its store culture into a customer-friendly one, despite the bonuses and store-rating systems touted by Conaway."

PRIMARY PRACTICE 4:

MAKE YOUR ORGANIZATION FAST, FLEXIBLE, AND FLAT

If you wanted to work at Kmart, you needed to know how to take orders—not just from customers, but from all the levels of command above you. Top-down management was the tradition handed down from the Kresge five-and-dime days, and it was still in effect during the early years of the Evergreen Project. Joe Antonini was a true believer in making the chain of command clear. That was evidenced early on when he took for himself the titles president, chief executive, and chairman of the board. There was to be no doubt about who was in charge.

During Antonini's tenure, the company's organization practice focused mainly on putting decision-making power in fewer hands, and those hands belonged to executives at Kmart's Troy, Michigan, headquarters.

One of his first moves was to restructure the company's entire merchandising operation. He put merchandising decisions for all 2,200 stores in the hands of headquarters people. They were thought to be in a better position to detect trends in product popularity than the people who ran Kmart's various divisions. The senior executive in charge of purchasing was also given responsibility for the stores' fixtures, displays, and packaging.

When efforts were made to make the Kmart stores more customer-friendly, the emphasis was on pushing individual store managers in that direction. The managers, after all, were responsible for everything that went on in their stores. They would know best how to motivate their employees. Not until late in the game did Kmart follow Wal-Mart's lead and seriously engage with individual store clerks.

Antonini's successor, Floyd Hall, was impatient with the hierarchical organization he had inherited—and with its poor track record. One of his major goals, he said, was to eliminate "silo management," his way of describing the self-perpetuating, turf-defending mini-empires that still ran much of the company. He said he wanted his people to work better across divisions—"cross-functionally," as he put it. The silos would have to be torn down.

One move in that direction was a conference of all the company's store managers, the first in the history of Kmart. Hall also reorganized the merchandise planning and replenishment department to improve communication among those involved with product allocation, purchasing, and distribution.

The trend toward a flatter organization continued when Chuck Conaway took over from Hall in 2000. "We have totally reorganized and flattened our field organization to eliminate redundancies and unnecessary staff support," he reported in 2001. His goal: an increase in accountability at the store level instead of the headquarters bureaucracy level.

A Conaway decision in spring of that year had a certain irony. The company was incurring a $195 million charge, he said, for a restructuring of its supply network. The new hub-and-spoke arrangement would do away with the separate systems so long in effect for the company's two main product lines. This was the very change that David Carlson, the chief information officer, had proposed back in the early 1990s.

There were many reasons for the failure of Kmart during the 1990s and thereafter, but among the most important was its inability to simplify the organizational structure, create a true exchange of information and expertise across divisional lines, and push the power down to where the customers and the most crucial action occurred—on the front lines.

SECONDARY PRACTICE 1:

MAKE TALENT STICK AROUND AND DEVELOP MORE

In keeping with its old-school organization and culture, Kmart had always been a firm believer in promoting from within. Management careers traditionally started in the stockroom. The Evergreen study demonstrated that such an approach to the talent management practice is characteristic of Winners. Aside from its being less expensive, it means dealing with known quantities, and thus avoiding unpleasant surprises. Internal promotion also encourages worker loyalty.

In other words, Kmart had it right. Then it proceeded to move in the opposite direction.

The reliance on outside talent began in earnest toward the end of Joe Antonini's stewardship, when he brought in a team of four outsiders to fill key positions. One of the newcomers was Charles Chinni, who had made his mark as an executive with R.H. Macy & Company. He was given responsibility for improving Kmart's merchandising.

Chinni turned out to be one of those unpleasant surprises. The goods he selected for Kmart's shelves were well suited to a department store, but they didn't sell at a discounter. The new CEO, Floyd Hall, was outraged. "There are literally hundreds and hundreds of items that don't fit," he said. The company eventually had to sell most of them for next to nothing. Hired in the spring of 1995, Chinni resigned in October of the same year.

Hall himself was an example of the trend toward hiring

outsiders. His successes at Grand Union and Target had made him seem the perfect candidate to save the floundering Kmart in 1995. Noting the high (and damaging) turnover rate among his managers, Hall gave them clear performance standards and issued stock options to those who met the standards. The outsider was seeing to it that the inside talent stuck around. At the same time, Hall totally overhauled the executive ranks, recruiting more than thirty experienced retailers. Yet neither the Kmart veterans nor the newcomers, Hall included, were able to stem the company's losses or prevent its further downward slide.

When Chuck Conaway took over the reins, he cleaned out the executive suite. A year after his arrival, just eight of the original forty-seven officers remained, and only one of that eight held a senior post. Most of the people he recruited were young, driven, and had worked for major retailers. Many were Wal-Mart veterans. As Conaway pursued his anti–Wal-Mart strategy, the suspicion soon arose that they had been hired for their knowledge of how the enemy operated.

Conaway's most important former Wal-Mart hire was Mark Schwartz, who was eventually named president and chief operating officer. Schwartz led the low-price charge on Wal-Mart. He was so confident the bargains would draw hordes of new customers that he purchased huge quantities of extra goods, the inventory soaring by $400 million in a single quarter. But the extra sales never materialized. Schwartz left the company just five days before it filed for bankruptcy protection in January 2002.

James Adamson, the chairman and CEO from March 2002

until January 2003, would have the last word on Conaway's talent management practice: "He had a little problem with selecting high-quality, talented people."

For most of the period covered by the Evergreen study, Kmart was unable to staunch the outward flow of talented employees, who were given little financial incentive to stay and saw little chance of rising through the hierarchy. Management kept the revolving door spinning with new teams of executive imports, many of them with little direct experience as discounters. It was not a winning policy.

SECONDARY PRACTICE 2:

MAKE LEADERS COMMITTED TO THE SUCCESS OF YOUR BUSINESS

For winning companies in the Evergreen study, the importance of hiring and retaining leaders who identified with the organization's success was self-evident. The steps they took to accomplish that goal—the mandates—varied considerably. For example, members of management were urged to demonstrate their commitment to the company by forging relationships with people at all levels. They were also expected to hone their ability to recognize problems and opportunities at an early stage.

The leaders of Kmart during the decade of the Evergreen Project were inheritors of a conservative, top-down, command-and-control organization, and by and large they did little to change it.

There was no true interchange of ideas between the executive suite and the managers of Kmart's stores, much less with the frontline workers in those stores. Ideas and innovation came from topside, and orders were to be obeyed without question.

There was little doubt that CEO Joseph Antonini, a longtime Kmart veteran, cared deeply about the company and worked hard in its service. But by 1995, it was evident that his efforts to get Kmart moving had gone nowhere. Operating earnings plummeted, the share price was static, and Kmart continued to lose ground to Wal-Mart and Target. The investor community was up in arms, many shareholders calling for Antonini's ouster. Meanwhile, the board of directors hesitated, trying such half-measures as stripping Antonini of his chairman's title and creating a new management team, most of whom were brought in from outside the company, to work under him.

In the spring of 1995, the board at last sent Antonini packing, but its actions and inactions—its leadership failures—had serious consequences. It had delayed the possible development of a new company-saving strategy. The hiring of the outside executives left the company in the hands of people who lacked intimate knowledge of the company's strengths and weaknesses, and made it all the more difficult to find a new CEO, since that person would be saddled with the outsiders.

Floyd Hall, who succeeded Antonini, was a determined and forceful executive who made some difficult and much-needed decisions, including the revamping of the board of directors. But during his first year in the job, Kmart's numbers only worsened, and its stock dropped almost 50 percent. As discussed earlier, one of the disasters of that period was the massive purchase of inappropriate goods by one of the outside executives, Charles Chinni, which had to be sold at enormous loss. Hall castigated Chinni, who soon departed the company. But many observers wondered why Hall himself had not made it his business to know what Chinni was doing and countermand it.

Nor was Hall inclined to personally reach out to customers and connect with employees. During his first six months with Kmart, when morale was at a low ebb—even then there was talk of possible bankruptcy—he made no particular effort to buck up the troops. In fact, they virtually never saw him. Some questioned his long-term commitment to the company, as he maintained his home in New Jersey, spending his weekends there and his weekdays at Kmart's Detroit headquarters. It didn't help morale when a photo of Hall in India appeared in *Time* magazine—he had taken off nine days to join a group of executives touring foreign climes—at a moment when rumors of bankruptcy were rife and the company was headed for an unexpectedly large third-quarter loss.

Kmart's failure in the leadership practice was dramatically on display in its longstanding, bootless competition with Wal-Mart. Billions of dollars were wasted trying to match Wal-Mart's low prices or attempting to challenge Wal-Mart stores in their own backyards. By the same token, the company's leaders wasted the human resources within Kmart itself. Instead of fostering a real dialogue with managers and employees on devising and implementing a winning strategy, the leaders looked to themselves alone, and they never found the answer.

SECONDARY PRACTICE 3:

MAKE INDUSTRY-TRANSFORMING INNOVATIONS

Given the old-fashioned, even stodgy, quality of its organization, it was unlikely that Kmart would be a leader in the innovation management practice, and the company didn't disappoint. Time after time, Kmart was the Johnny-come-lately where breakthroughs in business model or technology were concerned. Wal-Mart, Target, and other competitors had been there first.

The vast renovation of Kmart's stores undertaken by Joe Antonini at the start of the period studied by the Evergreen Project was the single major event of his time as CEO. Once again, Kmart was late. "We waited a little too long to start remodeling our stores," he told *Corporate Detroit* magazine in 1991.

Aside from redesigning the appearance of the stores, Antonini had another innovation in mind: he was going to introduce technology that would transform Kmart's supply chain with electronic registers and point-of-sale systems using satellite technology in the remodeled stores. Computerized inventories, for example, combined with daily delivery of merchandise, would cut way back on the big inventories that had plagued the company, freeing up stockroom space for the display of products.

The project was necessary, and at $2 billion expensive, but it wasn't going to force competitors to follow suit. They already had the systems in place. In the case of Wal-Mart, whose stores on average were ten to fifteen years younger than Kmart's, the technology had been in operation for a long time.

Fast-forward a decade. Chuck Conaway is now the chief executive. He is spending yet another $2 billion to improve Kmart's technology and distribution systems. Web-enabled scanners and point-of-sale registers are supposed to trim customers' checkout time by 20 percent. The innovation was not, however, industry-transforming, since Kmart's competitors had been there first.

When Kmart brought forth its Super K stores in 1992, they brought in substantially more revenue than the smaller stores. Offering groceries, pharmacies, and video rental kiosks along with the standard Kmart products, they attracted a broader range of customers than the company's usual low- and middle-income patrons. The Super K's were impressive, but they were not new. Wal-Mart already had similar stores operating around the country.

Most of the Winners in the Evergreen study demonstrated a capacity for developing beakthrough ideas and products; they also led their industries in technological innovation. Kmart's inability to match that record, to excel in the innovation practice, was yet another reason for its failure. Forced to compete with pioneering organizations like Wal-Mart and Target, it never did find a way to beat them to the punch.

SECONDARY PRACTICE 4:

MAKE GROWTH HAPPEN WITH MERGERS AND PARTNERSHIPS

In the 1980s and early nineties, as noted earlier, Kmart devoted considerable energy and capital to its specialty-store chains. The company perceived its ability to expand chains quickly as a core competency, which it had exercised so impressively in the fast and furious growth of Kmart itself.

Though the specialty stores did provide Kmart with much-needed extra income for a time, they eventually proved to be a burden. In fact, with few exceptions, Kmart's whole experience with acquired companies and partners illustrated its uncertainty when it came to implementing the merger management practice.

The Pace Membership Warehouse chain, discussed earlier, was purchased in 1989 and sold four years later. During that time, Kmart succeeded in increasing Pace's size all right, but at the same time erasing its profits. Growth unaccompanied by earnings is not the hallmark of Winners.

One of Kmart's partnership triumphs was its alliance with Martha Stewart, which began in 1987, when she became an "entertainment and lifestyle spokesperson and consultant." That led to the made-for-Kmart Martha Stewart lines of home furnishings, which became a key component of Kmart's selling proposition. They racked up sales of more than $1 billion a year, though even this success may be marred by Stewart's alleged involvement in insider trading.

Too often, though, Kmart's alliances were mishaps. One of the most damaging was a $4.5 billion agreement with the Fleming Companies, a distributor, under which Fleming would provide all of the food and consumable products for Kmart stores. "What makes this alliance so advantageous is that it is a perfect blend of strategies and cultures," said Chuck Conaway. "Kmart has focused strategically on its retail operations. Fleming, on the other hand, has focused strategically on the procurement and logistics component of its business. Our cultures connect and our core competencies fit 'hand-in-glove.'" Yet, by 2002, this "partnership made in heaven" had disintegrated in acrimony.

There were complaints about Fleming—that it lacked the warehousing needed to serve a national retail partner, and that it was having trouble getting goods to the stores on schedule. There were complaints about Kmart—that it was focused on undercutting Wal-Mart instead of battling to take market share away from drugstores and supermarkets.

Winning companies are able to use mergers and partnerships to achieve healthy growth because they have the right skills, mind-set, and management practices. Kmart was too inconsistent to gain that advantage.

Whither, Kmart?

During the period of the Evergreen Project, Kmart didn't excel at any of the four primary management practices. Nor did it excel at any of the secondary practices. As a result, it never did rid itself of the negative image of its past, the widely held perception that its stores were dirty and chaotic, with weak in-stock ratios and surly sales clerks. Efforts to stiffen its culture to support greater customer focus and company loyalty had only modest success. Beyond all such considerations, though, is the still-open strategic question: What role should Kmart play in the industry? Until that is resolved, its future seems clouded.

With the completion of our examination of Kmart as Loser, we move on to Part 2 of this book, where you will find four chapters devoted to an in-depth discussion of each of the four primary management practices of the 4+2 formula: strategy, execution, culture, and structure. In these chapters, we present illustrative case histories along with a fuller exploration and analysis of each particular practice and its accompanying mandates.

What we do not offer is a precise recipe for tailoring practices to best serve your company's particular needs. Our goal, rather, is to lay out the ground rules, a kind of template, that you can use for that task. In other words, instead of telling you what to do, we show the route taken by our large sample of successful companies.

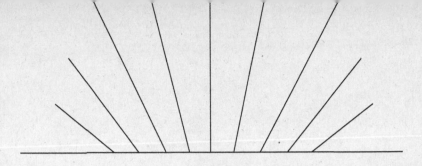

PART 2

The 4 in 4+2:
Primary Practices

4

Make Your Strategy
Clear and Focused

Success, they say, has many parents, and any number of reasons have been put forward to explain the remarkable success of Target. During the decade of the Evergreen study, and over the years since, the Minneapolis-based retail chain has risen to become the nation's second-largest discounter, behind Wal-Mart.

How did it happen? Target's climb can be understood in terms of its leaders' ability to clearly define and put into effect an ingenious, highly focused strategy. That will explain why Target has been targeted, in this chapter, as the main example for an in-depth discussion of the strategy practice, the first of the four primary practices that underpin the 4+2 formula. Chief among the other examples is L.A. Gear, a Tumbler in contrast to Target, a Climber.

In the pages ahead, these organizations will be examined to determine the extent to which they pursued one or more of the following strategy practice mandates, which were identified as hallmarks of Winners in our survey as well as our other analyses. Was their strategy built around a clear value proposition for their customers? Was their strategy based upon a deep understanding of customers, partners, and investors? Did they possess a talent for spotting and tracking potential changes in the marketplace? Did they demand massive growth of both their core businesses and a new, related business?

As we mentioned in the introductory chapter, among Evergreen's most interesting insights was the absence of correlation between Winners and the vast majority of the 200 well-accepted management practices we studied. Not that these practices were necessarily counterproductive—they simply were not *central* to the success that Winners enjoyed. In some cases, that conclusion plainly flew in the face of the received wisdom.

For example, there was no direct correlation with winning when the principal strategic goal of a company was to introduce numerous products, to outperform competitors in product quality, or to adopt the position of low-cost competitor. Such strategic positioning choices did not have a significant effect on a company's success or failure.

By the same token, in cases where Winners undertook a fundamental change in strategy, that change wasn't driven by a chief executive's vision, a change in management, a takeover attempt, or a consultant's advice. Nor was it greatly affected by a change in patent status or a desire to copy a competitor's strategy.

And the process that Winners used to develop their strategies was also not a key factor in these companies' success. Whether people from all levels of the organization were involved or long-range planning and budgeting was made an integral part of the process made no important difference in how winning companies arrived at their strategies.

One thing most managers can agree upon, at least in principle, is that growth of the core business should be the major strategic focus. But in the heat of the moment, with demands for greater support arriving hourly from all segments of the organization, too many leaders allow their resources to be used for lesser purposes while the core business languishes.

That doesn't happen in winning companies. They keep their strategic goals firmly in mind and tailor their budgets to fit. Target, for one, has been a master at keeping its eye on the main chance, which is to say, on its core business.

Now, let's examine the five mandates of the strategy management practice, one by one.

Build a strategy around a clear value proposition
for the customer.

A value proposition isn't so much a statement of what you want to be but of what you are. It exists at the interface between a company's ability to deliver a product or service and the perceived needs and desires of a targeted market segment. As the Evergreen analysis showed, a clear value proposition is an essential element of a successful strategy practice. And the value propositions of Winners are rooted in a deep, certain knowledge

4.1 Strategy: Winners *versus* Losers

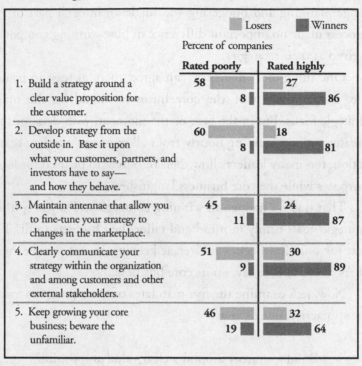

The chart shows how winning and losing companies were rated as regards the five mandates of the strategy management practice. Winners, for example, performed at their highest level on the growth mandate and at their lowest level in anticipating changes in the marketplace. Losers' worst rating was in establishing a clear value proposition.

Note: A poor rating equals 1 or 2 and a high rating equals 4 or 5 on a 5-point scale with a score of 3 being average. Some mandates and their scores are the composite of several survey items. The percentages do not add up to 100% because companies with average scores are not included. Losers include the scores of all companies in losing periods and Winners, the scores of all companies in winning periods. The differences between Losers and Winners are statistically significant at the 95% confidence level.

Source: Evergreen team analysis.

of their targeted customers and a realistic appraisal of their own capabilities.

Target: *Psychic comforts, bargain prices*

Successful value propositions may emerge from intense, lengthy examination of every facet of a company and an industry, or they may represent the intuitive insights of a single individual. In the case of Target, that person was John Geisse, a legendary merchant who, among other things, founded Price Savers and was a consultant to such retailers as Wal-Mart. "He was the one who decided upscaling was a possibility," said Thomas R. Grimm, the then chief executive of Sam's Club. "He felt there was more to discounting than just cheap merchandise."

Since then, Geisse's creation has come to encompass the Mervyn's and Marshall Field's department-store chains, as well as the Target division, which accounts for 1,100 of the corporation's 1,400-plus stores. Our major focus in this book, though, will be not on Target the parent company but on the Target division and its extraordinary success in fulfilling the mandates that make up the strategy practice.

Aside from inexpensive wares, what the Target division offers is a shopping experience that makes customers feel good about themselves. They can find the products they want at a price well below that of a traditional department store while enjoying many of the physical and psychic comforts that attend a department store visit. That, in essence, is the value proposition in Target's strategy. It draws a customer base that is 80 percent female with a median age of 44 and a median household income of $51,000.

Thirty-nine percent of its customers have finished college, and 43 percent have children at home.

Part of Target's allure is simply its physical environment. Most discount stores are crowded, noisy, bare-bones, and unpleasant. Target stores are pleasant, open, clean, and designed in a contemporary style. A feeling of spaciousness is part of the value proposition. Products are displayed attractively without the typical discount store clutter, and the aisles are wide enough to let two carts pass side by side.

Convenience is another crucial element in Target's value proposition. While Wal-Mart intentionally designs its enormous stores with a confusing floor plan so that customers will wander around for hours engaged in "discovery shopping," Target wants to help its customers get on with their lives. Its layout and signage make it easy for them to find their way around. Customers can read the three-sided aisle signs from any angle. With the price scanners that are available throughout the stores, shoppers can check item prices themselves, and use the accessible red phones to connect to customer service.

Of course, price is an essential part of the value proposition, but Target hedges its low-cost promise. While Wal-Mart offers "everyday low prices," Target advertises: "Expect more, pay less." In other words, customers will find higher-quality products than those at traditional discounters, but the prices will only be low, not super-low.

To deliver on the merchandise side of its slogan, Target relies primarily on goods created for its own aisles rather than on the national brands that are the traditional discounter's stock-in-trade. In fact, about 80 percent of the merchandise is private label. Top designers in clothing, furniture, and other areas make lines specifically for Target. The store also offers the second-tier lines of leading manufacturers—cookware by Cephalon, for example. In its SuperTarget stores, the company sells its own food line, Pantry's Pride. Its message to customers is this: we have high-quality goods that you cannot find elsewhere, and they are inexpensive.

The polite, efficient service provided by Target's employees, uncommon in the discount world, is the final piece of the value proposition. The company adheres to the idea that happy workers make for happy customers, and treats its employees accordingly. Their full benefits include medical and dental insurance, a $1,500 contribution toward adopting a child, and help in obtaining home loans. Everyone in the company is on a first-name basis and wears the red-shirt, khaki-pants uniform. In part because of its department-store roots, in part because Robert Ulrich wants it that way, Target's value proposition includes treating customers like guests.

L.A. Gear: *For the fun of it*

The original value proposition of L.A. Gear, as delivered by founder Robert Greenberg, was simplicity itself. Greenberg had been manufacturing sweatshirts and jeans. When Reebok scored with a line of fashionable aerobics shoes in the early 1980s, Greenberg was inspired to design and produce his own fancy sneakers for a narrowly defined and well-understood market: teenage girls. His products were made of denim or patent leather and adorned with rhinestones or fringes and they were affordable. There were no guarantees that the shoes would be more comfortable or last longer than competitors' products. They were intended for would-be Valley girls to wear for the fun of it.

The success of Greenberg's early products led him to create and market a full line of sneakers to appeal to a broad spectrum of customers—including high-performance sneakers for serious athletes. At this point, the brand's value proposition became confused and uncertain. Major advertising and marketing campaigns had established the company's logo, with its imitation of the Los Angeles city seal, in the public mind, and that image had little or nothing to do with the manufacture of tough, long-lasting, high-performance athletic shoes.

Greenberg's decision to include clothing and accessories in his company's value proposition further muddied the waters, adding an entirely new set of expectations to its value proposition. Now L.A. Gear was promising to be all things to all people, both trendy and affordable, on the one hand, and high-quality and high-priced on the other.

The strategy worked for a while, but toward the end of the 1980s it began to misfire. The economic downturn of the time was a contributing factor, but the confused value proposition also took its toll. Athletes and many of the retailers they visited never believed that a company that made "cool" sneakers for teenage girls could turn out stronger, technically superior performance shoes. There were complaints about the sneakers' quality, and it didn't help when one of L.A. Gear's performance shoes, worn by a Marquette University basketball player, lost its sole during a nationally televised game.

The clothing and accessories operations yielded little profit, while contributing to the company's loss of focus. "If I hadn't built all the paraphernalia into this company," Greenberg observed years later, "I probably wouldn't have had as much trouble as I did making a turn when the recession hit."

In September 1991, strapped for cash, Greenberg sold 34 percent of his company to Trefoil Capital Investors and lost control of the corporation. Mark Goldston took over as president and sought to simplify and refocus the value proposition. The clothing and accessories businesses were dumped. The number of shoe styles was slashed from 400 to 150. He even recognized that the L.A. Gear logo was not going to sell performance sneakers and replaced it with a new label, L.A. Tech.

Thus, high-performance products remained a major part of the mix, for a while at least. But after Goldston left the company in 1994, L.A. Gear further simplified its value proposition, gradually dropping all of its higher-priced adult lines and performance shoes. "It's a question of accepting who you are and liking who you are," said Robert Landes, executive vice president of sales and marketing in 1995. "It was very difficult trying to be Nike or Reebok."

The new-old strategy called for the company to manufacture shoes that were fun, fashionable, and affordable, at $35 to $60. In addition to children's wear, L.A. Gear would now focus on women between eighteen and thirty-four, forgoing the fickle young-teen market. The new products that year included a mesh shoe, to be worn in water and out, and a musical children's shoe.

The changes in the company's value proposition certainly served to clarify, but they failed, in the end, to save L.A. Gear from having to seek Chapter 11 protection in January 1998.

The Limited: *A narrow focus lost*

Yet another retail wunderkind that turned Tumbler was The Limited. Founded in 1963 with a single store and a $5,000 investment, it metamorphosed into an empire of thirteen separate chain stores by 1996, the final year of the Evergreen study. Its not-very-limited empire included such nationally known apparel names as The Limited, Express, Lerner New York, Henri Bendel, Lane Bryant, Victoria's Secret, Abercrombie & Fitch, and Structure. Its 5,300 stores brought in revenues of $8 billion.

The resident genius of The Limited, of course, was (and still is) Leslie Wexner, whom the *New York Times* has described as "one of the great merchant princes of the late twentieth century." He had a magical touch in devising new fashion concepts, as in his early-on decision to offer women separates to appeal to different lifestyles—a sweater for a romp in the country, a funky shirt for making the bar scene, and so on. He went on to invent or acquire chains of stores that filled particular market niches, particularly in women's wear.

Across its thousands of stores, The Limited's value proposition for the customer was clear, consistent, and compelling. Each store division was focused on a distinct target market, meeting a previously unsatisfied customer demand. With an amazing fecundity, Wexner regularly introduced a new species of store (Structure, for instance, with its European styles for men) or seized upon and elaborated an existing store (Victoria's Secret, for example, with its lacy lingerie, Victorian decor, and sweetly scented air). Despite the ever-growing number of store divisions under The Limited's flag, Wexner made sure the customer had no trouble knowing what was offered where, what kind of prices were charged, and which outlet was right for her (or his) needs.

But by the 1990s, Wexner seemed to be losing his touch. Sales growth had slowed, and profits dwindled. The troubles were felt, in particular, at the three big women's-wear divisions, The Limited, Express, and Lerner New York, which accounted for half of overall sales. At The Limited division, for instance, operating profits in 1995 were just 1 percent of sales, as compared to 17 percent six years earlier.

To be sure, the early nineties was a bleak time for women's-wear merchants all across the country; customers were simply not buying. But Wexner himself acknowledged that some of his key divisions had lost their way. Essentially, the company had wandered from its clear value proposition.

No longer could a customer be sure what her favorite store stood for. Express, designed for single, with-it shoppers, and The Limited stores, intended for suburban mothers, were selling many of the same items. Their brand identities had become blurred in the consumer's mind.

Meanwhile, Lerner New York, which served budget-minded career women, had been losing its customer base in the nation's malls to even less expensive discount stores. When Lerner sought to solve the problem by targeting a somewhat more affluent customer, the division found itself in direct competition with The Limited stores.

As Wexner recognized, it was time to return to the strategy that had brought his company its initial success. He needed to make certain that each division had its own niche target and distinct identity—and that those identities would be maintained and regularly refreshed. Otherwise, customer confusion would continue to reign, and the company, absent a clear value proposition, would continue to tumble.

> **Develop strategy from the outside in. Base it upon**
> **what your customers, partners, and investors**
> **have to say—and how they behave.**

About half a century ago, the Harvard sociologist David Riesman published his book *The Lonely Crowd*, in which he identified two kinds of personalities: inner-directed and other-directed. Simply put, inner-directed people tend to base their decisions and actions on their own experience and ideas; other-directed people are more likely to act in response to the views and demands of, yes, others.

For the most part, experts agree that inner-directed people are far more likely to be healthy and happy than those who are hostage to the ideas and attitudes of others. That formula does not, however, apply to retailers. As the Evergreen research made clear, Winners in every industry were guided by the words and actions of their customers, partners, and investors in creating their strategies. The strategies were, in fact, developed from the outside in.

That may sound simplistic, yet many retailers insist upon following their own "instincts" in devising their organization's strategies. They brag about their "feel" for the market. Even when a product line that they had embraced fails, they remain convinced that they had simply been "a little ahead of the wave."

Target: *A yearning for quality*

Target's founders made no such mistake. In designing their basic approach, they relied on conversations with potential customers and observations of shoppers' behavior. They observed that many women stayed away from discount stores, despite the low prices, because they were unhappy with the product selection, the service, and the ambiance.

Unlike the mass of discount customers, these middle- and upper-middle-class women could afford to do without bargains, but they still wanted them. That was the opportunity.

To tap that market, Target sought—and continues to seek—its own answer to the eternal question: What do women want? To find out, the company studied their shopping habits, interviewing hundreds of middle-class women. After analyzing their tastes in products and their lifestyles, an answer gradually emerged. These women would support a store that offered a pleasant, speedy shopping experience, higher-quality products than the goods available at traditional discount stores, and substantially lower prices than could be found at department stores.

That was the raw material for the strategy Target adopted and pursues to this day. The store design must be bright and attractive, with uncluttered aisles and clean floors, and the design must be constantly reexamined and upgraded in response to customers' changing needs and desires. The company invests millions of dollars per store on remodeling to keep its outlets in synch with the latest design prototype and maintain Target's branded "look."

When customers told the company that they were usually in a hurry, Target organized the stores to speed them along. The signage at the entrances, for example, offers very little information because the customers have no time to stop and read. The signs at the cash registers are more detailed, because the customers are waiting and have the time to read—and the company believes they are smart enough to retain the information for their next visit.

Customers also told the company that they preferred to do all their shopping in one store. As a result, Target provides an ever-widening range of product categories. At the company's Super-Targets, shoppers can buy groceries, have their photographs developed, fill their prescriptions, purchase new eyeglasses, and stock up on plants and gardening materials.

In its study of customers' attitudes, Target discovered that they were looking for a discount store that would go beyond a pleasant experience to make the shopping fun. That led the company to develop a marketing strategy that identifies Target as a chic, with-it enterprise and the stores as good-time destinations. The advertising advanced that premise brilliantly, with maximum use of the red-and-white bull's-eye, Target's logo, in funky pop-culture settings. The ads were fun, and they convinced many of those women who had vowed never to set foot in another discount store that this discount store was different; it was cool.

Suddenly, Target had cachet. Upscale customers compared savings and showed off their latest Target purchases—a new dress, a set of cookware, perhaps a television or DVD player. Of course, as customers made clear, cachet alone wasn't enough; the products would have to be quite impressive.

To this end, the company responded with an ingenious merchandising strategy: gradually, it dropped the national brands that other discounters stock in favor of exclusive products. Designer products, in particular, satisfied customers' yearning for quality while adding immeasurably to Target's upscale, with-it image.

Among the designer offerings are a line of small appliances and household goods by the renowned architect Michael Graves, and another by the designer Todd Oldham, who also provides Target with an exclusive line of his bright, funky clothes for the MTV generation. The hip fashion designer Mossimo Giannulli has an exclusive line for Target, while Cherokee sportswear lines cover everyone, infants to adults. In addition to his for-Target-only clothing, designer Philippe Starck is contributing a line of organic foods.

Perhaps the ultimate tribute to Target's other-directed strategy has been its customers' total acceptance of its cheap-chic, upscale identity. One example: the sudden, widespread use of the French pronunciation of the company's name, Tar-*zhay*. "[It's] a moniker the customer gave Target," said a marketing executive. "It isn't something Target invented. If you had to do our entire mission statement, that would be it. If you had to say to a buyer, judge your merchandising against that name, Tar-zhay, you would be getting where Target is."

L.A. Gear: *The market ignored*

In L.A. Gear's first years, strategy formulation lay totally in the hands and mind of Robert Greenberg, and his overwhelming goal was growth. "I love to build," he said after Trefoil took over his company. "That's why I get in trouble, building too much." When he saw an opportunity to expand, he spent relatively little time or effort determining whether potential customers were interested in what the company might offer.

The decision to enter the performance shoe field, for example, was not based upon surveys of the teenagers and adults who bought this kind of sneaker as to whether they were interested in another brand. The performance market was already crowded with small contestants in addition to Nike and Reebok. However, Greenberg forged ahead.

When it was Mark Goldston's turn to run the company, he was no less confident than Greenberg about L.A. Gear's ability to sell performance sneakers. "Nike and Reebok have less than 50 percent market share," he said. "There's more than $3 billion of unused volume out there."

Yet neither Greenberg nor Goldston ever succeeded in cracking the performance market. The customers were unconvinced that the company that had made its name by selling Valley Girl shoes was capable of producing top-flight performance footwear. And even after Goldston removed the L.A. Gear label, he was unable to persuade them otherwise.

Greenberg's decision to move his company into clothing and accessories was likewise unaccompanied by any serious investigation of his potential market. His assumption that the L.A. Gear name would carry the day proved to be sadly mistaken.

Teradyne: *"We know better"*

For Teradyne, a Boston-based manufacturer of automatic test equipment (ATE) for electronics and telecommunications, the handwriting appeared on the wall in 1985. After years of double-digit growth in lockstep with the U.S. semiconductor industry, Teradyne's sales were down. Japanese manufacturers were taking over the microchip market, and they were buying their test equipment at home, from Japan-based producers. In 1990, Teradyne had its fourth year in the red in five years. Its big, complex machines, which sold for millions of dollars apiece, were going begging.

The Asian shift was not the company's only problem. Since its founding in 1960 by two former Massachusetts Institute of Technology classmates, Nicholas Dewolf and Alexander D'Arbeloff, Teradyne had been known for its high-quality, technologically advanced products. By 1984, it had achieved annual sales of $453 million. But competitors like Advantest and LTX were overtaking the company on the technical front. And Teradyne suffered from two other major disadvantages: its prices were high, and its employees were arrogant.

In the company's book of corporate values, this statement appeared: "We should build for our customers what they need, not what they want." In a skit performed by employees at the annual Christmas party—titled "The Customer Is Always

Wrong"—a customer asks for a longer power cord for his new tester to reach the wall socket. The Teradyne salesman replies: "Move the wall." By all accounts, the skit was no exaggeration. Teradyne people always knew better than their customers what kind of testing equipment was needed and how it should be used.

The company's pricing policy, too, had a touch of arrogance. Convinced that their products were the best, Teradyne's leaders decided they could charge more than their competitors. They got away with it until the mid-1980s, and then they didn't.

That was when D'Arbeloff, the president and chairman, and his staff decided that the company would have to remake itself. "We saw that our customers didn't think as much of us as we did of ourselves," he told *Electronic Business* magazine. It was the beginning of a years-long transformation whereby the company for the first time really listened to what its customers wanted and crafted a strategy to meet the demand.

One thing the customers wanted was more reasonable pricing in line with the rest of the industry. Teradyne invested heavily in research and development to update its product lines and reduce prices.

Customers also wanted less attitude and greater responsiveness from Teradyne. The company surveyed its customers to find out just how to go about responding to those desires. One major change: the service department, which previously had operated as a profit center, was now expected only to break even—while providing far greater aid and comfort to customers. Customer focus became the centerpiece of the corporate culture.

To make its wares more attractive to a broader spectrum of

customers, Teradyne greatly increased its sales staff and adopted a global marketing perspective. It formed new partnerships with Japanese companies. At the same time, Teradyne greatly enlarged its offerings to customers, becoming the only company to provide products in all three key segments of the chip-testing industry.

With a strategy based upon the desires of its customers, rather than its own convenience and advantage, Teradyne was able to recapture its industry leadership. A company that was floundering when the Evergreen decade opened had found itself by listening to its customers and become a Climber.

Maintain antennae that allow you to fine-tune your strategy to changes in the marketplace.

It was hard enough to keep up with styles and trends when television was the hot medium. Now, with cell phones and the Internet showing the way, the changes arrive with mind-boggling speed. Everyone everywhere seems to be constantly in touch with everyone else. If a high-school junior in Manhattan puts a picture of himself and his buddies wearing string backpacks up on his website, we can expect that stores on Long Island will run out of the item within a day or two. The new tattoo on the bicep of a Chicago basketball star is likely to show up a week later on T-shirts in New Orleans.

In the blizzard of ideas and innovation posted on the Internet and spread by cell phone, spotting the new developments that will have an impact on a particular business is tougher—and more important—than ever. But as the Evergreen research made clear, Winners possess antennae sensitive enough to pick up early on the marketplace trends and changes that count, whether they take the form of a new technology or a competitor's breakaway product.

Winners typically monitored not just their immediate customers and competitors but customers and competitors in adjacent businesses. They recognized that competition creeps in on the edges, picking off your customers by, say, addressing needs you hadn't thought worth the trouble to address. Having gained a small foothold, these new competitors then start attacking your mainstream product line.

Keeping track of these potential rivals on the margins, and of all the trends in the markets and the relevant technical fields, is a daunting task, but one that Winners do not shrink from. They develop systems and programs to anticipate change, because they understand that their very existence depends upon their early comprehension of what's happening in the marketplace.

Target: *Help from a family friend*

When John Geisse created Target, he was already known in the retail industry as a master trend-spotter. He spent a lot of time strolling up and down Park Avenue and wandering through airports and malls to see what styles the trendsetters were favoring. Again and again, he was able to position his stores on the leading edge of a fashion wave.

Target's early leaders were also quick to recognize and take advantage of some of the larger trends that were sweeping the nation. One of them was a new enthusiasm for casual clothing and a more casual lifestyle among upscale Americans. Target identified the trend and moved rapidly to exploit it. The store also spotted, and thoroughly exploited, the new willingness of well-off shoppers to pick up a bargain or two in discount stores. It was a kind of latter-day slumming on their part, an adventure in the lesser regions. Target was the store that made it possible for them to have their discount-shopping adventure without having to be buffeted by the usual discount crowds.

Today, Target's trend-spotting strategy demands a constant, intensive effort in a number of directions. Its first line of defense against being surprised is a team of experts whose task it is to identify a rising wave while it is still a ripple.

The store also benefits from the entree to high fashion provided by its sister division, Marshall Field's. By studying customers' reactions to new lines in upscale department stores, Target can identify the styles that will, in slightly modified form, show up eventually in the nation's discount stores. That early heads-up makes it possible for Target to get its knock-offs into the stores months ahead of competitors. Robert Ulrich puts it more politely: "We can anticipate their lifestyle needs by interpreting current season fashions and presenting them in tightly edited assortments."

Some of Target's antennae are focused on its stable of individual and corporate partners. For example, Kayser-Roth, which supplies Target with a branded product, also serves as a good source of information about future trends. "They ask us what trends we see," says Jed Holland, a Kayser-Roth executive. "We have a department-store business and we like to tap into that, even though we don't offer those products at Target."

The designers who create exclusive lines for Target are on the front lines of fashion and style, and that makes them another rich source of clues as to what is coming. The fact that Target deals directly with them, rather than through middleman vendors as most discounters do, makes it easier to tap that source.

L.A. Gear: *Watching feet go by*

At L.A. Gear during its early years, Robert Greenberg was the trend-spotter-in-chief. His whole previous career had been predicated on discovering and making the most of marketplace changes, from the burst of public interest in roller skates (he built a shoe factory) to the popularity of the film *E.T.* (he sold $3 million in themed shoelaces). Like Target's founder, John Geisse, he spent many hours at airports and other public places watching what people were wearing. In Greenberg's case, of course, he had his eye out for shoes.

"I haven't seen the last minute of a movie in seven years," he told a reporter, "because I like to be the first one out of the theater so I can watch three hundred people walk by real fast. I spot trends that way." He expected his designers to do the same, urging them, for example, to look into funk dance classes for inspiration in creating new sneakers for aerobic activities.

In his last years with the company, Greenberg's trend-spotting skills seemed to weaken. Many of L.A. Gear's new lines were disappointments, including one endorsed by Michael Jackson. Teenagers ignored the black buckled shoes carrying the famed singer's name.

In his first year or two, Mark Goldston focused more on repairing the company's weak financial condition than on developing antennae to recognize change. However, some of the dozens of new styles he introduced thereafter were clearly designed to ride trends. The Kombat Gear line, for example, was his response to the switch by city teenagers from sneakers to leather shoes or hiking boots. Goldston described Kombat as an "urban warrior–type hiking boot."

Spotting a trend, of course, is only the beginning of wisdom. Winners know how to turn out the product that will best satisfy the new demand created by the trend. Losers don't. In the end, L.A. Gear was a Tumbler.

Flowers: *Turning rivals into customers*

For a contrast in the ability to spot marketplace changes and adjust your strategy to fit, consider Flowers Industries, a bakery giant. Back when Flowers was just a regional bread baker with only $20 million in market capitalization, its leadership recognized that its future was threatened. As a bit player in an industry increasingly dominated by giants, Flowers would not be able to compete. It would inevitably be bought and swallowed by one of the giants.

That was not what the Flowers family had in mind. As CEO McMullian told *Miller and Baking News* years later, the company had a strong "will to survive." So the family set the company on a different course. Over the following decades, it bought dozens of small baking companies throughout the Southeast. In effect, it survived the giants by becoming one of them.

Flowers Industries' antennae have never lost their acuity. Far ahead of most competitors, it realized that the appearance of bakery operations within supermarkets represented a major challenge to traditional bakeries. That insight led the company to another major strategic move. It decided to view the in-store bakeries as customers rather than as rivals.

Back in 1976, Flowers had bought Stillwell Foods, a processor of frozen vegetables and fruit products serving the Southwest. It parlayed its knowledge of that business into the business of producing and distributing frozen, ready-made dough to the in-store bakeries. Much of the company's growth in recent years has come from this area of its operations. Once again, its ability to spot changes in the market and alter its strategy to take advantage of them has served Flowers Industries well—and maintained its position as an Evergreen Winner.

Clearly communicate your strategy within the organization and among customers and other external stakeholders.

The first and most critical task facing any management, of course, is to develop a winning strategy. But a strategy in a vacuum benefits no one. For it to be implemented properly, it must be presented and explained first and foremost to the people who will be bringing it to life—your managers and employees. Yet that is only the beginning of wisdom.

As the Evergreen research showed, the ability to share their strategies with customers was a hallmark of winning companies. Both for business clients and for the public at large the communication of a company's basic goals and intentions is an essential step in accomplishing those goals. By sharing its strategy a company paves the way for its products and sells itself to its customers. Beyond that, it invites its customers to become partners in the chain that leads from raw materials to finished products to sales. Winners are communicators.

Target: *Hitting the bull's-eye*

In ways both obvious and subtle Target has assiduously conveyed its cheap-chic strategy to its customers. On the obvious side, the company has for years used print and television advertising to inform customers and potential customers just what it has in mind for them. Images of stylishly but inexpensively dressed women were powerfully linked with the Target name and the red bull's-eye logo. The ads played a key role in convincing the public of the unlikely reality of a company that could deliver high-quality goods at very low prices in a clean, neat, welcoming environment.

In a triumph of the advertising craft, honored as such by *Advertising Age*'s Marketer of the Year award, Target went on to create a series of TV spots showing sleek blondes serving red bull's-eye-shaped molds of Jell-O and dancing around a room papered with a repeating pattern of the Target logo. The spots were an instant hit with the public as well as the trade. As *Advertising Age* put it, Target has "established its logo nationally as an advertising icon in a class with those of McDonald's arches and Nike's swoosh."

The design and details of the stores themselves represent a more subtle means of communicating the Target strategy to customers. By making the sites bright and open the company has fulfilled the promise of its ads, that the customer would feel comfortable in a with-it, upscale atmosphere. At the same time, the design reinforces the other half of the strategy: there is no effort to add elaborate trappings as though the store were a fancy department store or anything other than an upscale discounter.

To make sure that its major suppliers are in cahoots with its strategy and its immediate needs Target has adopted a collaborative planning, forecasting, and replenishment system (CPFR). This Internet-mediated groupware platform allows Target to instantly share the latest information about its goals and operations with vendors. If sales of a vendor's item suddenly rise or fall, for example, the vendor can immediately adjust its production and delivery schedules to meet the new situation.

L.A. Gear: *Good image, wrong product*
Back in those halcyon days of 1989 when L.A. Gear's sales were soaring toward $500 million a year, up from $9 million five years earlier, the company's leaders were convinced that the single most important element in its success was not its product line but its strategy to sell customers on a particular corporate image.

"It's the Los Angeles life style," Elliot J. Horowitz, the executive vice president, told the *Los Angeles Times* that year. "It's fun, colorful, fresh, and young."

The strategy was to make everything about the company fun and lively, from its palm-tree logo to its funky sneakers, and for a while it worked. Then the company moved away from its core business to plunge into performance shoes for male athletes. With that drastic change in strategy, L.A. Gear was now communicating a mixed message with its logo. Its new male customers had no interest in image, especially one linked to women's products; they wanted quality and performance. Yet, it took the company two years to remove the palm-tree logo from some of its shoes for men.

By 1995, L.A. Gear had abandoned its men's shoe lines and was struggling to reestablish its much-weakened women's shoe brand. The strategy message to customers was clearer now, and considerably changed. The L.A. lifestyle was still the focus, but it was a more sophisticated image now, pitched not to those fickle teenagers but to women between the ages of eighteen and thirty-four in search of "affordable fashion." It came too late to save the company from bankruptcy.

In its dealings with retailers, L.A. Gear failed time and again to clearly communicate its strategy and intentions. As early as 1991, retailers were complaining to Greenberg that the company was allowing—even encouraging—the sale of its less popular sneakers at deep-discount outlets and swap meets. In other words, while presenting itself as a producer of quality, full-price shoes to the retailers, it was going behind their backs to dump the same shoes for next to nothing.

Two years later, Goldston, now in charge, told *Sporting Goods Business* that the company had changed its ways: "We have a very open, interactive dialogue with [retailers], which is, I think, a departure from what they knew before from the company." But a year later, retailers learned that the company had (1) made a $240 million deal to supply Wal-Mart with its branded shoes, and (2) ushered out Goldston just three weeks before the start of a major back-to-school advertising campaign to introduce L.A. Flak, a new shoe that had been Goldston's baby.

Retailers were upset over having to compete with the 800-pound gorilla discounter on yet another product, and also concerned about the timing of Goldston's departure. "I just hope this doesn't mean that the board is not supporting the Flak concept and the future direction of L.A. Gear," Mitchell Modell, president of the Modell's Sporting Goods chain, told *Footwear News*. Once again, L.A. Gear had failed to communicate changes in strategy to its customers and other stakeholders.

Keep growing your core business; beware the unfamiliar.

In every corporate boardroom, the word "growth" sets hearts beating faster. Company leaders talk about profitable growth, but they dream about bigness—it's hardwired in the psyche. As a sign of progress, as proof that the organization is vital and alive, growth buoys the human spirit. Beyond that, it is one of the chief measures by which the markets judge a company; a growth strategy has a way of keeping the stock price bubbling.

The problem is, many companies go about it the wrong way: they seize upon every promising opportunity to expand. They push into unfamiliar markets. They acquire organizations with which they have little in common by way of product or culture. Confusion reigns, performance falters, profits evaporate.

The Evergreen research results (see Exhibit 4.2) underline the key role a growth policy plays in creating Winners. In fact, the most successful organizations have adopted stretch strategies that aim at doubling the core business over a five-year period, which requires a 15 percent growth rate each year. Over a ten-year

4.2 Growth: Winners *versus* Losers

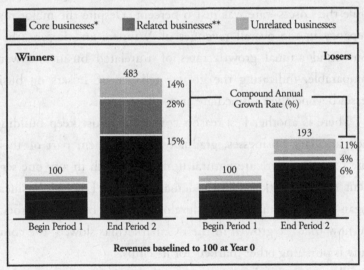

* Core businesses are those businesses (primary and secondary 4-digit Standard Industrial Classification) contributing the majority of 1986 revenues.

** Related businesses are those businesses whose primary Standard Industrial Classification is the same as that of the core business.

Sources: Compustat, Evergreen team analysis; Dr. Harbir Singh, the Wharton School, University of Pennsylvania.

period, they also develop a second, related business equal in size to their current company by moving into a related product market, a new customer segment, a new channel, or a new geographical market.

The chart on the preceding page shows how Winners and Losers have increased their revenues over the decade of the Evergreen study. Winners grew 483 percent, versus 193 percent for Losers. One of the striking differences between Winners and Losers can be seen in the compound annual growth rates of their core business and of operations related to that business. Winners, for example, had a 15 percent compound annual growth rate, while the Losers' rate was just 6 percent. Despite the major discrepancy in the overall revenues of Winners and Losers, their compound annual growth rates of unrelated businesses were comparable, indicating the greater reliance of Losers on businesses beyond their immediate areas of expertise.

There is another key reason companies must keep building their ancillary businesses, gradually making them part of their core business: there are natural limits to growth in any one segment of the market. When demand for its DRAM business began to falter, Intel had its developing CPU business to focus on; now that the growth in the PC market has slowed, the company is pursuing other markets for its chips.

That moment when a company discovers that a competitor is about to remake the marketplace, or that its core product is about to be commoditized, is inevitably a turning point. There is a temptation to rush into new businesses to make up for the looming loss of income, but that can easily lead to the weakening of the company's focus on its core value proposition and induce a long decline. In fact, the situation is usually not out of control: the company may have an extended period of profitability as less resolute competitors take flight, and it may be able to reinvent its core so that profitability can continue while the company pursues opportunities for growth in related areas.

As a general rule, though, Winners stay Winners because they start building their next growth businesses before the growth potential of their core business shows signs of disappearing. The dynamically evolving strategic focus on growth is the formula for business success.

Target: *A push into financial services*

Target is constantly seeking new ways to apply and extend its upscale-discount core strategy. Perhaps the most outstanding example of that effort is the SuperTarget chain of stores, in which food is added to Target's customary mix.

When the first SuperTarget opened in 1995, some analysts and industry experts warned that it was too little too late. Wal-Mart's Supercenters and Kmart's Super K stores were already well launched with their elaborate grocery sections and special services, such as banks and pharmacies. The theory was that the low-margin groceries would attract new crowds of customers, who would stay to buy higher-margin goods. Even though it would be arriving late, Target was determined to go ahead with its own one-stop-shopping entry.

The company has been happy with the results. SuperTarget customers visit the stores 4.5 times a month, while customers of the standard Target format make 3 visits a month. For 40 percent of their customers, SuperTargets are the primary grocery destination, and 60 percent of the grocery customers buy other goods. As of the summer of 2002, there were 75 SuperTargets in 17 states, and there may be as many as 350 operating by 2010.

The SuperTargets average 175,000 square feet, 50,000 more than the standard Target, but they are entirely consistent with the look and premise of the smaller stores, including their discounted prices, uncluttered environment, convenience, and high-quality products. And, of course, the Target cachet for style and fashion extends to all of the SuperTargets' added offerings, particularly its groceries.

The food sections operate under the Archer Farms brand, a Target creation. The chocolates are by Fannie May, and the bread comes from La Brea. Sushi and kosher food are available, as are fine wines and microbrews. Of course, there is an ample sampling of organic food, as well as a Starbucks coffee shop. As indicated earlier, Target stores do not generally try to match Wal-Mart in terms of price, and that goes for SuperTargets as well, with the exception of those SuperTargets located close to Wal-Mart stores.

Target's forceful move into the area of financial services represents another successful application of its stretch strategy. The company applied all of its merchandising skills along with imaginative loyalty programs to convince 20 million customers to sign up for and use the Target Guest Card, its chain-wide credit card, issued by Retailers National Bank, a Target affiliate. The card accounted for about $4 billion in sales in the 2001 fiscal year, while creating an enormously profitable loan portfolio. Later that same year, Target took a calculated leap into a whole new dimension of financial service, becoming the first U.S. retailer to offer its customers a microchip-enhanced Visa "smart card." Like the guest card, it was issued through the Retailers National Bank.

The smart card represented a substantial risk for Target—and a major investment. To accommodate its arrival, the company had to install, in all its hundreds of stores, point-of-sale terminals. Aside from adding in-store convenience, the smart card gives customers a new shopping-with-credit vehicle, the use of which is not restricted to Target stores, and it is accompanied by substantially expanded rewards programs. Target offers the card to new customers, while also trying to persuade its best customers to switch over from the store card.

Smart cards are capable of storing huge amounts of information, thousands of times more than the usual magnetic stripe cards—typically, information about the holder's medical history, personal banking background, and shopping preferences. The cards are also more reliable than their striped predecessors, and capable of performing many more functions.

By pioneering the smart-card technology in the retail sector, Target is positioned to win a host of new customers from among the millions of people who hold other Visa smart cards but have no stores in which to use them. At the same time, the new card is increasing the size of Target's remunerative loan portfolio by up to $2 billion a year. And now that the company has access to all that new information about customers' interests and preferences, it can focus its promotions precisely to meet the needs of its smart card users.

Acquisitions are often part of a stretch strategy, since they represent a short route to dramatic growth. But the acquiring company sometimes finds that the attitudes and culture of the new arrival are so different from their own that the deal is doomed to fail. When Target goes shopping for growth, it takes a cautious approach. A recent example was the company's purchase of the rights to thirty-five former Montgomery Ward stores; thirty of them were rapidly remodeled and reopened as Targets. The acquisition, Ulrich said, "was an excellent opportunity for Target to purchase sites in a number of premier markets, including California, where prime real estate is particularly difficult to find." The new stores are flourishing.

L.A. Gear: *A leap into the unknown*

At L.A. Gear, growth was a prime goal of the founder, Robert Greenberg, and thus a prominent part of the company's overall strategy. Too often, though, the actual expansion was ill-considered and badly executed.

The move into men's sneakers was a prime example. Up to that point, L.A. Gear's core business had been a sensational success on the basis of its expertise in designing and marketing lively sneakers for teen girls and young women. Performance footwear might be considered a "related new business," but, in this case, the company had little or no expertise in the design and production of such products. It had no in-depth knowledge of what the customers for these sneakers wanted or whether they would welcome a totally new brand, particularly one with a feminine image.

And L.A. Gear knew that it would be entering into what was arguably the most competitive area of the shoe business.

Over the years, the company sold a great volume of performance sneakers, but not enough to make up for the enormous effort and investment they required. By the time L.A. Gear had been pared back down to its core business, the company was on the brink of bankruptcy.

The Limited: *So big, so out of control*

If ever there was an organization committed to a stretch strategy, it was The Limited. Leslie Wexner was a genius at spotting untapped niches for his company to enter, and a wizard at getting these new outlets up to speed.

During one six-year period, ending in 1988, the company bought Lane Bryant, Lerner, Henri Bendel, Abercrombie & Fitch, and Victoria's Secret. And at the same time, it was developing its own entries: during the Evergreen decade, they included Cacique, which sold lingerie; Limited Too, for young girls; Bath & Body Works, which sold body-care products; and Structure.

In each case, Wexner was deeply involved, giving new additions his undivided attention, adding the special touches that made them inviting to customers. But once they were truly launched, he tended to lose interest as he looked for new challenges. "I think temperamentally I've always lived in my own world," he told the *New York Times,* "and that world is very much in the future. I don't get much pleasure out of today."

That loss of focus undermined the effectiveness of Wexner's

stretch strategy. After their initial success, the new outlets too often showed flattened sales and profitability. During the period of the Evergreen Project, for instance, The Limited division sought to meet the needs of its original customers as they aged, becoming more affluent and involved in careers—but the division's buyers continued to purchase the T-shirts and jeans that had been appropriate a decade earlier. Meanwhile, Express had lost its focus on its young, swinging customers and was offering clothes for an older, more sophisticated consumer.

As the experience of The Limited suggests, a stretch strategy may be one of the hallmarks of a winning strategy, but it cannot stand alone. The company that achieves substantial growth must also possess the ability to manage the large, mature business that results. The Limited's failure to master the second half of that equation during the years of the Evergreen study turned it into a Tumbler.

What Comes Next

To sum up, the Target division excels at keeping its strategy clear and focused. Its leaders have developed a value proposition that powerfully supports its strategy, precisely addressing the needs of its "target" customers. The company has built its strategy upon the words and actions of its customers, partners, and investors, relying upon well-developed antennae to scope out and adjust to marketplace changes and trends. Furthermore, Target, constitutionally unwilling to rest on its laurels, has adopted a stretch strategy that assumes it will grow at an ever-faster pace.

Meanwhile, L.A. Gear has managed to transform its amazing initial success into failure by wandering from its core strategy, overextending its value proposition, and paying too little heed to its customers. Similarly, The Limited has wandered from its original and successful strategic focus and turned Tumbler.

In the following chapter, we move ahead to the second primary management practice identified by the Evergreen Project: make your products customer-focused and execute flawlessly—or "execution" for short. There, you will find the important mandates that were followed by Winners. You will also meet a remarkable organization called Duke Energy, an exemplar of the execution practice.

5

Execute Flawlessly

Most of our days as businesspeople are spent making incremental decisions about small, familiar matters, yet every so often, inspired by an idea or an unexpected turn of events, we find ourselves at a fork in the road. One path will take us (and our company) where we have gone before; the other will carry us toward a different future rich in promise and uncertainty.

In 1994, Richard B. Priory, then president of Duke Power, stood at such a crossroads. He was convinced that the power industry would eventually be deregulated, and he feared that his organization would not be prepared for the brutal competition that would follow. He might easily have put that concern aside: deregulation wasn't imminent, and Duke, based in Charlotte, North Carolina, was doing quite well. Like so many regional energy companies in the regulated era, it was a virtual monopoly whose guaranteed rate of return delivered painless profits. But instead of maintaining the status quo, Priory took the path unknown, a decision that would lead to drastic changes in every aspect of the company's operations—and rocket Duke into the top tier of the nation's power elite.

In this chapter, Duke serves as the prime example of a business that has achieved superior execution (the second of the four primary practices that Winners and Climbers excelled in during the decade of the Evergreen study). For them operational excellence, so essential to meeting the standards of today's ever more sophisticated customers, was not easily arrived at. Like strategy and the other primary practices, flawless execution can only be achieved through intense and continuing study, considerable ingenuity, and constant effort—along with a willingness to flout some old management chestnuts.

The fallen status of the chestnuts was evident in some of the Evergreen study's findings. Contrary to the familiar notion that companies should outsource the execution of as many activities as possible, we found that there was no relationship between the degree to which a company embraced outsourcing and its financial performance. Success did not hinge on the extent to which a company invested in technologies and in systems like enterprise-resource planning, supply-chain management, or customer-relationship management. It did not make much difference to its bottom line whether a company adopted a total-quality-management program or some other execution-oriented initiative.

In the 1890s, long before there was a Duke Power—or a Richard Priory, for that matter—there was an entrepreneur named James Buchanan Duke. Together with his brother Benjamin he organized the American Development Company and started buying up land and water rights on the Catawba River in South Carolina, with an eye to producing electricity for the expanding textile industry. Over the next several years, the brothers Duke were active in a series of companies formed to make that vision real. The first generating station of what would become known as the Duke system opened for business on April 30, 1904. Six years later, James "Buck" Duke was named president of the Southern Power Company, which was renamed in his honor in 1924. He died the next year.

Today, the deregulation Richard Priory wanted to prepare for is happening on a state-by-state basis. In the Carolinas, it will affect the wholesale market first; the time when retail consumers there will be able to pick and choose among competing suppliers is apparently some years away. However and whenever it occurs, though, Duke Energy will be ready. It has a strong footprint in both the regulated and unregulated spheres. As of the final year of the Evergreen Project, 90 percent of the company's revenues and more than half of its profits were generated by its competitive businesses.

Duke Energy's utilities serve 2 million customers in its region. It is a leading producer of natural gas, runs a 12,000-mile pipeline network, and sells gas products and electricity wholesale. It owns merchant power plants around the country, including nuclear facilities, and is a leading builder-for-hire of fossil-fuel plants. It also trades energy on a global basis. And it has major plant construction projects and pipelines in Australia and Latin

America, along with more than a million retail customers in Canada.

In other words, Duke has within its precincts the tools and talent to compete in terms of price and quality at virtually every level of the energy business, a vertical integration that was given major impetus in 1997, when the company bought PanEnergy and thus gained expertise in the gathering, processing, storage, transport, trading, and marketing of natural gas.

Much of Duke Energy's growth during the Evergreen years was in the wholesale energy field, but its operating performance was buttressed by the company's remarkable improvement in its regulated retail operations. Like the other Winners and Climbers in the Evergreen study (see Exhibit 5.1), Duke Energy met the following mandates that led to flawless execution: deliver products and services that consistently meet customers' expectations; empower front lines to respond to customer needs; constantly strive to improve productivity and eliminate all forms of excess and waste.

Let's take each in turn.

Deliver products and services that consistently meet customers' expectations.

As the Evergreen research revealed, winning companies like Duke excelled at the backstage of business, developing the high-performance systems and processes that turned out the on-camera products. Their skill at the operational, execution side was dedi-

5.1 Execution: Winners *versus* Losers

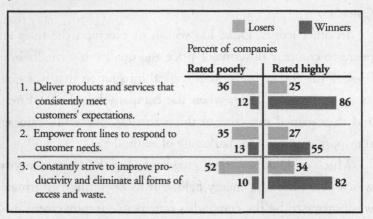

	Losers	Winners
	Percent of companies	
	Rated poorly	Rated highly
1. Deliver products and services that consistently meet customers' expectations.	36 / 12	25 / 86
2. Empower front lines to respond to customer needs.	35 / 13	27 / 55
3. Constantly strive to improve productivity and eliminate all forms of excess and waste.	52 / 10	34 / 82

The chart shows how winning and losing companies were rated as regards the three mandates of the execution management practice. Eighty-six percent of the Winners, for example, were rated highly on meeting customers' expectations, while 36 percent of the Losers rated poorly. A solid 82 percent of Winners rated highly on the productivity mandate, while 52 percent of the Losers rated poorly.

Note: A poor rating equals 1 or 2 and a high rating equals 4 or 5 on a 5-point scale with a score of 3 being average. Some mandates and their scores are the composite of several survey items. The percentages do not add up to 100% because companies with average scores are not included. Losers include the scores of all companies in losing periods and Winners, the scores of all companies in winning periods. The differences between Losers and Winners are statistically significant at the 95% confidence level.

Source: Evergreen team analysis.

cated to the mandate of meeting their customers' expectations. Note, however, that they did not commit themselves to delivering perfect products or services.

Contrary to some popular prescriptions, we found (see Exhibit 5.2) that Winners did not always deliver truly extraordinary product or service quality relative to their peers. They did not make it a top priority to try to delight their customers with

5.2 Quality: Winners *versus* Losers

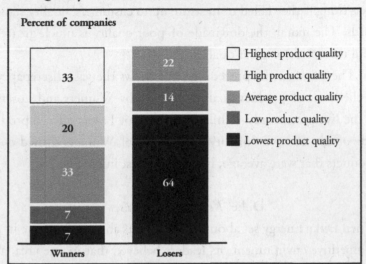

Sources: Dr. Stan Leibowitz, the University of Texas at Dallas; industry literature.

the best possible quality, or to exceed their expectations. They understood that the benefits of product quality are asymmetric: unless perfection is part of their strategic value proposition, companies do not gain a sustained economic benefit by offering the very best quality.

However, Winners did consistently deliver the quality their customers expected. More important, they rarely delivered poor quality. Most customers cannot discriminate and don't really care about a level of quality that goes beyond their needs and desires. But all customers can recognize a poor-quality product or service that fails to meet their expectations, and when that happens their trust in a company evaporates.

Winning companies understood that they were sure to lose everything if they failed to measure up to customers' quality standards. The moral: the downside of poor quality is much greater than the upside of great quality.

The chart on the preceding page shows the vast discrepancy in the levels of product quality achieved by Winners and Losers in the Evergreen study. While 78 percent of Losers offered products of low or lowest quality, 86 percent of Winners turned out products that were average, high, or highest in quality.

Duke: *Keeping its promises*

When Duke Energy set about examining its ability to operate in a competitive environment, its leaders believed that in one area, at least, there would be little need for change. As Jimmy R. Hicks, senior vice president of electronic transmission recalled, "Our quality of service was already pretty high. [But] once we started to look, we found plenty of opportunities for improvement." As the Evergreen content-analysis research revealed, winning companies constantly raise the bar on their service level.

At Duke, leaders discovered that the company's promises to customers to complete a job in a specified period were fulfilled only 74 percent of the time. One of the problems was that the corporation had never bothered to determine just how long its various service tasks took to complete. When a customer called in a request to the telephone center, the operator might routinely assure the customer that the problem would be resolved that day without really knowing what was involved.

In a competitive environment, Duke's leaders knew, customer satisfaction would loom large. So they established a new goal: 96 percent of the orders would have to be finished by the day promised.

The first step toward that goal was to get a clear fix on how long a particular service order took to complete. That made it possible to give customers an accurate estimate as to when their service would be restored.

In some cases, when the repairs were extensive, Duke simply adapted to the customers' needs. When the streetlights in a neighborhood fell dark, callers hoped that repairs could be finished within three days. Duke set itself the goal of fixing 95 percent of streetlight problems within that period. They calculated that only 5 percent of the outages involved underground repairs, which required bringing in heavy equipment and a longer time frame.

The various service tasks were analyzed in depth, and a target time was established. The members of every repair team were thus on notice as to how long a job should take, and at the end of the month the team received a scorecard showing how successfully it had met the company goals. At the same time, the company continuously tracked customer satisfaction. Employees could see how their efforts were increasing customer approval, and thereby company revenues; they were also rewarded financially for meeting and exceeding their targets.

In 1997, Duke was rated first in the nation in customer satisfaction among electric utilities by *Fortune* magazine. One reason was the company's design and construction of a state-of-the-art, 24/7 telephone service center outside Charlotte. It replaced a dispersed approach whereby a large number of customer-service groups were spread across the Carolinas.

Duke responded with equal energy and intelligence when some customers showed a preference for dealing with the company online, rather than through the telephone service center. It put together a top-flight website at www.dukepower.com. It allows home customers to examine their bills and account history and obtain explanations of the various items. They can also request repairs, pay their bills, and even get loans for new heating or cooling equipment, all online.

For small businesses, the site makes it possible to explore their energy efficiency and consider new approaches. Owners can receive an energy analysis showing how their energy use compares to others in similar businesses and whether particular changes would reduce energy losses.

One of the major goals of Duke's initiatives was to improve performance and productivity on every level of its operations practice, and in this the company succeeded well. The details of that success will be discussed later in the chapter. Suffice it to say here that the company's larger purpose was to bring costs down— for Duke, and, hence, for its customers, meeting and even exceeding their expectations.

Smithfield: *Quality control in Hogville*

Another fine example of flawless execution is Smithfield Foods, the world's largest hog producer and pork processor. During the decade of the Evergreen study, Smithfield never varied from its intense focus on producing the high-quality pork products its customers wanted, while delivering them in a variety of forms and under a variety of brands. Its sales and earnings grew handsomely, despite such profit-depressing developments as increasing federal regulations, food-safety challenges, and the usual boom-and-bust cycle of over- and underproduction that afflicts that industry. The company was an Evergreen Winner.

Joseph W. Luter III, the chairman and CEO, is the third generation of his family to preside over Smithfield Foods since its founding in 1936 in what can truly be called a hamlet—tiny Smithfield, Virginia. It was he who introduced vertical integration, putting the company into the hog-raising business to lessen its dependence on Midwest farms and improve product quality. He also acquired a bevy of companies to increase production and reduce fixed costs, and to build its portfolio of brands.

The quality control achieved through integration helped Smithfield gain a major stake in the lucrative Japanese market. Typical of Smithfield's determination to meet customer expectations was its willingness to satisfy the desires of its Japanese customers in terms of cuts of meat and packaging. Many another company would have insisted that Asian customers accept the product in its U.S. version.

Another example of Smithfield's focus on customer desires was its reaction to the public demand for leaner, healthier meat. In 1991, Luter bought exclusive rights to develop and market in the United States a long, extra-lean hog bred by the National Pig Development Company of East Yorkshire, England. This NPD pig, as it is known, aside from its leanness, can yield up to three pounds more ham meat and up to four pounds more boneless loin product.

Over the next year or so, some 2,000 NPDs were transported across the Atlantic, some by boat, others in the world's largest cargo plane, the Russian AN-24. That led, in short order, to Smithfield Lean Generation Pork, a new line for the company's flagship brand. Smithfield says that, cut for cut, the new line has 35 to 60 percent less fat than traditional pork. As of 2002, NPD sows accounted for 55 percent of Smithfield's total herd, and the lean line was selling at a rate of 100 million pounds a year.

Empower the front lines to respond to customer needs.

Businesspeople have recognized forever that the moment when the customer interacts with a company employee is crucial to the organization's success. Traditionally, the moral that managers took from this fact was: keep your frontline employees on a tight rein; teach them to come running when they encounter anything out of the ordinary. Today, as the Evergreen research showed, winning companies take a very different tack. They understand that the frontline people themselves must be given the authority to make real-time decisions, along with the training that will help them make the right ones.

Peter Drucker, one of the fathers of management theory, wrote some years ago about the different structural arrangements that the various parts of any company require. Managing foreign-currency exposure demanded total centralization, for example, while customer service demanded almost complete local autonomy, to an extent "going way beyond" traditional decentralization. "Each of the individual service people must be the 'boss,'" he wrote, "with the rest of the organization taking its direction from him or her."

Duke: *A new breed of decision makers*

When Richard Priory and his team began Duke's transformation, the company was a traditional top-down, hierarchical organization. The leadership group concerned itself with every facet of the company's processes, from design to execution. That arrangement had a negative impact on customer service. It meant that frontline workers were dependent on their supervisors, both before and during a job. When unexpected questions or problems arose at the job site, decisions were delayed while the service person tried to contact his supervisor for advice—and the supervisor tried to contact her manager.

Beyond the delay factor, Duke found that the command-and-control approach failed to tap the potential of its frontline people. They were order-takers with little or no incentive to raise their performance level or use their own initiative—and that also had a negative impact on their dealings with customers. Decisions made at long range were often less effective than those made by on-site employees. As the Evergreen survey and content-analysis showed, it is those very real-life interactions that winning companies relied on to develop brand loyalty.

Duke turned its operations upside down. All of its hundreds of tasks were analyzed from the customer's vantage point—the billing process, for example, was measured in terms of its accuracy. Then the company instituted a clear and precise division of labor. Henceforth, in keeping with the mandate to empower frontline workers, the execution of a process would be the responsibility of a frontline team. The supervisors' frontline role was limited to making sure the teams had the necessary resources. Their chief responsibility would be the continuous redesign of the processes themselves.

Now the real-time interaction between the frontline people and the customer took on a very different cast. The employees, equipped with the information needed to do the job well and empowered to deal with problems that might arise, were more confident and content in their work. Customers described themselves as more satisfied with both the quality of the work and the friendliness of the workers.

This organizational change was not, however, gained easily. Frontline people needed to be convinced of the advantages of the new system. They had to be trained to follow new process maps. Many were uncomfortable at first receiving assignments from a central scheduling unit instead of their supervisors. By the same token, many supervisors found it hard to relinquish their managerial role.

An unexpected consequence of the reorganization was a falling-off of service to some customers. Builders, for example, had become accustomed to working with supervisors to see that new houses had their electricity hooked up in time for buyers to move in. Now the supervisors were no longer available, and Duke's initial work-scheduling system turned out to be flawed. Many builders were disappointed. "While we were designing and refining our work processes," Jimmy Hicks said, "we damaged the trust and intimacy we had built up over the years." It took a while before the damage could be repaired.

Once the new organization got through its growing pains, though, the results were impressive. Morale within the company improved markedly, and customer-survey scores rose to new highs.

Home Depot: *Technology aids interaction*

Duke Energy came late to its determined focus on customer service; at Home Depot it was built into the operation from the beginning. That was in 1978, when Bernie Marcus and Arthur Blank, after having been fired from Handy Dan, the home-improvement chain, decided to enter the business on their own. They proposed to provide home handymen and women with whatever tools and materials they might need in one store and to deliver such helpful, friendly one-on-one service that customers would never even think of going anywhere else.

How important is that level of service to Marcus and Blank? Important enough to actually cannibalize a successful store in order to open another outlet nearby rather than overtax the first and risk damaging its trademark customer-friendly environment.

Too many customers spoil the formula. "Your store could do $800 a foot," Blank, the president, told *Building Home Supply Centers*. "But the reality is that at some point, you're running a store that is abusive to your customers, abusive to your associates, and abusive to the products that are in the store. It's just too much intensity."

The solution: a second store to bleed off volume from the first. Short-term, the cannibalization policy damages comparable-store sales. Not a problem, Blank insisted: "It doesn't hurt us internally, it hurts us in terms of the way we're viewed by the financial community." In the long run, the policy increased total sales and profits.

To make sure that customers receive loyalty-inducing service, Home Depot installed state-of-the-art technology, including computer-assisted ordering to keep inventory under control and get goods to the stores when needed and organized so that they can be put away easily. Otherwise, employees get so busy handling merchandise they stint on customer service. "The critical factor," Marcus told *Chief Executive*, "is to be able to receive the merchandise, get it on the shelves, and still have people on the floor of the store taking care of the customers."

Walgreen: *Above all, convenience*

Another company that invests in technology to give employees—particularly pharmacists, in this case—enough time with customers is Walgreen, the nation's largest drugstore chain and a Winner in our study. Walgreen has grown large and its brand all-powerful by catering to the convenience of its customers, transaction by transaction.

To be sure, low cost and desirable products were essential elements of the strategy, but what set Walgreen apart in particular, and built brand loyalty, was the impressive variety of ways it found to make shopping easier. Its 1989 annual report insisted that "nothing is more important to Walgreen's long-term success than convenience," and that has turned out to be gospel. The average customer buys two items and spends well under ten minutes in the process—think of an office worker on a thirty-minute lunch break.

While competitors stuck to their malls or shopping strips, relying on neighboring stores to bring customers in, Walgreen established free-standing outlets in high-traffic, heavily populated areas where it was the sole or major tenant. That made it possible for customers to park close by, rather than walking a long way at a mall. Many of the Walgreen outlets actually offered drive-through shopping.

By going it alone, the company was also able to offer its in-a-hurry customers a wide variety of non-drug items without having to compete with grocers or other retail outlets at the malls. Most Walgreen aisles are chockablock with the likes of chips, bread, soda, milk, and beer, not to mention shampoos, greeting cards, toys, and electric fans.

Walgreen parted with its rivals on a number of other matters. All through the decade covered by the Evergreen Project, the drugstore industry was undergoing massive consolidation. Companies needed to leverage their size to negotiate prices and attract customers with the rise of third-party reimbursement programs. Deep-discount drugstores and mail-order pharmacies were cutting deeply into the margins of traditional drugstores.

In that ever more hostile environment, many drugstore chains that had spent the 1980s diversifying found themselves dragged down by their non-drug holdings. By 1986, however, Walgreen had already divested itself of almost all of its non-drug businesses, which ranged from menswear to restaurants. It had also, during that time, bought its share of small and midsize drugstore chains. Now it took a different path, turning its back on diversification, focusing exclusively on the drugstore business, and expanding internally with stand-alone sites while its rivals continued along the acquisition trail.

As Walgreen built itself into a nationwide chain, its dedication to customer convenience became ever more clearly associated with its brand. Its technology helped in that cause, speeding up checkout lines and enabling its pharmacists all across the country to access any customer's prescription records. That made it possible for a Walgreen customer away from home on business or vacation to get his or her prescription filled in any of the thousands of Walgreen outlets.

Constantly strive to improve productivity and eliminate all forms of excess and waste.

The goal is to achieve perfect operational execution, constantly improving systems and processes, hiring better people, routing wastefulness and inefficiency. This mandate was followed by all winning companies, as the Evergreen research showed; but, in this case, perfection did have its limits.

Winners recognized that there was no way they could be truly flawless, outperforming their competitors on all operating parameters. Instead, they determined which processes were most important to meeting customers' expectations and focused their energies and resources on making these processes as efficient and productive as possible.

Duke: *The case for interchangeability*

For Duke Energy's repair people, the particular trucks they went out in each day were like second homes. They put up family pictures and good luck charms and stocked it with the tools and equipment they most frequently used. No one questioned that arrangement until Richard Priory set the reinvention of the company in motion with its call for increased productivity in every corner of the operation.

The "privatization" of the trucks, as it were, became a problem during a storm or other emergency when normal scheduling was impossible and trucks were assigned to different workers. Unfamiliar with the vehicle, the workers had no idea where particular tools and equipment might be stored. Some trucks were packed full of every conceivable piece of equipment; others carried a limited sample. The workers' ability to deal with crisis conditions was thus compromised.

The company announced a plan to standardize the materials carried by the trucks, making them, for all intents and purposes, interchangeable. Line people protested. They were afraid that the tools they most preferred would not be included in the standard supply. They complained that they were being deprived of vehicles they thought of as their own, which they had broken in and kept clean.

In the end, interchangeability was adopted. It enabled the

company to reduce the size of its truck fleet, eliminating excess with no loss of productivity and no lessening of its efficiency in an emergency or when a vehicle was out of service for maintenance.

A few years later, the trucks' productivity was further enhanced with the installation of mobile data terminals in each vehicle. Line people could now immediately type in an order on a terminal in the truck, entering it in the company's mainframe and thereby avoiding the need to have the dispatcher retype the order. With the introduction of the mobile terminals, the company was able to reduce its dispatcher locations from twenty to four.

The tale of the trucks is just one example of the many productivity increases Duke Energy obtained after reexamining its operating processes with a critical eye. Another example: the streamlining of the company's reaction to customer-service requests.

In the old days, a customer's telephone call would lead to a printout at one or another operating center. A clerk at the center would move the request from the printer to one of a handful of boxes, depending upon what day the service call was to take place. On the appropriate day, the paper would be moved to the box of the line person assigned to the job.

The paper trail was long and slow, and subject to error. And it was further complicated by the fact that the company was divided into thirteen geographical areas, and each of those thirteen operations did things a bit differently, depending upon its size and the nature and capacity of its staff.

Now an electronic information system spirits the customer's

request, whether received via telephone or Internet, directly to the master schedulers at the central operations unit.

The schedulers—known as "assemblers" at Duke—assign people to handle the request. And because the schedulers now know how long any particular job takes, they are able to provide employees with enough work to accurately fill their days. In the past, employees had been assigned a task with no thought given as to how long it would take: they might complete it in an hour, or spend six hours and leave the job unfinished. By giving people a full day's work, the company substantially increased overall productivity.

To make the new system work, schedulers had to have a precise picture in advance of the human resources available for assignment on any given day. The traditional approach to vacations and sick leave had been typically free and easy: the employee worked it out with his or her supervisor. That soon yielded to standardization, with employees' requests sent not to supervisors but to the central office, which can see the whole picture. Maintaining a balanced workforce on any given day has, by itself, greatly raised productivity.

As the Duke Energy story makes clear, achieving operational excellence requires considerable soul-searching and a major investment of time and money to bring a company's performance to new heights—and keep it there.

To meet customers' expectations as to when a repair would be completed, for example, Duke analyzed all of its service tasks in depth so that it could accurately determine how long any task should take. It was then able to make realistic promises to customers, and keep those promises an outstanding 96 percent of the time.

Duke's interactions with customers were greatly improved when the company gave frontline employees the training, information, and authority they needed to take responsibility for customer contacts. In so doing, the company tapped new levels of creativity in its employees while speeding up and improving service to customers.

Duke Energy's success in cutting costs and improving productivity was fostered, in part, by its patience and long-term perspective. Rather than engage in the kind of occasional, draconian campaigns that antagonize and exhaust everyone in an organization, Duke pursued improved productivity as an ongoing initiative that was simply a key part of its daily operations.

Campbell Soup: *A drastic solution*

One of the most thoroughgoing and successful warriors against waste and excess among the companies studied by the Evergreen Project was Campbell Soup during the 1990–96 tenure of David Johnson as chief executive. When he arrived at the company's home base in Camden, New Jersey, its sales were flat, its profits in decline, its market share dwindling, and its stock price in the doldrums. Many of the heirs of John Dorrance, the inventor of condensed soup, who held a majority of the stock, wanted to sell the company to the highest bidder. Johnson, a noted turnaround artist, had been brought in to see that didn't happen.

"Crisis was inevitable," he said at the time. "There were too many inefficiencies." He immediately turned his attention to cutting costs and raising productivity.

Within just nine months, he closed down or sold twenty plants, cut the 51,700 workforce by 15 percent, put unprofitable overseas businesses on the block, and ditched dozens of unprofitable product lines. He also introduced the company to zero-based budgeting.

Each year, Campbell's had used the fall tomato harvest as an occasion for a special promotion for its tomato soup. Inspired by Johnson's budget move, the soup marketers reconsidered the promotion. Since the company used tomato paste rather than fresh tomatoes in its soup, the campaign was canceled, thereby saving 10 percent of the soup marketing budget. As an executive told *Fortune* magazine, "The 10 percent is the elimination of the stupid."

To bring efficiency to Campbell's manufacturing plants, he insisted that the plants surviving his ax bid for the business that had been handled by the deceased operations. It forced the plant managers to focus as never before on cutting costs and improving productivity overall in order to get and hold on to the extra work. Operating efficiencies soared.

The new CEO was soon dubbed "Quantification Johnson," not only because of his bottom-line goals but because he insisted that executives and managers be held accountable to the numbers. In the case of marketers and manufacturers, they were judged by their competitors' numbers.

By trimming waste and inspiring unprecedented efficiencies, Johnson accomplished a minor miracle. Between 1990 and the end of the 1994–95 fiscal year, Campbell's profits rose at an annual rate of 18 percent, while return on sales skyrocketed from 0.1 percent to 9.6 percent.

Target: *Discipline, the key to creativity*

When Target's CEO, Bob Ulrich, is asked why his company has succeeded so well, he gives discipline high marks—discipline in operations, strategies, and finance. "Our consistency of execution," he says, "gives us the flexibility to be creative in our merchandising, our marketing, and our brand identity."

A prime example of Target's flawless, customer-focused operations can be found in its approach to technology. In the 1970s it broke new ground in its market with storewide electronic cash registers that monitored inventory and accelerated service. It was ahead of the pack in its nationwide rollout of electronic scanning in the 1980s, and, as we saw in the last chapter, in the adoption of smart credit cards.

In each case, however, the company managed to avoid two pitfalls that plague technical initiatives in so many companies: it installed technology for the right reason, and it tested it thoroughly before adoption.

As is the case with winning companies in general, Target understood that superior operations and distribution-system technology can create sustained value only if they enable a company to reduce costs and increase productivity. There are no gains from being a pioneer per se. At Target, technology projects were driven by clear performance-improvement benchmarks rather than by milestones marking adoption rates and the like.

Target spotted the technologies early on and then put them

through a gauntlet of tests and pilot studies. Only after the new processes had proven themselves would Target introduce them throughout the chain. As a result, they invariably worked just fine, improving operations without disturbing other processes or inconveniencing customers.

When Target first decided to create an Internet presence, it proceeded in its customarily thorough manner, painstakingly examining its options and studying the experience of less cautious, unsuccessful competitors. In 1998, it bought Rivertown Trading, a catalogue and direct-marketing firm based in Woodbury, Minnesota. That provided Target with the call center and distribution capability it needed to operate a commercial website.

A year of planning and testing passed before Target.com was launched, and it was a gentle start with just 2,000 items for purchase. They were high-margin products that were generally not to be found at Wal-Mart, and were user-friendly for the distribution center. Some analysts complained that Target's Internet approach was too slow—at one point, Ulrich acknowledged that for a time "we looked like Luddites"—but gradually the company introduced more products and more customer aids, including its bridal and baby registries, the world's largest. Today, the Target's Internet sites work just the way they are supposed to. As a result, the company has become the online leader among discounters.

Target is also using Internet-mediated buyer auctions to improve its purchasing operations. The company was among the founding members of the Worldwide Retail Exchange and remains one of its most aggressive participants.

In these auctions, Target can invite bids from a number of suppliers at the same time, and the bidders have a limited deadline for responding. Generally speaking, the goods the company seeks are high-volume, high-margin products like paper bags, hangers, or coffee filters. They are of particular interest to Target because they can easily be transformed into private-label products. The suppliers can see what their competitors are bidding and have a chance to lower their bids.

From the suppliers' point of view, the auctions are less than popular, since they are bidding against each other. On the other hand, they do create a level playing field—which makes it possible for new vendors to break into the game.

From Target's vantage point, the auctions are a money-saving machine, but they also represent an extension of the company's long-term policy of dealing directly with suppliers and cutting out the buyer middleman. Aside from the cost savings, that gives Target greater direct control of every aspect of the product, a giant step toward making sure that the supplier fulfills the customer need Target has identified. In addition, the auctions introduce the company to new vendors who can make fresh contributions to improving execution.

What Comes Next

As the Evergreen Project discovered, successful companies know how to execute flawlessly in providing customer-focused products and services—the second of the primary practices in the 4+2 formula. In the chapter just ahead, you will find a detailed discussion of the third primary practice: make your culture gung-ho for performance. The mandates revealed as essential by Evergreen research emphasize the importance of such issues as team loyalty and pay-for-performance programs. Home Depot and Campbell Soup are among the company examples used to show how Winners go about designing and supporting performance-oriented corporate cultures. Polaroid serves as an example of how not to do it.

6

Build a Performance-Based Culture

Among the more intriguing results of the Evergreen study was the emergence of culture as one of the four primary practices. In some quarters of the business world, culture is just beginning to be taken seriously as an aspect of management on a par with, say, operations. Yet, as the Evergreen Project made clear, Winners get that way because virtually everyone in the organization is performing at his or her highest level. Gregory Peck had it right in that great old World War II film *Twelve O'Clock High* when he announced, "I want maximum effort." Maximum effort brings victory in corporate wars, too.

In this chapter, the discussion focuses on the means to that end, the four mandates that successful companies follow to achieve a high-performance culture. The major example is that champion of the do-it-yourself movement, Home Depot. Before and during the decade covered by the Evergreen Project, the retailer demonstrated exceptional skill and ingenuity in creating a culture dedicated to performance and the customer.

Along with the other Winners, Home Depot abided by the culture mandates, inspring all to do their best, rewarding achievement with praise and pay, creating a challenging and satisfying work environment, and establishing and abiding by clear company values.

6.1 Culture: Winners *versus* Losers

		Losers	Winners
		Rated poorly	**Rated highly**
1. Inspire all to do their best.		47	25
		5	91
2. Reward achievement with praise and pay-for-performance, but keep raising the performance bar.		63	15
		3	87
3. Create a work environment that is challenging, satisfying, and fun.		51	22
		11	77
4. Establish and abide by clear company values.		44	24
		13	72

Percent of companies

This chart shows how Winners and Losers performed on the four mandates of the culture-management practice. Ninety-one percent of the Winners, for example, were given high ratings on the first mandate, "inspire all to do their best." Among the Losers, 63 percent received poor ratings on the second mandate, "reward achievement with praise and pay, but keep raising the performance bar."

Note: A poor rating equals 1 or 2 and a high rating equals 4 or 5 on a 5-point scale with a score of 3 being average. Some mandates and their scores are the composite of several survey items. The percentages do not add up to 100% because companies with average scores are not included. Losers include the scores of all companies in losing periods and Winners, the scores of all companies in winning periods. The differences between Losers and Winners are statistically significant at the 95% confidence level.

Source: Evergreen team analysis.

There is another characteristic of Winners that separates them from their competitors: they apply a stretch yardstick to their performance. It is built into their culture.

Too often, companies fool themselves into believing they are doing well because they have better results than in the previous year. To be sure, year-to-year improvement is nothing to take for granted, but it is an insufficient measure. The only way to meaningfully define an organization's progress is to compare it to the record of its competitors.

To the degree that a company lags behind others in its competitive arena in the measures that count the most—whether it be in sales or shareholder return or selling, general, administrative expense—to that degree it is falling behind. An SG&A cutback of 2 percent in a given year is no cause for celebration if your immediate rivals have achieved a 3 percent cutback.

Many Winners, such as GE or Oracle, reinforce that competitive stance with posters and pep talks that define the goal as "crushing the enemy." When Microsoft's Bill Gates expressed such sentiments in his e-mails, they were presented as evidence in the U.S. Justice Department's antitrust suit against his enterprise. Yet a high-performance culture doesn't limit itself to defeating immediate competitors. It constantly raises the bar, aiming at surpassing top-ranked companies in any and every industry. Once the business has overmatched its industry rivals in, say, the effectiveness of its logistics, the culture asks: "Why can't we do it better than Federal Express?"

And when such stretch goals turn out to be unreachable, it

serves to alert the winning company to another potential opportunity. If some organization outside its industry is so clearly superior in some particular area, why not outsource the task? Excellence is excellence, whether a function is handled in-house or by a supplier.

That kind of go-for-broke culture thus yields an incidental, but far from negligible, benefit to its company. It can lead management to make better decisions about which operations to handle and which to outsource.

One of the more surprising results of our research was the lack of correlation between some of the various categories into which experts tend to put cultures and the success of the winning companies surveyed. In other words, the corporations viewed their cultures as neither hierarchical nor cooperative, competitive nor collegial, but preferred descriptions such as "action-oriented" or "risk-taking."

But before we consider the culture practice mandates in detail, let's take a closer look at our prime illustrative example, Home Depot.

By 1986, the start of the Evergreen decade, seven-year-old Home Depot was already a substantial enterprise with 60 stores, 6,600 employees, and $1 billion in sales. By 1996, it had 512 stores, 98,100 employees, and sales of $19.5 billion. By any definition, its growth had been meteoric—and yet it had only begun. As of 2001, a mere five years later, the number of stores and employees as well as the sales volume had risen by more than 150 percent. Its financial results had broken records, year after year.

The reasons were not hard to find. To begin with, Home Depot was something new in the world. In 1991, Bernard Marcus, one of the founders, described the home-improvement industry in the era before Home Depot for *Chief Executive* magazine: "Everybody was used to very high margins. . . . All you had to do was open up your door, abuse the customer, sell them products at a very high price, cherry-pick the merchandise, close your store, and go home and count your money."

Home Depot introduced a huge assortment of products, low prices, and record-high level of customer service. Over the years, the service level, too, has improved exponentially. The stores all have design centers staffed with professionally trained people who offer free advice on home-improvement projects, up to and including computer-assisted kitchen and bathroom design. There are free how-to clinics for adults on Saturdays and Sundays at every store, as well as free workshops for children. Tools and other equipment can be rented on a try-before-you-buy basis. Trucks can be rented to carry purchases home. The list goes on.

What made the formula click, though, and enabled the company to achieve ever higher levels of performance, was a corporate culture that inspired everyone to do his or her best. A position as an "associate"—the term universally and democratically applied to everyone from janitors to executives—was not just a job; it was a calling. There were rowdy Home Depot pep rallies, Home Depot mottoes and traditions, Home Depot community volunteer groups. There was a Home Depot cheer and a Home Depot color (orange—at the rallies, associates spoke of themselves as being "orange-blooded"). In ways both subtle and obvious, the culture was designed to inspire employees to ever-greater efforts on behalf of peak corporate performance.

Now let's examine the four culture mandates followed by Winners like Home Depot.

Inspire all to do their best.

Ever since the first manager hired his first employee, the same questions have hovered over their relationship. Is the employee simply to follow orders unthinkingly, or is he expected to suggest better, more efficient ways of doing the job? Is he supposed to be little more than a wage slave, or is he expected to identify with the goals of the organization? Consciously or unconsciously, the leaders of every organization answer those questions through their treatment of employees and their own standards of behavior. Their actions are the major ingredients in the stew of notions and emotions known as a corporate culture, which, in turn, determines the attitudes employees bring to their work.

As the Evergreen Project demonstrated, winning companies constantly sought to design and support a culture that promoted high levels of individual and team performance, and that held employees, not just managers, responsible for corporate success. Along with that responsibility, employees and managers were empowered to make many more independent decisions, and urged to seek out ways to improve company operations, including their own. The ideal culture nurtured feelings of loyalty toward the employee's team and the company as a whole.

Home Depot: *Partners in a greater cause*

The Home Depot culture considers the interaction between customers and associates as the ultimate moment of truth. Customers must have pleasant, rewarding experiences; associates must feel proud of their role in the encounter. The culture and the company emphasize the importance of satisfying both ends of that equation. The message: care about the customer; care about your fellow associates. In that way, the interests of the company can best be advanced.

In that process, the associates—individually and in specialized teams—are encouraged to take risks, try new approaches, make decisions without checking with department heads or managers. As one of the company's frequently proclaimed mottoes has it, "If you don't make dust, you eat dust." At Home Depot, the *status quo* is never enough.

The culture also assumes that associates will have a sense of ownership, defined by Arthur Blank, a cofounder and longtime president of the company, as a feeling on their part "that they own the stores, that they own the merchandise, that they have total responsibility for the customers in their aisles, and that they create the value."

The sense of ownership as well as the decision-making and risk-taking behavior are also expected of store managers. In most retail chains, the merchandise is identical, and the way it is laid out is identical from one outlet to another. "We give the store people a lot of room to initiate their own response to how they think they want to move merchandise," said Marcus. "You can go from store to store to store, and you will never see the same items in the front of the store. It may cost us money in some areas, but it creates excitement."

Yes, empowerment can create chaos. But Home Depot's leaders insist that, in their case, it mainly yields positive results, by inspiring the troops to greater effort and higher levels of performance overall. In fact, that was an observation made of virtually all the Winners in the Evergreen study.

The risk-taking behavior was balanced, at Home Depot, by a firm hand on the financial tiller and an insistence on business fundamentals. "The critical thing," Marcus said, "is to mix the elements—the entrepreneurial spirit with the necessity for controls."

How has Home Depot managed to develop and sustain its culture? The founders, Marcus and Blank, have played a major role, continually spreading the serve-the-customer, serve-yourself message through in-house television appearances and endless personal tours of stores around the country. It was rare to find both of them in their offices at the same time. Within the Home Depot culture, they were accorded the kind of reverence that Sam Walton received from his Wal-Mart clan.

The founders also used their store visits to mix informally with associates to determine what was happening on the front line. Their main object, they said, was to find out what was going wrong—the goal being to improve, not simply maintain. Board members were also expected to visit stores, as many as seven each quarter, posing as shoppers and then identifying themselves and chatting with employees in the break rooms. They, too, were supposed to spread the culture message. "You can't enforce a corporate culture," Marcus said, "if you are so out of touch that you don't even know if it's effective or if it's changed."

Through satellite and voicemail connections, some with question-and-answer capability, company leaders kept associates across the nation informed of business developments and spoke to rumors or other concerns employees might have. Any change in policy was also widely announced and explained.

To inspire existing employees and educate newcomers in the ways of the Home Depot culture, the company provides a variety of training programs. Many of them include the competitive, gung-ho approach that has long been a staple of the Home Depot culture.

There are the oracular commandments: "We never walk by a customer without speaking," or "Only a store manager may ever say no to a customer." There are the seminars intended to "instill a sense of teamwork and reinforce competitive spirit" at which managers play at being fighter pilots, attacking the enemy, "Lowesnia," a not very veiled reference to the Lowe's home-improvement chain. There are tours of The Legend, a museum described by the company as "chronicling the history of The Home Depot and illustrating the values that set us apart."

That sense of apartness—of being special and different from outsiders, of being engaged in a battle with competitors for the hearts and wallets of the public—has always been central to the Home Depot culture. The associates saw themselves as partners in a greater cause, and they enabled the company to achieve remarkable growth and profitability.

Campbell Soup: *Rallies and scoreboards*

When David Johnson became Campbell Soup's chief executive in 1990, he quickly made it clear to everyone in the company that its hidebound, *status-quo* culture would have to change. "The shareholder is the prime, supreme, and first of all stakeholders," he announced. Earnings, dividends, and share price would have to rise—and keep rising.

Typically, for "Quantification Johnson," he focused on a numerical measure: he pushed employees to lift net earnings faster than the competition. The comparison was to be made not with the company's previous record but with that of the enemy. "Numbers always tell the story," he said.

And the way he went about inspiring the culture change had elements of the gung-ho Home Depot approach. Scoreboards were set up all around the company showing how Campbell's net profit compared with that of other food companies. Signs appeared showing the Campbell red-and-white soup logo with the words "We're Number One!" across it. Suddenly, the phrase "team spirit" was cropping up with great frequency in conversations executives and managers had among themselves and with frontline employees.

Johnson pursued his culture-altering mission at formal gatherings and during informal encounters. He also sought to connect with the company's far-flung 44,000 employees at pep rallies around the country.

At these events, he would speak at length, describing recent developments within the organization and plans for the future. But the heart of his talk, delivered with fierce intensity in the accent of his native Australia, would be aimed at energizing the corporate culture. The greatest satisfaction in a job, he would often say, lay in the feeling that it had been done to the best of one's ability. In fact, it was to be a cardinal rule of the new corporate culture that one's reach should always exceed one's grasp.

Implicit in that kind of go-for-broke culture was the need to take risks, both at the corporate *and* the employee level. As every employee knew, when you take a chance on a new idea or a different way of doing things in a corporate setting, you put your job at risk. But the culture as Johnson redefined it covered that contingency. Failure was not a firing offense as long as the risk had been reasonable and the goal of sufficient value. What counted was performance.

Reward achievement with praise and pay-for-performance, but keep raising the performance bar.

Ralph Waldo Emerson, the great nineteenth-century American writer and philosopher, had it right, in theory at least: "The reward of a thing well done is to have done it." But when it comes to our jobs, we also look for other, more tangible and obvious rewards. We have to earn a livelihood, and the greater our income, the more comfortably we and our families can live. In fact, though we may find psychic satisfaction in doing our jobs well, a pay raise is probably going to inspire us to do them better.

As the Evergreen Project's research showed, Winners concurred with these views, using financial rewards to urge their employees to greater heights of performance. At the same time, they did not fail to pay tribute to the psychic side, developing programs to give productive employees public recognition of their achievements and opportunities for promotion.

Home Depot: *Ownership as incentive*

At Home Depot the greatest emphasis was placed on creating a sense of belonging and identification among employees. During the Evergreen Project years, the company, which was non-union, paid most employees no more than the industry average. But part of their income was in the form of shares in Home Depot, a further effort to give associates a feeling of ownership and to tie their fortunes more directly to those of the company. During most of the Evergreen decade, the value of the shares soared.

Even the salary schedule was not cast in stone. "We pay people what they're worth," Bernie Marcus said. "Just because two people have the same job description doesn't mean they get paid the same wages."

As an example, Marcus cited an electrician with twenty-five years' experience, who would receive more money than another with just a year's experience. Not only was he doing the job better, but he was training the other electrician, and all those around him, to improve their work.

At its rallies, Home Depot honored associates who had initiated new programs or found better ways to do their jobs. During their frequent visitations of stores, the company founders always went out of their way to praise local innovators and their innovations.

Campbell Soup: *Pay for performance*

At Campbell Soup, too, the achievements of individuals and teams were celebrated at pep rallies. Risk-takers learned that they would be publicly honored if their new approach worked.

The major focus, though, was on linking compensation to the progress of the organization. Every kind and variety of pay incentive the company offered—including its matching contribution to the savings plan—was tied to the performance of the individual, the company, or both. As the company's earnings went, so went your nest egg.

The higher your position in the organization, the greater the percentage of your income that depended upon the degree to which you in your particular area and the company overall met specific earnings and sales targets. In the case of CEO David Johnson, that was what determined more than 75 percent of his compensation.

As of 1996, there were 1,200 employees eligible for bonuses of one sort or another if they could jump through particular financial hoops.

For about 300 of them, his top aides, Johnson devised another means of encouraging them to do their best for the company. Depending on their position in the hierarchy, he demanded that they own anywhere from one half to three times their base salary in Campbell Soup stock. In 1996, when Basil Anderson was hired as chief financial officer, he had to borrow $700,000 to meet that requirement.

Johnson constantly raised the bar on his goals for Campbell Soup. He often talked in terms of "20-20-20," by which he meant an annual 20 percent net profit-per-share increase, a 20 percent average return on equity, and a 20 percent average cash return on assets.

When Campbell's financials actually climbed to the top of the food industry, he told his troops that the company was "best in class"—he had once raised sheepdogs and greyhounds and entered them for prizes at county fairs. Now, he informed them, they should be shooting for "best in show." The performance bar had been raised again: henceforth, they were to be judged by the measure of such consumer-goods icons as Coca-Cola and Gillette.

Create a work environment that is challenging, satisfying, and fun.

The end is a high-performance culture, but the means cannot be so draconian and the atmosphere so dour that employees lose enjoyment in their work. It is a fine line between a high-performance culture and a high-anxiety culture, and leaders cross it at their peril.

The importance of maintaining a pleasant, satisfying workplace was underlined by the Evergreen research, which found that Winners, as a group, conformed to this mandate.

Home Depot: *"We want extroverts"*

Home Depot, for example, built its culture on the conviction that the emotional state of its associates would determine the outcome of their encounters with customers. Its hiring policy is quite explicit. As Bernie Marcus has put it, "We want extroverts, people who like other people." Then he added: "Work should be fun . . . and I think that comes through on the floor of the store. . . . When I walk around, if I see sour faces, if someone can't take a joke, I know we have a leadership problem."

In its statement of values, under the heading "Living Our Values," the company claims: "The key to our success is creating an environment where all associates feel that they are respected, their contributions valued, and they have equal access to growth and development opportunities."

Workplace informality can also support a positive encounter with a customer. The universal use of the word "associate" conveys the leaders' desire to make employees feel important and to erase the traditional caste and class distinctions that denigrate frontline people. It helps staff members feel good about themselves.

Informality finds other expressions at Home Depot. For example, since the focus is on person-to-person interaction, memos are frowned upon. Executives are addressed by their first names. They often dispense with ties in the office and never wear them when visiting stores. It all helps to make for a relaxed, friendly, productive environment.

To better maintain that environment, the company has sent its assistant store managers to one-day programs to help them become "more effective leaders." The assistant managers are the people primarily responsible for coaching store associates in the ways of the culture. The three main areas covered are teamwork, increased trust, and improved communication skills. As part of the communication program, the assistant managers learn to better "confront negative behaviors and provide effective positive reinforcement."

When Home Depot opens a new store, it is faced with the task of creating an enjoyable work environment while also instilling the culture in the new associates. To make that happen, the company sees to it that from 15 to 30 percent of the employees are seasoned Home Depot veterans. As Bernie Marcus put it: "You can't change someone's philosophy by putting out memos or showing them a video."

When the new store is located in an existing Home Depot market, Marcus added, "Our customers actually help spread the culture to new employees."

Polaroid: *The case against paternalism*

We talked above about the fine line between a high-performance culture and a high-anxiety culture. Edwin Land, Polaroid's amazingly innovative and charismatic founder, walked that line like a high-wire artist. He created a culture in which employees were treated to such advanced management practices as profit-sharing, job rotation, and reimbursement for education. He virtually guaranteed them lifelong job security. He urged them to join him in a ceaseless, exciting search for perfection in every product the company produced. The people of Polaroid, he assured them, could do anything and be anything beyond those of any other company in the world.

At the same time, for all his immense personal charm, Land was a paternalistic autocrat, insisting on total control, driving his employees as hard as he drove himself, which was often to the point of exhaustion. He could also be stubborn, arrogant, and demanding in his day-to-day contacts with managers and workers. His definition of corporate performance had everything to do with being the best, and nothing to do with making money. As a result, the culture measured itself by its technical achievements, not its customer relations or its bottom line.

Land decided what goals to pursue, with little concern for the marketplace. "I don't do product research," he said. "I'll go and invent something and spring it on the world, and people will love it."

For years, Land's formula worked. He invented the instant camera, and consumers loved it. He made less and less expensive versions, models that took color pictures as well as sepia, and sales soared. Wall Street saluted, sending Polaroid stock to what was in 1972 an amazing ninety times earnings and a spot in the Nifty Fifty. That was the year he brought forth the SX-70, a folding camera that produced an instant print that "self-developed" in broad daylight—right before your eyes. It represented a whole assortment of breakthrough inventions, from motor drives to lenses to film.

Despite its remarkable technology, the SX-70 was a sales disappointment, in part because of technical problems. The next ten years were hard on Edwin Land and Polaroid. He pushed through, for example, an expensive instant movie system that could not compete with existing products and had to be dropped, at a cost of $80 million. Land seemed to have lost his touch, and he stepped down as chief executive in 1980.

As of 1986, the first year covered by the Evergreen study, Polaroid was coasting along on its instant camera and instant film sales. But the future was uncertain, and the very essence of the company had changed. Land's successors sought to modify and even scrap many elements of the culture. It no longer worked without the founder at the helm.

In 1990, Harvey Greenberg, the manager of a Polaroid plant, recalled his first days at the company: "When I arrived here in 1984, the charge that I had given myself was to change the culture." Employees complained that supervisors never answered their questions or responded to their suggestions. A topside decision on production issues would take more than a week to reach frontline employees.

"I came here believing that for people to be committed to their work, they need to know everything about that work they possibly can," Greenberg said. That was not happening.

The excitement and challenge that Edwin Land had engendered was also missing. Polaroid was no longer turning out breakthrough products; competitors were nipping at its heels. By 1994, the culture had turned staid and cautious, and Greenberg and CEO I. Macallister "Mac" Booth, a company veteran, were desperately trying to refocus it on risk-taking and high performance in the service of technological excellence.

When Gary Dicamillo took over as CEO in 1996, it was evident that his predecessor had failed. Polaroid's big technology bets, Dicamillo said, had been "skewed heavily to things that were going to be five years, maybe ten years, down the road." He intended to bet on smaller projects with more immediate returns, and spend his resources on repackaging existing products.

Dicamillo was also concerned that Polaroid's culture was still insular—"inward-looking," as he put it—and he planned to rely much more on partners and engage in joint ventures and acquisitions. Part of that new outward-looking culture would be a deep concern for matching products to customers' needs, a concept signally lacking for more than a decade, he said.

The toylike I-Zone instant camera, introduced in the fall of 1999, was a much-needed commercial success, but it did not sit well with many employees. As David Laituri, manager of design strategy, commented a few months later, "The key idea at Polaroid now is that it's not the quality of the image that is important. It's how you use it." In other words, Polaroid and its culture were no longer dedicated to creating the best possible product, simply one that sold.

All through the years of the Evergreen study, Polaroid struggled with strategies that were in one way or another a mismatch with its original culture. The excitements and satisfactions that had inspired employees when the company was pioneering the instant camera technology had leeched away. Polaroid was barely making ends meet. Working there was not much fun.

Establish and abide by clear company values.

Not since the darkest days of the Teapot Dome scandal in the 1920s and the antitrust movement a decade later has the business community been viewed with such opprobrium as it is today in the wake of the Enron, WorldCom, and Andersen debacles. Never has it been so evident that good behavior promotes good business—and that weak or nonexistent values will, in the end, destroy lives and ruin enterprises. The Evergreen research supported that view, demonstrating that the Winners among the companies studied abided by the mandate to establish and live by a strong value system.

Of course, it isn't enough merely to recognize that fact. The values of a company should be thought through and written down in clear, forceful language and made an essential part of the culture management practice. They should be presented to all employees and made easily and permanently available to them. Implicitly or explicitly, they should be part of every communication the company sends employees and every interaction between employees.

Home Depot: *Walking the talk*

Home Depot has identified seven core values, ranging from "excellent customer service" to "creating shareholder value." Of particular interest here are two others, "doing the right thing" and "giving back."

The first is elaborated in this fashion: "We exercise good judgment by 'doing the right thing' instead of just 'doing things right.' We strive to understand the impact of our decisions, and we accept responsibility for our actions."

Under "giving back," the company said: "An important part of the fabric of The Home Depot is giving part of our time, talent, energy, and treasure to needs in our community and society."

Lending concrete reality to that value, the company has provided millions of dollars in grants to hundreds of organizations in four areas: affordable housing, at-risk youth, the environment, and disaster preparedness and relief.

Team Depot, made up of thousands of volunteer associates, also focuses on those areas. These individuals work side by side with at-risk youngsters, for example, to rehabilitate housing for homeless and low-income families. They build safe playgrounds. Through clinics and seminars, they educate customers in dealing with emergencies—and help with supplies and expertise in the event disaster strikes.

The volunteer activities of Team Depot in the communities where Home Depots are located are a powerful response to the very vocal critics of the company's expansionist strategy, which they say drives smaller competitors out of business. Team Depot also powerfully supports the Home Depot culture as a whole, a constant example of how individuals, working alone and in teams, can take pride in their contributions to the larger good.

Campbell Soup: *No wiggle-room*

An outstanding example of a Winner's commitment to the "values" mandate can be found in Campbell Soup's booklet, "World-wide Standards of Conduct," developed in the early

1990s. The values set forth by the company are expressed firmly, with no wiggle-room. The language is clarity itself, and, where necessary, examples are offered as an aid to comprehension. And the booklet is all-inclusive, covering an employee's conduct with everyone from fellow employees to customers to political candidates.

In a foreword, the booklet says it reflects Campbell's "commitment to comply with the spirit as well as the letter of all laws which affect our operations." It then adds: "When you have special concerns, you are strongly encouraged to go to higher levels of management without any thought of reprisal." If any employees had their doubts about how seriously the company took its values, that invitation to whistle-blowing should have set their minds at ease.

As behooves a food company, the first item listed in the booklet is quality. Here is an example of the tone: "Quality is never compromised—shortcuts or half-hearted efforts in building quality assurance into Campbell products—at any stage of development, manufacturing or distribution—jeopardize our team performance. They also violate consumer trust and, therefore, cannot be tolerated. Such action should be reported right away."

The booklet goes on to discuss "Conflicts of Interest," "Competitive Practices," "Dealing with Suppliers and Customers," and "Selling and Promoting Our Products." Some of the items have particular resonance these days. "Trading in Company Securities," for example, forbids the purchase or sale of shares based on information not available to the general public. Such proprietary information should not be shared with people "outside the company, including spouses, friends and family members."

Under the heading "Accuracy of Company Records," the booklet urges readers "to be alert for irregularities—things like 'off-the-book' funds, money laundering and fraudulent payments, false entries and misleading statements or omissions in accounting records." Under the heading "Employment Practices," the company says it will not tolerate "behavior that fosters an environment of harassment or 'jokes' based on physical or cultural differences." (That zero-toleration policy is explicitly extended to suppliers.)

After each major category, the reader is asked to report violations of the company's standards. And the last sentence (all in capital letters in the booklet) reinforces that request: "The company will not tolerate any action against any person who, in good faith, reports known or suspected violations of the law or these worldwide standards of conduct."

All Campbell employees are expected to have read and understood the standards booklet. Each year, the directors, officers, and key employees of the company must sign a statement of compliance with the standards.

The promulgation of values can't guarantee that an organization's workforce will behave appropriately. It will, however, at the very least, put employees on notice that the organization won't countenance illegal or inappropriate behavior, and that it expects them to be vigilant in helping to prevent it. That is what Campbell Soup set out to accomplish, and it succeeded admirably.

What Comes Next

As this chapter suggests, the place of the corporate culture in the firmament of management practices has risen to the first rank. The Evergreen Project demonstrated that it was in the four practices that all Winners excelled. In the next chapter, we consider the fourth and final primary practice in our 4+2 formula, organization structure. There the emphasis is not so much on feelings and motivations, but on hard decisions about how the elements of an enterprise should fit together. Part of the answer provided by the Evergreen research can be deduced from the chapter's title: "Make Your Organization Fast and Flat."

7

Make Your Organization
Fast and Flat

Theoretically, there is nothing wrong with bureaucracy *per se*. Some procedures and protocols—which is what bureaucracy is all about, after all—are absolutely necessary to the smooth functioning of any large organization. But there is such a thing as having too much of a good thing. When an excess of bureaucracy puts roadblocks in the way of progress, when it dampens employees' enthusiasm and leaches away their energy, it becomes a clear and present danger to business success.

Superfluous bureaucracy is a tax on the value your employees create. It leads to impatience, which eventually devolves into an unhappy acceptance, which, in turn, breeds indolence.

The Evergreen Project found that excellence in the structure management practice was one of the four primary distinguishing marks of Winners—and that they were dedicated to trimming away every possible vestige of unnecessary bureaucracy. It was a full-time job.

In every business there is a natural drift toward complexity.

The urge to add permanent new rules and procedures to existing processes reflects a desire to quick-freeze current results. It can also reflect a manager's desire to fix his or her control of the process in concrete. Winners are aware of this bureaucratic drift and have established systems to prevent it.

The insurance company USAA calls this discipline "painting the bridge." Once you finish painting a bridge, prudent maintenance requires that you go back to the other side and start painting it all over again. So it is with bureaucracy: once you examine all of the core processes of the company and scrape off the bureaucratic barnacles, it is time to return to the first one and begin again. Otherwise, processes become more and more complex.

One company that is dedicated to maintaining a tight ship, structurally speaking, is Nucor, a manufacturer of steel and steel products based in Charlotte, North Carolina. Its lean management structure and highly decentralized operations have helped turn this one-time "niche" operator into one of the nation's largest steel producers. Nucor is the principal corporate example examined in this chapter; the structure practices of Home Depot, Campbell Soup, The Limited, and Teradyne are also explored.

As was often the case, the Evergreen Project cast cold water on some traditional views as to what distinguishes successful companies from unsuccessful ones. The project found that there was no particular structure that separated Winners from the rest. Whether the structural elements of a company were organized according to function or geography or product made little difference. By the same token, it did not matter much whether or not a winning company gave its business units profit-and-loss responsibility or if new businesses could adopt structures and processes distinct from the corporate norm.

Like the other Winners, Nucor adhered to three organizational mandates: Eliminate redundant organizational layers and bureaucratic structures and behaviors; promote cooperation and the ex-

7.1 Organization: Winners *versus* Losers

	Rated poorly	Rated highly
1. Eliminate redundant organizational layers and bureaucratic structures and behaviors. Simplify, simplify, simplify.	40 (Losers) / 19 (Winners)	40 (Losers) / 67 (Winners)
2. Promote cooperation and the exchange of information across the whole company.	37 (Losers) / 18 (Winners)	35 (Losers) / 60 (Winners)
3. Put your best people closest to the action and keep your frontline stars in place.	52 (Losers) / 17 (Winners)	27 (Losers) / 67 (Winners)

Losers ▢   Winners ▪

Percent of companies

This chart shows how Winners and Losers performed in terms of the three mandates of the structure management practice. Sixty-seven percent of the Winners, for example, had high ratings on their ability to minimize bureaucracy and simplify their structures. In the worst showing in relation to this practice, 52 percent of losing companies rated poorly in fulfilling the mandate to focus talent on the front line.

Note: A poor rating equals 1 or 2 and a high rating equals 4 or 5 on a 5-point scale with a score of 3 being average. Some mandates and their scores are the composite of several survey items. The percentages do not add up to 100% because companies with average scores are not included. Losers include the scores of all companies in losing periods and Winners, the scores of all companies in winning periods. The differences between Losers and Winners are statistically significant at the 95% confidence level.

Source: Evergreen team analysis.

change of information across the whole company; put your best people closest to the action and keep your frontline stars in place.

Before we move on to analyze these in detail, though, let's take a look at Nucor and its path to success.

Properly speaking, the company had its genesis back at the dawn of the U.S. auto industry with one Ransom E. Olds, who, in 1901, turned out the nation's first mass-produced car, the Oldsmobile. Three years later, Olds left the company he had founded and started another, the Reo Car Company, in Lansing, Michigan. Eventually, a division of Reo merged with a company called Nuclear Consultants, forming the Nuclear Corporation of America, and in 1962 Nuclear bought a manufacturer of steel joists named Vulcraft.

Under the leadership of F. Kenneth Iverson, Vulcraft was making a profit, while Nuclear was operating in the red. In 1964, facing bankruptcy, Nuclear named Iverson president. He moved the headquarters to Charlotte, North Carolina, and dumped half of Nuclear's businesses. Steel would be the new focus, and that called for a new company name: Nucor. Within two years, the company, under Iverson, was in the black, and he proceeded to move beyond steel fabrication into steel production.

But rather than follow in the footsteps of the big integrated companies, which started steel production with iron ore and coal, Iverson, a metallurgist by training, bet his company's future on a new technology, the mini-mill. These plants start out with metal scrap and use electrical furnaces to convert it to steel. The big steelmakers could not come close to matching Nucor's low production costs and prices, and Nucor gradually took over a major share of the market for low-end items such as I-beams and decking.

In 1989, Iverson once again bet on a new technology, the thin-slab process, in order to move Nucor into the more lucrative field of flat-rolled steel, which is used in auto parts. In the traditional plant, individual ten-inch-thick slabs of steel were reheated and put through rollers again and again to bring them down to a one-inch thickness. The thin-slab approach was based upon a continuous process that turned out two-inch-thick slabs that were slimmed down by just four rollers. Nucor realized major savings in terms of energy and labor, giving it a 20 percent cost advantage over the integrated companies.

By 1994, Nucor had grown into an important force in its industry with sixteen operating facilities in eight states, more than $2 billion in sales, and some 6,000 employees. The company's willingness to try new technical approaches played a big role in that progress as Nucor invaded virtually every area of steel production during the Evergreen decade. Just as vital, however, were the company's employee strategies and policies, which were distinctly not in the mainstream. Its employees, for example, were insistently non-union; Nucor built its plants in rural areas, where people tend to have low wages, a strong work ethic, and an antipathy toward unions.

Half or more of Nucor's mill employees' salaries came from bonuses based on performance. Under the bonus system, a group of people engaged in a complete task, such as the rolling team in a thin-slab operation, is given a standard—say, a certain number of good-quality tons of steel rolled per week. The members of the group are paid extra each week depending upon the degree to which the group exceeds that standard, and there is no roof on how much extra they can receive.

However, during economic downturns, which come with some regularity due to the cyclical nature of the construction industry, everyone in the company is subject to a program called "Share the Pain." It calls for a pay reduction of 20 to 25 percent for hourly employees. For department heads, the cut is 35 to 40 percent, while it can reach 70 percent for company officers. Nucor never laid off an employee for lack of work during the period of the Evergreen study, and the "Share the Pain" program made that possible.

There will be more on Nucor's inner workings in the pages just ahead, as we move on to a discussion of the mandates of the structure practice.

**Eliminate redundant organizational layers
and bureaucratic structures and behaviors.
Simplify, simplify, simplify.**

Simplifying the structure of a company yields many benefits, not least the ability to make decisions rapidly. Too often, promising ideas get hung up in bureaucratic traffic, slowly inching their way from desk to desk. By the time the idea is approved, the opportunity may have passed, or been seized upon by a competitor.

Winners consider ideas speedily, setting reasonable limits to deliberations. They are able to do so, as the Evergreen survey research showed, because they have kept the layers of bureaucracy to a minimum.

There is an added advantage to maintaining a trim, fast-decision structure. Because these companies have not invested so much time and management energy committing to an idea, they have an easier time reversing course if necessary. When a decision carries a heavy bureaucratic freight, there is a tendency toward what has been called "escalating commitment to a course of action," and that can all too easily lead to a tumble.

Nucor: *All of management in four layers*

During the Evergreen period of study, Nucor was the epitome of a trim organization. The usual management trappings and personnel department activities had been pared to the bone. In that regard, the whole company philosophy could be summed up in a phrase: less is more.

A visitor to the headquarters of this billion-dollar operation back in 1991 wasn't long in getting the message. The office was in rented space on the fourth floor of a building on the outskirts of Charlotte, with no sign to announce its presence. The entire corporate staff, secretaries to chief executive, comprised just twenty people.

At Nucor, there were just four layers of management, as compared to nine or more at the major steel companies. The Nucor four: foremen, department heads, plant managers, and president/chief executive. That streamlined structure, in turn, was possible only because of the power and responsibility that CEO Ken Iverson and his aides pushed down the line to the plant managers and on to the foremen and frontline people. Before the idea of managers as coaches became part of the consultants' lexicon, Nucor was actually putting it into action.

In an interview with *HR Magazine* in 1994, James M. Coblin, manager of personnel services, put it this way: "We tell managers we don't want you to manage anything, we don't want you to call a meeting, we don't want you to write letters, we don't want you to copy people."

Managers were expected to be available to frontline teams to answer questions and provide support and resources as requested—and wait for the teams to ask for help, since the teams themselves were assumed to be ready and able to resolve most problems. Managers were told to "lead by staying out of the way." And like the coaches in Major League Baseball or the National Football League, the managers either got along with their teams (their "players") or had to look for new ones.

Jim Coblin cited an example of a manager operating as coach. There was a mysterious rash of lost hard hats among members of the melting crew at a certain plant, and someone discovered that local teenagers had suddenly taken to wearing Nucor hard hats.

The plant manager thought it no coincidence, but he did not mention his suspicions when he called in three members of the melting crew on a Friday afternoon. He talked about the missing hats, pointed out that they were expensive, and asked his visitors to solve the problem by Monday. As they were leaving, he added, "Think about it real hard because whatever you tell me, that's going to be the rule at this plant for as long as I'm general manager."

On Monday, the crew members offered their solution: the company would henceforth provide new employees with hard hats, but after that, when employees needed another, they would have to pay for it. "That's the toughest hard-hat rule anywhere at Nucor," Coblin said. "If you coach employees and let them make decisions, they will be tougher on themselves than any manager would ever dream of being."

Nucor was impatient with anything that hinted of bureaucracy or show business. "We don't have a mission statement," Iverson said in an interview with *Management Review* in 1992, "because most of them amount to a tribute to motherhood. Most employees don't know what it is or what it means." Anyone who wants to know Nucor's mission, he added, need simply ask an employee.

Job descriptions were something else Nucor had no time for. "They tell you what you cannot do," Iverson said. I don't want to limit people that way." In addition, he thought that job descriptions wasted a lot of time and produced nothing but paperwork. Worse, they quickly went out of date. In other words, better no job description than a wrong one.

Regular performance appraisals were also frowned upon at Nucor. Documenting poor performance made sense, but why waste staff time documenting the overwhelming majority of employees who were doing a good job, and why take up those employees' time going over the appraisals? Aside from being useless, Coblin said, "I give it an A-plus on its ability to raise the tension level and to be a topic for gossip and divisiveness."

Nucor's ways of simplifying operations may not be right for every company, but they surely provide food for thought. The results in terms of efficiencies and performance have been impressive. The same could be said for the steps taken by Campbell Soup's David Johnson after he became CEO in 1990.

Campbell Soup: *An end to fiefdoms*

Like so many old, family-owned institutions before it, Campbell was riddled with independent fiefdoms. These silos were armed and dangerous, veteran bureaucratic battlers that had, over time, developed their own ways of doing things and fought off any sort of change or innovation as a matter of principle. Their motto: don't rock the boat.

The company's product divisions such as Swanson frozen foods, Pepperidge Farm baked goods, and Franco-American pastas and sauces went their own ways, with little or no concern about—or input from—corporate headquarters. But within months of his arrival, Johnson declared war on the entrenched bureaucracy, shifting individuals and assignments. Managers who failed to live up to his rigorous performance standards were let go, and that included quite a few executives who had been resting on their laurels for decades.

Among the principles Johnson brought to Campbell Soup was a passion for simple, straightforward, consumer-oriented structure. That soon became evident throughout the company, particularly in the Campbell North American division run by Herbert M. Baum. Within months of Johnson's arrival, Baum was erasing the traditional business-units organization built around the individual brands—Swanson, Godiva Chocolatier, Vlasic pickles, Mrs. Paul's seafood, and Pepperidge Farm—and replacing it with an organization geared to consumer-focused markets, which he called "sectors." The six sectors were soup, convenience meals, fresh foods, grocery, condiments, and Campbell Canada. Each sector had its own sales planning, promotion, and financial personnel.

As Baum described the workings of his new, Johnson-inspired organization to *Food & Beverage Marketing* in August of 1990, it enabled the sector directors to concentrate on pushing their particular brands in the marketplace, without direct responsibility for such operations as manufacturing and logistics. The directors could weigh in on those matters through what were known as "centers of competence" attached to the various non-sales operations.

The goal was to focus Campbell far more closely on winning brands. Losing or marginal products, which the company had been introducing at a feverish rate over the previous decade, were pared down. Johnson wanted the company's resources spent in the areas of its core strengths because, he insisted, that was where profitability would lie. And as the events of the next year demonstrated, he was right on target.

Baum's new-look organization was also flatter than its predecessor, with just ten directors reporting to him instead of the previous twenty-three. The number of levels between the highest and lowest echelons was reduced to four.

Another part of the Johnson canon was his insistence on simplifying the structure to allow people to work at what they did best. In 1987, Campbell Soup had created the position of "category general manager." The intent was to give marketers a chance to become generalists—that is, to run all aspects of a category, including acquisitions, finance, and manufacturing.

In some ways, the move was a success. The general managers' management skills improved, and operating costs were cut. But it soon became evident that they were spending less and less time and energy on the areas of their greatest talent, namely building brands and marketing.

"I began to see them coming to me and talking about variable fill weights and statistical process controls," said Herb Baum, "things that people in the plants were far better equipped to manage. We began to drift in terms of consumer marketing, because we were making financial people out of them."

So the position of category general manager disappeared. The responsibility for marketing decisions was given to the marketing manager, and the financial decisions went to the business manager. With everyone concentrating on what they knew best, the company's performance level quickly rose—and so did its profitability.

Johnson's insistence on simplifying and rationalizing the corporate structure was not confined to others. Within a year after he took over as chief executive, he had trimmed the number of managers reporting directly to him from fourteen to eight.

Promote cooperation and the exchange of information across the whole company.

Even when a company is not held hostage by independent fiefdoms—the silos of longtime privilege occupied by staffers jealous of their prerogatives and turf—it can suffer from boundary problems. Particularly in large businesses, where divisions and departments within divisions compete for limited corporate resources, there is a strong temptation to circle the wagons. Technical discoveries and best practices are held close to the vest. Why help other divisions look better in the eyes of top management?

The same sort of information hoarding is too often encountered on the front line, where loyalty to a team or a section within a department can run high. In that case, however, the major reason tends to be more emotional than tactical. The us-versus-them feelings can develop around an especially popular foreman, or they simply reflect the competitive, macho level in the work environment.

Wherever and however the impenetrable boundaries come to pass, they pose a clear danger to the performance of the company as a whole. As the Evergreen research demonstrated, many Winners spend considerable time and energy on meeting the terms of this mandate, establishing programs to open up the boundaries and get divisions and departments cooperating and exchanging information.

In some companies, staff members are specifically assigned to perform that function, acting as a kind of human sponge, absorbing news of corporate-wide value on their rounds of the departments. As discussed in chapter 4, Target has a system in place to monitor the reaction of customers to new fashions in the company's upscale department store division; it gives Target a head start on knocking off the latest styles. No boundary problems there.

In other organizations, regular meetings are scheduled at which the heads of divisions or departments are called together by top management to exchange ideas. That happens at The Limited, as we observe below. It does not happen at Nucor.

Nucor: *Walk the shop floor*

Meetings were not Ken Iverson's style. He gave the division and department managers responsibility for running the business, and since cooperation and sharing among the divisions and departments were in the best interest of the company as a whole, the managers were expected to find ways to make that happen— formally, informally, whatever. They, in turn, could rely on the loyalty of the frontline people, and their willingness—eagerness, even—to contribute to Nucor's financial well-being. "What Nucor management has been able to do," *Iron Age New Steel* commented in 1995, "is get its workers to identify their own interests fundamentally with those of management."

The closest thing Nucor had to a human sponge was Iverson himself. He made regular tours of the divisions, where, given his metallurgical training, he was a knowledgeable listener. Division and plant managers were also expected to be out in the shop on a regular basis, not just listening to problems but also keeping an eye out for technical developments or new best practices that might have wider application throughout the company.

Campbell Soup: *Coordinate or cash out*

When David Johnson came to Campbell Soup, its divisions made no effort to exchange ideas or share resources; a tomato-paste plant in California, for example, never bothered to make its technology available to a tomato-paste plant in Mexico.

In fact, the divisions were more likely to compete than cooperate. On one occasion, the soup company actually ran a joint marketing promotion with Nabisco crackers, unaware (or unconcerned) that Pepperidge Farm was trying to sell its own brand of crackers.

Johnson insisted on a high level of knowledge-sharing and cross-fertilization among the various departments and divisions, and he served notice that the parochialism of the fiefdoms would no longer be countenanced. He insisted that every division had to have a representative at every corporate meeting, a drastic change.

"He will not for a minute tolerate turf," said Herbert M. Baum, the chief executive of Campbell North America, adding, "and this place had walls." Johnson never stopped trying to flatten those walls.

The Limited: *Decentralization's dangers*

When last met, in the chapter on the strategy practice, The Limited and its founder, Leslie Wexner, had joined the ranks of the

Tumblers. The distinct identities of each of its stores had been lost, along with their customers. The company had grown so big so fast that it had outrun its management structure.

In the beginning, there had been good and sufficient reason to give the leaders of the different store divisions their head. The fashion world, after all, is built on creativity, which requires and thrives on freedom. Once Wexner had kicked off a new division, with all of the obsessive attention to detail that he was famous for, he handed the reins over and turned to the next challenge. But over time, as the different divisions took hold and grew prosperous, they lost their edge. Instead of relying on the suppliers and their savvy nose for fashion trends, store executives made style decisions; bureaucracies slowed down the company's ability to react rapidly to fashion changes.

As Wexner told *Fortune* in 1994, in a most diplomatic manner, "I believe in entrepreneurship, but we went too far in decentralizing the businesses. I essentially said to the presidents of the various divisions, 'You'll figure things out.' We didn't give them enough support."

The "support" took the form of a new organizational structure and new management disciplines. Among the latter was a monthly meeting at which the leaders of the divisions talked over common problems and shared ideas. Before, the divisions had been suspicious of each other, seldom sharing information or anything else. In some cases, as noted earlier, they had actually been in competition with each other.

Grace Nichols, who headed up Victoria's Secret, described the problem for *Fortune:* "In the past, we would never say to another president, 'I know you're having problems. Here's what I did when I encountered that.' We didn't know each other well enough. Now, I think we're starting to feel more comfortable in sharing our views."

**Put your best people closest to the action and keep
your frontline stars in place.**

Businesspeople of a few decades ago would surely have scratched their heads over this mandate. The notion that your best workers should be pushed down toward the trenches, rather than up toward the top of the chain of command, would seem wrong-headed. Yet the Evergreen research found that most winning companies followed this mandate. The stark contrast between the old view and the new is one measure of the revolution that has overtaken management thinking in recent years.

How is it possible that successful companies would place such emphasis on the front lines? Why do they want to put their most promising people in operating rather than staff positions? These companies are simply following through on their conviction that their futures rest not on the brilliance of their executives but on the dedication and inventiveness of their managers and employees. To tap their potential, to free them to create and innovate, Winners have restructured themselves, cutting away levels of command, banishing bureaucracy, all in the interest of getting leaner and faster and frontline-driven.

How seriously are the companies committed to their frontline-first policies? They not only move their stars toward the action, they also strive mightily to keep their best frontline people in place.

Nucor: *Saying yes to new ideas*

As noted above, Nucor has been a devout advocate of pushing the decision-making power and responsibility downward through the organization. Its infinitesimal headquarters staff sends a message: there isn't all that much work that needs doing at the top. The paucity of management layers sends another message: we want to cut the distance between us in management and you on the front line. We're here to serve you so you can serve the company better.

For managers, Nucor offers the ultimate challenge—the chance to run their own show with minimal interference from above. But that's not the only attraction. Managers are encouraged to come up with new ideas, and then encouraged to try them.

Iverson sometimes would give a talk entitled "Good Managers Make Bad Decisions." "When somebody makes a bad decision when he's tried something new," he explained, "to say that is negative is wrong. You should congratulate the employee on trying something new." Even though he may think an idea won't work, Iverson added, "we almost never say no. You want people to generate ideas."

As with their frontline people, a major share of managers' incomes came in the form of performance bonuses. In the case of department heads, for example, bonuses were geared to the profitability of their divisions. For the eager, hungry manager, that offered not only an opportunity to excel, but to get rich doing it. And if the company's profits dwindled in a given year, the manager had the consolation of knowing that the executives were taking an even bigger hit.

All things considered, the Nucor structure both moved talented managers into the hot seat and made it worth their while to stay there.

For frontline employees, too, there were special inducements to get them to remain in place. As long as Nucor did well, and its teams performed well, the bonus system would provide them with far more take-home pay than their counterparts in nearby towns. And their jobs were secure, even when other steelmakers were laying people off.

The egalitarian culture represented another major attraction. "Some companies give lip service to the idea," Iverson said, "but we really make an effort to eliminate the distinction between a management person and anybody else who works for the company."

All employees, top management included, had the same health-care program, the same holidays, and the same amount of vacation. There was no executive dining room (Iverson entertained luncheon visitors at a delicatessen across from headquarters), no reserved parking spaces. There were no company cars, airplanes, or boats, and everyone traveled economy class.

A story Iverson would often tell reveals a lot about him, his company's employee philosophy, and the reasons why frontline people tend to stay.

In the 1980s, Iverson decided that in the interest of equality, all employees should wear the same color hard hat in the plants. In many steel companies, blue hats were for workers, white for foremen, green for department heads, and gold for the president.

An exception had to be made for maintenance personnel, he acknowledged, since they have to be easy to spot in a steel mill; they were given yellow hats, but everyone else wore green.

Not everyone was happy with the decision. "I got letters from foremen saying, 'You can't do this to me. My white hat is my authority. I put it on the back shelf of my car when I go home, and everybody knows I am a foreman at Nucor.'"

Many companies would have ignored the complaints. Nucor put together a series of discussions around the idea that your authority does not derive from the color of your hat but from your leadership qualities.

Nucor's personnel policies are often tough-minded. Arrive at work fifteen minutes late and you lose your production bonus for the day. If you are thirty minutes or more late, you lose your bonus for the week. If production stops because a machine breaks down, workers are not paid for that time—they are held responsible for its maintenance. Workers who are out sick for less than three days are not paid.

Such rules are part of the company's obsession with speed and productivity. But they were also a reflection of Iverson's overall philosophy: "We give the worker the training, and furnish the equipment, and then, in a real sense, the team is in business for itself." For frontline workers, that is part of the challenge that helps keep them on the front line.

Home Depot: *HQ keeps hands off*

A similar focus on the front line has been a hallmark of Home Depot since its founding—the front line, in this case, being the individual stores. Authority and responsibility were pushed down-ward, away from headquarters, and the best people worked close to the action. The organizational structure supported that philos-ophy. As of 1995, the company had five divisions serving geo-graphical regions in the United States, based in California, Florida, New Jersey, Illinois, and Georgia. Many of the functions normally handled on the corporate level such as training, buying, and mer-chandising were given over to the divisions. For example, there was no central buying—the merchandising group within each division did the job based on the circumstances in its particular market.

But even the divisional officers were expected to provide support, rather than dictate to, the store managers. It was up to the managers, founder Arthur Blank said, to make sure "we're priced right, we're assorted right, we're doing all the correct things we need to do." Store managers ordered the product, most of which was shipped directly to them from vendors. If managers wanted to try out a major new display or marketing idea, they cleared it not with headquarters in Atlanta but with their division.

The ambitious among the best and brightest at Home Depot have always understood that an assignment to the corporate staff is not necessarily the optimal route to the top. The company wants them running stores and divisions, where the action is.

To hold on to its frontline stars, Home Depot has relied in large measure on its performance-based culture (described in chapter 6). The rallies, the cheers, the community work—they give associates a powerful incentive to continue working with their team. The company also binds employees with a program that rewards them with shares of company stock.

Teradyne: *A taste for teamwork*

Another company that put a premium on jobs close to the action was Teradyne, the maker of automatic test equipment (discussed in chapter 4). After years spent going its own way, with little attention paid to customers, Teradyne reinvented itself and its culture.

Among the changes was the decentralization of the company's sales and service organizations to move them nearer to the product lines. Before, customers had to go through several layers of bureaucracy to get their products serviced. "I would kill half a day to persuade them over the telephone that the machine was really broken," one Teradyne customer said. "Now when you call, somebody is on your floor in fifteen or twenty minutes."

By giving responsibility for customer relationships to local sales managers, the company made its intentions clear. The action that counted most, now, was no longer in the lab or the boardroom, but wherever the customer was. And the company proceeded to assign its best people as close as possible to that action.

The reinvention of Teradyne also included the introduction of special teams to the operation. That was commonplace among Winners and Climbers in the Evergreen study. Aside from the greater efficiencies achieved with teams, companies like Nucor, Home Depot, and Teradyne understood that the feelings of friendship and loyalty that develop among team members can go far in keeping top-notch frontline employees from wandering.

What Comes Next

This chapter on the structure management practice completes the in-depth discussion of the four primary practices that every Winner and Climber subscribed to: strategy, operations, culture, and structure. In the chapters to come, we move on to explore the four secondary practices, at least two of which were followed by every Winner and Climber. The four are: talent, leadership, innovation, and mergers and partnerships.

We start with the talent practice, the topic of the next chapter. There you will find policies followed by many of the top companies in the Evergreen survey in their endeavor to "make talent stick around and develop more."

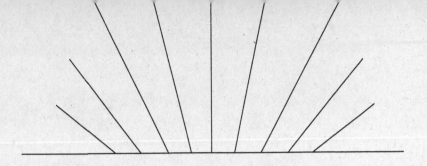

PART 3

The 2 in 4+2:
Secondary Practices

8

Make Talent Stick Around and Develop More

The talent management practice is the first of the four secondary ones in the 4+2 formula for sustainable business success. The Evergreen Project found that Winners succeeded by excelling in at least two of the four secondary practices, in addition to all four of the primary ones. It also discovered that the Winners' commitment to those secondary practices was every bit as intense and purposeful as their focus on the four primary practices.

About half of the Winners excelled in the talent practice, and these companies dedicated major resources, human and financial, to building an effective, innovative workforce and management team. They also showed a distinct preference for developing their own stars from inside the organization and an ability to retain their top talent.

During each five-year period of the study, Winners, in general, lost an average of thirty-five members of their executive team; Losers lost an average of fifty-six. Winners hired outside chief executives half as frequently as did Losers. The difference between those Winners who excelled in the talent practice and the Losers was even greater.

Why the discrepancy? It seems clear that Winners were far more cognizant of the value of talented, committed employees in creating a high-performance organization. They understood that these attributes are best nurtured by providing employees with broad educational and training opportunities—and that once an outstanding talent pool is in place, they would be able to follow a policy of promoting from within.

At a time when business increasingly relies on mid-level and frontline employees for greater initiative both as innovators and decision makers, employees' attitudes toward their jobs, their supervisors, and the company as a whole have become a matter of major concern to management.

"Workers today expect their jobs themselves to be meaningful," Ken Iverson, CEO of steelmaker Nucor, wrote in a 1993 article in *Planning Review.* "They expect to participate in decisions, particularly those concerning the work they perform. They expect to know where the company is going and how it expects to get there. If management does not develop programs that satisfy those expectations, the company will not be successful in the long run."

The existence of a talent-rich environment also tends to attract able people from outside a company. No organization can have too much talent, and Winners pursued it outside as well as inside their ranks, even though new hires tend to be more expensive. In so doing, they rejected the false premise that companies must choose between promoting from within and hiring outside talent. Winning companies did both. By the same token, they ignored the false dichotomy between a high-performance culture and "being good to our people." Once again, they did both.

The Evergreen study downgraded some talent practices and achievements that are often presented as being essential to corporate success. The quality of the human-resource staff, for example, and the existence of fast-track management development programs, formal mentoring programs, or 360-degree performance review systems were not significant determinants in creating a winning organization.

Companies in the Evergreen study that stood out on talent management demonstrated special skill in satisfying four mandates: they filled mid-level and high-level jobs with strong inside talent whenever possible; they created and maintained top-of-the-line training and educational programs; they designed jobs that intrigued and challenged their best performers; and their managements were intimately involved in developing and finding new talent.

Fill mid- and high-level jobs with internal talent whenever possible.

Question: What do talented employees and loyal customers have in common?

8.1 Talent: Winners *versus* Losers

	Losers ▥		Winners ▨	
	Percent of companies			
	Rated poorly		**Rated highly**	
1. Fill mid- and high-level jobs with internal talent whenever possible.	56	11	20	77
2. Create and maintain top-of-the-line training and educational programs.	50	13	21	75
3. Design jobs that will intrigue and challenge your best performers.	47	14	25	71
4. Become personally involved in winning the war for talent.	48	17	30	73

This chart shows how Winners and Losers parted company in their performance on the four mandates of the talent management practice. For example, 77 percent of winning companies won high ratings for filling mid- and high-level jobs with internal talent. But on that mandate, 56 percent of losing companies rated poorly.

Note: A poor rating equals 1 or 2 and a high rating equals 4 or 5 on a 5-point scale with a score of 3 being average. Some mandates and their scores are the composite of several survey items. The percentages do not add up to 100% because companies with average scores are not included. Losers include the scores of all companies in losing periods and Winners, the scores of all companies in winning periods. The differences between Losers and Winners are statistically significant at the 95% confidence level.

Source: Evergreen team analysis.

Answer: It pays to hang on to them, because they can be awfully difficult to replace.

Some organizations that will go to almost any lengths to retain a customer are unwilling to expend remotely the same energy to hold on to a skilled, seasoned manager. Often, there is a sense of hurt or even anger on the part of the manager's superiors that he or she would even consider leaving.

As the Evergreen research made clear, winning companies don't take that tack. They devote major resources to preserving in-house talent and developing their own stars. It is so much cheaper than going out into the marketplace and buying stars, particularly since you have no way of really being sure what you have bought. Talented people already under your roof are a known quantity.

Valspar: *Making room to move up*

One corporation that has a strong commitment to filling job openings from within is Valspar, a paint and coatings producer based in Minneapolis. This organization, which traces its origins back to 1806, has a remarkably broad portfolio of products, ranging from decorative and protective coatings for wood, metal, and plastic in industrial markets to inks for rigid packaging containers to automotive refinishers. It has 6,500 employees in more than eighty locations worldwide, and its track record has been impressive. As of 1996, the end of the Evergreen period of study, Valspar's return to shareholders had grown at an average rate of 30 percent for fifteen years.

Much of the corporation's growth over the last few decades has come from a string of acquisitions, more than twenty-five in all, that were diverse enough to make Valspar recession-resistant. Details as to the strategy and tactics followed by the company's longtime chief executive, Angus Wurtele, will be presented later, in the chapter on the merger practice, but one point needs to be raised here: when it makes an acquisition, Valspar does not act like a holding company, leaving the newcomer to its own devices. Rather, it merges the purchased organization's facilities and technology into the parent's operation. "Most important," as one Valspar executive put it, "we integrate key people from the new company's management. There is no clique from the original company. We're all part of a team."

That policy raised a potential problem for talented parent corporation people, whose promotions might well have been held back by the arrival of senior employees from all those acquired organizations. Partly in response to that situation, partly to increase its coatings market share, Valspar has combined its acquisition efforts with a major program to achieve internal growth.

"Acquisition by itself is not healthy," Bob Pajors, the company president, told *Corporate Report Minnesota* in 1989. "People will not be satisfied without internal growth. Employees have to know that there's a place for them to move up, too."

Schering-Plough: *An inside bias*

Another longtime proponent of filling job openings with existing employees is Schering-Plough, an impressive Evergreen study Winner, with headquarters located, appropriately enough, on Galloping Hill Road in Kenilworth, New Jersey. Originally the U.S. subsidiary of Schering AG, a German pharmaceutical and chemical company, Schering was nationalized by the U.S. government in both World Wars I and II, finally becoming a private,

U.S.-based company in 1952. Its 1971 merger with Plough, a consumer-products manufacturer based in Germany, led to a fourfold increase in sales over the next decade. Before and during the first period covered by the Evergreen Project, Schering was an active acquirer of disparate companies, but by 1992 its pharmaceutical division was turning out such a flood of successful products—and requiring such a large financial investment—that the company decided to sell off its electroplating, industrial chemicals, and natural-substances divisions and concentrate on drugs.

There was one set of acquisitions, however, that Schering never turned its back on. Earlier than most of its competitors, Schering management recognized the potential importance of biotechnology for the drug field. The expertise it gained from its purchases in this area have borne rich fruit, making possible some of its most successful products.

Today, Schering's main areas of research include allergic and inflammatory disorders (its best-selling product is Claritin), cancer, and cardiovascular disease. It has 30,000 employees around the world, many of whom have been with the company more than thirty years, and that is no accident. Schering works at keeping them, in part, by helping their careers along.

Between 75 and 80 percent of Schering's vacancies are filled from inside. As the company's website puts it: "We make strong efforts to fill open positions with qualified internal candidates." Job opportunities are posted and described on the site and potential candidates are urged to submit a job bid. And to keep its people moving upward, Schering expects supervisors to meet at least once a year with their team members to formally discuss work performance and the possibilities of job advancement.

Create and maintain top-of-the-line training and educational programs.

It is all well and good for companies to proclaim their intention to promote from within, but the promise is meaningless unless they offer the training that can prepare employees for promotion and then encourage them to enroll.

The growing importance accorded promotion-oriented training and education represents a sea change in management attitudes. It was once assumed that upwardly striving employees were totally responsible for preparing themselves for higher-level positions, and many companies still hold to that view. But as managers and frontline people have been given more authority and responsibility, worker continuity and company loyalty have taken on far greater importance.

Schering-Plough provides a host of educational opportunities. It offers 90 percent tuition reimbursement for relevant undergraduate and graduate courses. Its training programs range from sales to management, with special classes in language, math, and secretarial skills, for example. More than 2,000 employees a year take courses in production practices.

Employees who have bonded with the organization are far more likely to give their best efforts to their jobs. And the company that helps employees rise through the ranks, supplying training and educational assistance as needed, is well positioned to be bonded with.

Flowers: *A step toward management*

At Flowers Industries, a *Fortune* 500 baking company, the sense of continuity and company loyalty is strong at all levels of the organization.

Flowers Industries was founded in 1919 by two brothers, Joseph and William Flowers, in the south Georgia town of Thomasville. They and their children presided over a steady corporate expansion, acquiring and creating bakeries throughout the Southeast. Major and continuing investments in technology have made its dozens of facilities among the industry's most efficient. The company turns out hamburger buns for Burger King and private-label breads for Kroger and Winn-Dixie, snacks for vending machines and wholesale-club retailers, and frozen goods that are marketed across the country. Its brand names include Cobblestone Mill, Nature's Own, and Mrs. Smith's.

Flowers is long on tradition and loyalty. "I think the average tenure here of the management team is something like twenty-three years," said C. Maxtin Wood III, a company executive during the years of the Evergreen study. "That gives us a spirit of trust and compatibility, a sense of direction and teamwork, that I don't think can be matched anywhere in the industry." And that teamwork permeates the whole company, he explained, partly because it gives employees the chance to improve their skills and their jobs.

Aside from the more usual training and educational offerings, two of the company's programs suggest how committed it has been to giving employees a boost.

The first was designed to provide workers in their modern,

high-tech baking plants with detailed knowledge about all the operations and equipment on the production line. The program prepares them to become baking technicians, who focus on improving operations rather than simply laboring on the line.

"Here is a person who has been selected and trained, who is highly motivated and well compensated, and here is the first step toward management on the operations side," Wood said. "The next step up the ladder is management."

Under the second program, Flowers sold its delivery routes to workers who had the requisite training and experience, not to mention the financial wherewithal (though the company offered lenient payback terms).

"Here is the opportunity to own your own business, be as creative as you want with that business, and to create as much money as you possibly can for your family," Wood explained. The independent distributor system represented the ultimate in giving employees a leg up.

Seagate: *Teaching Thais to take over*

At Seagate Technology, the world's largest manufacturer of disk drives, the company underwrites the full tuition cost for employees taking work-related college courses; about 40 percent of the total workforce is enrolled. Seagate also offers its own courses—the usual assortment on topics like management development and computer training, and a few more esoteric, like cross-cultural management and English. That is because a majority of Seagate's employees work in manufacturing plants outside the country, in Singapore, Thailand, and Malaysia, not to mention Scotland and

Ireland. As of 1996, the end of the Evergreen decade, the company had 21,500 assembly-line people and 5,500 support people in Thailand alone. (In the United States, employees are scattered around six research-and-development centers in addition to the corporate headquarters in Scotts Valley, California.)

The disk-drive business is known as the "extreme sport" of the technology industry. Once or twice a year, new discoveries ratchet up the amount of information disks can hold, antiquating current models and sending their prices plummeting. (Seagate lately boasts a drive capable of storing information equal to what you would find in a stack of typed pages three times the height of the Empire State Building.) To make those discoveries, disk companies like Seagate must employ thousands of technical experts in fields ranging from physics and fluid mechanics to information theory and aerodynamics. At the same time, because of the price swings, disk companies must be able to cut costs to the bone and keep cutting if they are to compete successfully.

On the domestic front, Seagate must provide the training and educational support that its technical people demand on their way up the corporate ladder. Overseas, to keep host countries friendly, Seagate established elaborate training and mentoring programs to prepare local workers to take over managerial and management roles. Every year, the company brings hundreds of overseas workers to one or another company site in the United States, where they spend months being trained in production techniques for new products.

The process of preparing these employees for higher-level

jobs was well advanced in 1996 as Pornchai Piemsomboon, a Seagate vice president in charge of a plant in Thailand, made ready to open another. "When I first came to set up the Teparuk plant," he said, "we had fifteen expatriate staff. That's down to four now." At the new plant, he added, there would be just one staff member from outside Thailand. By investing in its international workforce, Seagate has been able to attract and retain the best talent across the globe.

**Design jobs that will intrigue
and challenge your best performers.**

When George Allen became the head coach of the Los Angeles Rams in 1966, the team had gone through seven straight losing seasons. In Allen's first year, the Rams won eight of their fourteen games, and the next season posted an 11-1-2 record, topping the National Football League's Coastal Division. In 1971, Allen moved on to coach the Washington Redskins, which had just a single winning season over the previous fifteen years. All seven of his seasons there were winners. His amazing regular-season record with the two teams: 116-47-5.

Allen was a technical innovator—the first coach to put major emphasis on special teams, a pioneer in the use of the blitz, zone coverage, and the nickel defense. He was also a keen strategist—his "The Future Is Now" motto described a decision to make trades to obtain veteran players, sacrificing future draft choices.

But beyond those skills, Allen was a motivator. He found

assignments for his veterans that would call upon all their some-times waning abilities, and challenge them to perform at their peak. The better they responded, the more responsibility he gave them. In his mind, getting the job done better was what counted. That was what the Football Hall of Fame recognized when it inducted him as a member.

On a different playing field, Evergreen found that many of the winning companies studied followed a mandate not unlike George Allen's coaching philosophy. They made sure to keep their best performers interested and challenged in their work.

This mandate rests on an unstated assumption, namely, that bright, talented people want to be challenged, that they subscribe to Allen's dictum: "The achiever is the only person who is truly alive." One way to keep them achieving, once they have mastered one assignment, is to give them another that has greater responsi-bility attached. There are few things that so focus the mind on a task than the knowledge that whatever happens, it is on your head.

The decentralization and empowerment policies followed by companies like Valspar, the paint and coverings company, and steel-maker Nucor are intended, in part, to keep good people intrigued.

Valspar: *Small is better*

During the 1970s, Valspar found itself with a number of small, less productive older plants. Rather than build expensive new facilities, the company decided to rehabilitate the old ones. Out of that dol-lars-and-cents decision emerged a conviction that has governed Valspar ever since: small is better. Since the object was to maintain the "we-can-do-it-all" spirit found in small companies, Valspar simply put a ceiling on the size of any of its plants. They would not employ more than 250 people, which was thought to be the limit for employees' getting to know each other by their first names.

Valspar gives these units—there were already sixty-five profit and cost centers in 1989—substantial autonomy and responsibility. Under those entrepreneurial conditions, the company has realized rising profitability, and its best people have been constantly challenged to find their own solutions to all the new and unpredictable problems any organization faces.

Nucor: *Turning it over to teams*

At Nucor, too, the organizational structure pushes authority downward, giving managers and frontline people the opportunity to exercise the full range of their talents—pushing for better performance, trying out new tactics and ideas, cutting costs, urging other members of the team to greater effort.

On a visit to a Nucor mill in 1995, a visitor watched a team put spangles of different shapes and sizes on strips of galvanized steel. The team had figured out a way of tailoring the spangles by varying the air pressure used to dry the steel after its zinc bath. By eliminating a separate process, the discovery substantially speeded up production.

When the team's coup was described to the plant's general manager, Larry Roos, he laughed. "I find that happening all the time around here," he said. "There are many improvements in cost, quality, and production that are going on that I don't even know about. They just happen, and they don't have to be rubber-stamped."

CEO Ken Iverson put it this way: "We give the worker the

training and furnish the equipment, and then, in a real sense, the team is in business for itself." Along with the performance-based bonus plan, discussed earlier, the empowerment system leads teams to take over any and all functions that affect their operational success.

For example, Nucor teams don't leave it to headquarters to train newcomers. Team members do it themselves to make sure production doesn't suffer, and given the pressure from their new colleagues, trainees tend to sink or swim quickly.

The system works on many levels. Three years into the Evergreen decade, Nucor was turning out 980 tons of steel a year per employee; the industry average was 420 tons. Nucor's costs were $60 a ton, while the industry's was $135.

The system also serves to attract talented new people and bind employees to the company. When a mill placed a single help-wanted ad, it drew more than a thousand applicants. When a union organizer started distributing pamphlets at a mill gate, supervisors had to protect him from angry employees.

Nucor's ability to intrigue and challenge its talented employees by empowering them has paid the company huge dividends.

Become personally involved in winning the war for talent.

In most large organizations, the task of hiring the best and brightest falls to the human-resources department. They are the people who write the want ads, conduct the campus interviews, and deal with the headhunters.

That approach might have sufficed back in the days when employees were viewed as interchangeable cogs in the corporate wheel, who simply followed orders and collected paychecks. But that time is long past. Once organizations began relying on front-line people and managers as idea-producing, decision-making partners, a company's talent bank took on far greater significance. As suggested above, Winners focus on the grooming of talented in-house employees for higher-level jobs. But the Evergreen research also indicated that senior executives in many winning companies were very much aware of the recruitment imperative and were themselves involved in helping their organizations win the war for talent. They were convinced that this task was simply too important to leave entirely in the hands of the human-resources professionals.

When Schering-Plough Healthcare Products moved its sales and marketing staff headquarters from Alabama to New Jersey, for example, David E. Collins, the president, had his company's talent bank in mind. "We did it first of all because that is where the industry is concentrated," he said, "and for us to recruit the kind of folks to make us competitive, we felt we had to be at the heart of the action."

Seagate: *Hunting for "smart people"*

Seagate's founder and CEO Al Shugart is an inveterate recruiter, forever on the lookout for talent, moving people around his huge chessboard, the personnel roster of the California-based disk-drive manufacturer.

One of the major turning points in the company's history

came in 1989, when it bought Imprimis Technology, a subsidiary of Control Data. Shugart, never at a loss for enthusiasm, called it "the acquisition of the century from a technology standpoint." Up to that point, Seagate had simply waited for some other organization to come up with a new disk-drive version and then relied upon its low-cost production to take over the market. But product cycles had gotten so short there wasn't time for the company to recoup its production costs before another innovation appeared. With Imprimis in the fold, Seagate now had both ends covered, innovation and production.

Shugart was also attracted to Imprimis by the quality of its workers. He needed the company, he said, not just for the technology but "for the smart people they brought to the party." Shugart never stopped looking for smart people.

Amyl Ahola, an Imprimis executive, left Seagate not long after the merger, but he stayed in Al Shugart's mind. Two years later, Ahola received a phone call, inviting him to return. "Al says, 'I don't know what I want you to do, just come back and work,'" Ahola recalled. And he did.

Shugart has no hesitation about his role as a talent hunter. "I have the easiest job in the company," he once said. "I just hire smart people."

Cardinal: *Holding on to managers*

Another CEO with an eye out for potential new hires was Robert D. Walter of Cardinal Health, a drug wholesaler based in Dublin, Ohio. Back in 1971, as a twenty-six-year-old with a Harvard M.B.A., Walter ran a leveraged buyout of Cardinal Foods, a food wholesaler with a supermarket customer base. It had sales of $21 million a year. He sought to grow with acquisitions, but the industry had already consolidated. In 1980, Walter bought a pharmaceutical distributorship and liked the business so much it became his central focus; he has since acquired more than a dozen companies, starting with other drug wholesalers' until he had nationwide coverage for his customers, mainly independent drugstores and hospitals. As of 1996, the end of the Evergreen decade, Cardinal's sales were $8.9 billion, and its net income was $111.9 million.

All through his buying spree, Walter pursued his talent hunt. The only companies he bothered with were those that were well operated and had managers who would stay in place and keep the shop going after a buyout. "The kings in our company are the guys out there running their fiefdoms," Walter said.

Even when one of his bids for a company failed, an infrequent occurrence, Walter often came away with some new hires. That happened in 1993 after he bowed out of a bidding war for Durr-Fillauer Medical, a drug wholesaler headquartered in Alabama. At that point, Walter knew Durr very well, and within a few months after the bidding ended he succeeded in luring five of its managers to jump ship and cast their lot with him.

Cardinal Health was a clear Evergreen Winner, and that was due in no small measure to its leader's continuing focus on finding the right people to run his company.

What Comes Next

In the chapter just ahead, we examine the overall role of corporate leadership as a factor in the success of an organization. Specifically, we discuss the leadership management practice of the winning companies in the Evergreen study, with special attention to four mandates that were pursued by those Winners that excelled in this secondary practice.

The next chapter also offers a number of company examples, including some names familiar from previous chapters such as Schering-Plough and Campbell Soup, enterprises that have managed to attract, develop, and retain some of the country's most effective leaders.

9

Make Your Leaders
Committed to Your Business

In the wake of the corporate scandals of the new millennium, it has become fashionable in some quarters to belittle the very notion of the powerful chief executive who embodies his company and determines its fate, for good or ill. Yet, there are few events of greater significance to an organization than the selection of a new chief executive.

In a study conducted by one of the authors, it was shown that CEOs on average influence 15 percent of the total variance in a company's profitability or total return to shareholders. To put that in perspective, the same study found that the decision by a company as to whether it will remain in its current industry or move to another likewise accounts for a 15 percent variance in profitability. In other words, the choice of a chief executive is crucial.

The celebrity CEO came of age at a time when business news was suddenly of mainstream concern as millions of new investors flooded the soaring stock markets. CEOs who showed up well on television, who could mesmerize stock analysts, became all the rage. The subsequent business scandals and the dizzying drop of the markets drastically altered the dynamics. Imperial CEOs were now seen as being irresponsible, greedy, or both.

Of course, these charming, magnetic, larger-than-life figures were never the norm among successful corporate leaders. As Jim Collins puts it in his book *Good to Great,* the chief executives of winning companies are often "charismatically challenged." They have other attributes.

The best CEOs, for example, are able to communicate their vision so convincingly that others will adopt that vision as part of their personal agenda. They also have great integrity, in word and action. When their company is confronted by a moral dilemma—a product defect, for instance—there are no hesitations or excuses. These CEOs simply announce a recall or whatever move best resolves the problem. In other words, they walk the talk.

Angus Wurtele, the longtime chief executive of Valspar, made it a policy to immediately inform employees when a plant was going to be closed or a layoff was coming, giving them months, and in some cases years, to prepare. "I know the conventional wisdom is not to say anything until just before," he said. "But our experience never verified that fear." It was a matter of principle and of good business practice, he added.

When leaders demonstrate their true and firm commitment to their beliefs, they reinforce their leadership roles. Their employees see that the chief executives live by their words, that they can be trusted, and that trust is precious, particularly when times turn hard. No one wants to hear bad news, but it goes down better when it comes from a person you trust.

As the Evergreen Project showed, there are some common beliefs about leadership that actually have very little to do with a company's becoming and remaining a Winner. For example, a leader's decision-making style, whether he or she makes most decisions independently or in collaboration with the top management team, did not matter in terms of winning. Nor does any such correlation exist as concerns the personal characteristics of the CEO, whether he is patient or impatient, visionary or detail-oriented, secure or insecure. It also made little difference to a company's success whether senior managers relied on quantitative or qualitative assessments in making key decisions.

The Evergreen Project's Winners that excelled in the leadership management practice shared a dedication to the following mandates: inspire management to strengthen its relationships with people at all levels of the company; inspire management to hone its capacity to spot opportunities and problems early; appoint a board of directors whose members have a substantial financial stake in the company's success; closely link leaders' pay to their performances.

In the pages ahead, these mandates are discussed in some detail and presented along with examples of companies that followed—or failed to follow—their precepts.

9.1 Leadership: Winners *versus* Losers

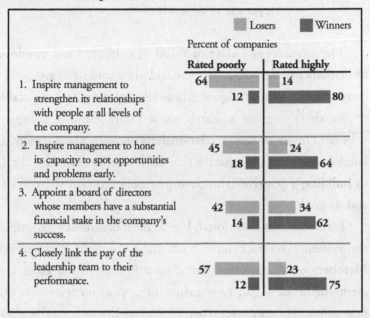

This chart shows how Winners and Losers performed on the leadership management practice. In some cases, the differences are striking. On the first mandate, "Inspire management to strengthen its relationships with people at all levels of the company," 80 percent of Winners received high ratings, while 64 percent of Losers received low ratings. By the same token, 75 percent of Winners were rated highly on the fourth mandate, "Closely link leadership team's pay to their performance," while 57 percent of Losers were rated poorly.

Note: A poor rating equals 1 or 2 and a high rating equals 4 or 5 on a 5-point scale with a score of 3 being average. Some mandates and their scores are the composite of several survey items. The percentages do not add up to 100% because companies with average scores are not included. Losers include the scores of all companies in losing periods and Winners, the scores of all companies in winning periods. The differences between Losers and Winners are statistically significant at the 95% confidence level.

Source: Evergreen team analysis.

**Inspire management to strengthen its relationships
with people at all levels of the company.**

The attitudes and state of mind of managers and employees can enhance or demolish the best-laid plans and strategies, and no company can afford to ignore these all-important imponderables.

As the Evergreen research made clear, winning companies believe in fostering strong relationships between management and employees. They understand that such relationships are the key to building a positive attitude in the ranks toward the company and its goals.

Particularly in traditional, hierarchical organizations, employees typically interact only with their immediate supervisors. Members of management are distant figures whose faces ornament the house organ or occasionally appear on television business shows. For employees, top executives live only in the stories, often apocryphal, passed down from one level of the company to the next, and in the decisions, delivered from on high, that directly affect the workplace. The distance the employees feel from management will help determine how those decisions are received, and how employees feel about their jobs.

When leaders seek to close that gap, when they take the time to connect with lower echelons, they strengthen and even redefine the economic net that links every level of a company. When CEOs present themselves as flesh-and-blood people, as fellow employees rather than as masters, they can foster positive attitudes that translate into improved company-wide performance.

All that is not to suggest, of course, that top management

should seek to become bosom buddies of every foreman and clerk in the organization. That is as unnecessary as it is unlikely. But by making regular visits to outlying facilities, by appearing occasionally on factory floors, by making more appearances on the intranet, chief executives can communicate to employees their personal interest and their concern for the well-being of everyone in the enterprise.

Campbell Soup: *Getting to know you*

When David Johnson was chief executive of Campbell Soup, he constantly found ways to reach out to employees, to let them see him in all his flamboyant enthusiasm—as a man who saw problems as challenges and setbacks as spurs to success. Some years ago, a study of 450 CEOs by a California consultancy found that about 70 percent of them were introverts. Johnson was definitely an exception. He was about as different from the standard buttoned-down M.B.A. corporate executive as could be imagined—an informal and accessible individual. "I want to rip out the bureaucracy," he once said, "the pretense, the corridors-of-power syndrome, the games that are played."

At the frequent rallies he organized to communicate directly with the troops, he sometimes dressed in a red-and-white apron and a white chef's hat, identifying himself as "top spoon." He was the captain of the cheerleading squad, praising achievers, laying out the current situation, calling upon everyone to work harder and do better so they could feel good about themselves and their company.

"We could stop and rest if we wanted to," Johnson told a

reporter in his typical gung-ho manner. " 'Why wear a hair shirt, why make a rod for our back?' people ask. I tell them, 'Because that's life. That's fulfilling your potential as an individual, as a management team, as a company.' "

Johnson's success as a motivator was the stuff of legends at Campbell Soup. He was particularly effective with his staff and managers, whom he sometimes took on wilderness trips to build a stronger *esprit de corps*. In fact, phrases like "team spirit" came to be sprinkled liberally through the conversations of headquarters executives.

"I want us to think like a small company," Johnson often said. People get to know each other very well in a small business, and he expected his staff to spread his ideas and inspirational messages through increased face-to-face contacts all through the company. Executives got the message. If Johnson believed that stronger relationships would help deliver greater profitability, they were going to make that happen. And it did.

Nucor: *On the floor, talking about anything*

The giant steelmaker Nucor also expected its management to connect with all levels of the organization. Ken Iverson demanded it of his executives, and showed the way himself, making regular tours of the company plants and making himself available to workers for question-and-answer sessions.

If Iverson felt that he wasn't getting to the bottom of an issue on one of his visits—if employees seemed to hesitate to confide in the chief executive—he arranged for surveys, and then abided by the workers' preferences. In one case, a survey found that steel-mill workers and joist-plant employees both favored random drug testing, but differed on the details. The mill people, most concerned about safety, felt offenders should be immediately dismissed. The joist-plant people thought offenders should get a second chance. Iverson granted each group its wish.

The headquarters' focus on improving relationships is also played out at the individual Nucor plants. At the Crawfordsville mill, smack in the middle of Indiana cornfields, the then general manager, Larry Roos, pretty much said it all: "I think it is very important for everyone to know that we are accessible and can talk about anything, from production problems to who won the Indianapolis Colts' game Sunday. I get lots of feedback from the managers, but I know a lot more about what's going on by being out there talking or listening to everybody. You break down some of the idea that there is a big difference between management and people. There is no difference between management and people—we all run the place."

The then manager of the mill at Crawfordsville, Kevin Young, walked through the facility twice a day, morning and afternoon, stopping to chat with anyone and everyone he encountered along the way. "I get a handle on what's going on, listen to people's problems, and help foster communications between areas," he said.

Seagate: *"They know who I am"*

At Seagate Technology, Al Shugart, the founder and CEO, covers more miles in reaching out to connect with employees than most top executives. In his case, of course, he must reach out from headquarters in California to company facilities all over Asia, not to mention those in Europe and the United States. Every quarter, Shugart flies off to tell local employees how the company is doing. And he expects his aides to follow a similarly open management style.

Ronald D. Verdoorn, general manager of the extensive Thai operations, made it his business to spend time on plant floors. "Everyone from the operators to the managers said, 'Hello, Ron, how're you doing?' They know who I am."

Contacts between employees and managers have also been institutionalized at the Thai plants by means of their "quality communications groups." Fifteen representatives elected by employees meet regularly with middle- and upper-level managers to pass on complaints and problems, offer solutions, and describe innovations proposed by factory-floor personnel.

For managers, said Brent Bargmann, another executive, "we need the feedback. For operators, they have a voice in how things are run." The sessions also assure that the operators understand messages from management. The danger, said Bargmann, is that "vital information can be watered down in levels of management."

At Seagate, as at Campbell Soup and Nucor, strengthening management's relationships with all employees was both desirable and necessary. It felt good, and it helped make these companies Winners.

Inspire management to hone its capacity to spot opportunities and problems early.

Chief executives and their top aides, generally speaking, know how to deal with the immediate problems of their organizations. Having come up through the ranks, they have a feel for what makes a company tick, and they are comfortable in their ability to resolve its day-to-day difficulties. But Winners don't allow their managements the luxury of simply coping with the now; they convince their top people to focus as well on the future.

The Evergreen research revealed that among winning companies excelling in the leadership practice, a major emphasis was placed on improving management's ability to anticipate change and its potential impact on the organization.

The means to that end are many and various. Some companies create special groups assigned to stay abreast of changes in everything from politics to demography. Sometimes the crystal-ball gazers are outside consultants with academic credentials. Whatever the mechanisms employed, the goal is the same: to make certain that the organization isn't blind-sided by new government regulations or social trends, and to alert the company to just-over-the-horizon business opportunities.

Schering-Plough: *Spotting the promise in OTC*

During the decade of the Evergreen Project, Schering-Plough, the New Jersey drug company, demonstrated its ability to foresee opportunity and forestall threat. Again and again, the company led the field in spotting new trends and developing the products to take advantage of them.

Schering management recognized, for example, that a number of long-term and short-term trends were pointing toward a boom in the over-the-counter (OTC) market. The soaring cost of prescription drugs, for example, was driving more and more people toward less expensive OTC products. The public's growing interest in self-medication was another factor. And, since older people buy a disproportionate percentage of OTC products, the aging of the population would automatically increase sales.

To take advantage of these trends, Schering's leaders lit a fire under its product-development teams to come up with new OTC products. At the same time, they made a command decision to begin shifting some of the company's prescription-only products into the over-the-counter category. They moved rapidly and early, becoming the first in the industry to complete such a shift with the unveiling of Coricidin R in 1951. Over the next years, they reproduced that success with products like Afrin and Chlor-Trimeton in 1976, and Lotrimin in 1990.

All through those years, Schering's management had mobilized the company's prescription and R&D branches to help spot changes or special needs among consumers. A number of new, made-for-OTC products emerged and sold well. But the OTC shift items were the real coup. By 1991, midway through the Evergreen decade, the company had brought out almost three times as many shifted products as its closest competitor.

Campbell Soup: *An eye out for new flavors*
When David Johnson arrived at Campbell Soup, he drastically changed the company's approach to consumer research, the science or art of predicting what customers will buy. "We threw a lot of products out there in the eighties without adequate pre-research," said Paul N. Mulcahy, who was vice president for marketing services. Johnson demanded a maximum of forward-looking studies to get an early jump on trends, positive and negative.

In the product-development area, the company now relies on its Global Consumer Foods Center to spot changes in eating habits and new flavors around the world.

"We look for new ingredients and tastes that appear in the literature," said Michael Fallon, director of U.S. grocery soup product development. "We note the frequency of mention, and when those reach a critical mass, we take the trend into product consideration."

Another group keeps an eye out for nutritional trends, both among health experts and in terms of public demand, and seeks to improve existing products or create new ones.

Appoint a board of directors whose members have a substantial financial stake in the company's success.

As the events of the last few years have so abundantly demonstrated, too many boards of directors of U.S. companies don't take their jobs seriously. They rubber-stamp the decisions of the chief executive. They never question the reports and opinions of lawyers and accountants, on or off staff. They seem to view themselves as indulgent uncles and aunts, content with whatever snippets of information they receive and disinclined to ask awkward questions.

One way or another, boards play a significant role in the fate of their companies. Their responsibility for selecting the chief executive, all by itself, is clearly crucial. CEOs, as indicated above, have a 15 percent impact on the ups and downs of an enterprise's profitability.

From time to time, over the years, there has been a clamor

about the weakness of corporate governance. At one point, the furor was over the excessive use of inside directors, and "reform" meant bringing more outsiders onto boards. But the question remained, Just how seriously would these independent directors view their board membership? Would they put loyalty to the board leaders who appointed them above their loyalty to the company itself? Would they go with the flow or be willing to buck the tide?

Evergreen's research showed that Winners shared the conviction that the best way to inspire directors to take a truly informed and active role was to make sure they had a major financial interest in the company (see Exhibits 9.2 and 9.3). In other words,

9.2 Board Compensation: Winners *versus* Losers

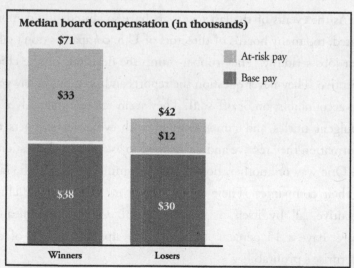

Source: Dr. Donald C. Hambrick, Pennsylvania State University.

the directors' personal money had to be at risk. When it was, directors tended to select and support superior chief executives.

The chart on page 212 shows the contrast between Winners and Losers in terms of the size and makeup of board members' remuneration. Directors at winning companies received an average of $71,000 a year, split almost evenly between base pay and at-risk pay. Directors at losing companies received an average of only $42,000 a year, of which only $12,000 was at-risk pay.

The chart below shows the remarkable change during the decade covered by the Evergreen Project in the combined ownership stake of outside directors of winning and losing companies. In 1986, the outside directors of winning companies, as a group, had a stake of $26 million, on average, while the figure for Losers was $6 million. Ten years later, the stake among winning

9.3 Board Ownership Stake:
Winners *versus* Losers

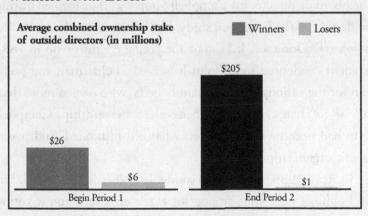

Average combined ownership stake of outside directors (in millions)

Winners   Losers

$205

$26

$6

$1

Begin Period 1   End Period 2

Source: Dr. Donald C. Hambrick, Pennsylvania State University.

companies had soared to $205 million, while it had dropped to $1 million for Losers.

Valspar: *Looking out for the company*

Angus Wurtele, the then chairman and CEO of Valspar, strongly pursued this mandate during the Evergreen decade. As he told the Harvard Business School Club of Minnesota in 1989, after being honored by the group: "If the management and directors of a company have only token ownership, they will look out for themselves first, shareholders second."

At Valspar, directors' stakes in the company are far from token. Wurtele saw to that with a variety of programs, including stock-option plans, incentive programs, and profit-sharing. As of 1989, directors, senior managers, and other insiders owned a remarkable 35 percent of the company's outstanding shares.

Campbell Soup: *A minimum stake of 3,000 shares*

The board of directors at Campbell Soup was transformed during the decade of the Evergreen study. For many years it had been led by John T. Dorrance, Jr., son of the young chemist who in 1897 invented condensed soup. John Jr. served as chairman and point man for the various Dorrance family heirs, who owned more than half of its shares. Under his benevolent stewardship, Campbell Soup had become a quaint, somewhat old-fashioned, and paternalistic organization.

In April 1989 he died, and suddenly everything changed. His big holdings were split among his three children, and a voting trust he ran for a group of nephews and nieces reverted to their individual control. Many of the Dorrance relatives were dissatisfied with the company's financial returns, which lagged far behind its peers. John Dorrance had cared about keeping the company intact and in the family; the new owners were more concerned about their own investment, and they listened with interest to takeover proposals from several organizations.

The board of directors knew that there was only one way to keep the unhappy family members from selling the business. Somehow, the board would have to find a leader who could rapidly increase profitability and total shareholder return. They found David Johnson, and he made it happen.

Along the way, the board recognized that it would have to play a far more active role in the enterprise. During the 1990s, it became the poster company for strong and effective corporate governance. Its rules and regulations were among the strictest and most demanding in the business world.

Within one year of their election, for example, board members must own 1,000 shares of Campbell stock; by their third year they must own 3,000 shares. Seventy-five percent of their pay takes the form of Campbell stock, either in actual shares or in options. The repricing of options to accommodate a falling market is prohibited.

Only one current Campbell executive, presumably the chief executive, is permitted membership on the board; everyone else is to be an independent. No former company executives are allowed. No interlocking directorships are permitted, as when a Campbell executive would become a board member of another company and an executive of that company would join the Campbell board.

At least twice a year the board must examine and evaluate the performance of the chief executive, who is not allowed to attend these meetings. Neither is the CEO permitted to serve on the governance committee, which is responsible for evaluating the performance of the board and of each of its committees, nor on the audit or compensation committees.

Their substantial financial stake in the company has spurred the directors of winning companies like Campbell Soup and Valspar to choose CEOs who will maximize the worth of that stake.

**Closely link the pay of the leadership team
to their performance.**

The stock price of a company is not, of course, the only measure of its progress. There are times when share price fails to mirror a company's real performance—a fact that became all too evident in the New Economy boom of the 1990s that metamorphosed into the bust of the initial millennium years.

Unlike board members, members of top management need to be rewarded for their achievements in dollars as well as shares. But at the end of the day, the executives' remuneration should reflect their performance against a set of preset corporate goals.

All three aspects of the Evergreen research showed that the winning companies excelling in the leadership practice followed that prescription. In most cases, the goals were defined in terms of profits or stock price. In all cases, if targets were missed, bonuses were not forthcoming.

Nucor: *Sharing the pain*

During the Evergreen decade, officers at steelmaker Nucor received base salaries that were lower than those paid in the industry as a whole. They had no employment contracts, retirement programs, or annuities. Their entire bonus depended on that year's return on stockholders' equity. If the company earned, say, 8 percent on stockholders' equity, there would be no bonuses. Apart from the bonus, about 4.5 percent of earnings was put into an incentive compensation pool for officers.

The bonus plan peaked at a 24 percent return on shareholders' equity. At that point, officers received twice their salary in cash and the equivalent of their salary in stock. On the other hand, an economic downturn could play havoc with their income, shrinking it by 65 to 70 percent.

Ken Iverson, the CEO, made $460,000 in 1961. When the company's return on stockholders' equity dropped below 8 percent in 1982, his total remuneration was $108,000.

"Is that fair?" he asked in an article for *Planning Review.* "Absolutely! The general managers and the corporate management make the decisions that determine whether or not Nucor is successful. If we make wise decisions, we receive bonuses. If we make poor decisions that affect the entire company, we share the pain."

Campbell Soup: *Miss your target, miss your pay*

At Campbell Soup, the payment rules for its top executives, like those for its board members, rely strongly on giving them a large financial stake in the company. As discussed earlier, the top 300 executives must own Campbell stock at a value ranging from one-half to three times their base salaries.

But unlike directors, executives are paid according to their personal job performance. A large percentage of the executives' income is tied to their achievements as measured by the financial results of the units they supervise. In the case of the chief executive, for example, more than 75 percent of his or her pay is linked to company results.

Bonuses and long-term performance awards are tied entirely to meeting specific dollar and percentage goals for growth in earnings, cash, and sales. Even the amount the company contributes to the corporate savings plan depends on a quantitative measure: the company's performance compared to that of its competitors.

Incentives tied to performance characterized many of the Winners among the companies studied in the Evergreen Project. The appeal to the personal interests of employees is a powerful motivator.

What Comes Next

The third of the four secondary management practices identified in the Evergreen study is innovation. Many of the winning companies excelled in this practice, including Walgreen, Schering-Plough, and Avery Dennison. How they went about it—how they followed the three mandates of this practice—is described in the following chapter.

10

Make Industry-
Transforming Innovations

What passes for technical achievement in most companies—
marginal, incremental improvements in existing products,
for example—would never satisfy organizations that excel in the
innovation management practice. Their eye is on the main chance,
an altogether new product idea or technological breakthrough
that has the potential to transform their industry.

At such companies, this goal drives every aspect of the organization. Leaders echo the words of Sony's former U.S. chief executive, Mickey Schulhof: "If we stop innovating and stop bringing
new electronic devices to market, we'll die." Frontline people and
managers alike understand that the message is to be taken literally. The very premise upon which many organizations exist is the
expectation of breakthrough innovations, one after another.

One measure of Sony's seriousness is the fact that it invested
9 percent of its sales in research and development. Competitor
Matsushita invested just 4 percent of sales in R&D. The difference helps explain why Sony was able to develop such break-

through products as the lightweight camcorder, and why the corporation was able to outpace its rivals.

Based upon the copious literature on corporate innovation, you might expect that most of the winning companies in the Evergreen Project would have excelled in the innovation practice. In fact, as Exhibit 10.1 indicates, a bare majority did so—a tribute to its demands and difficulties. Innovation is not to be entered into lightly.

Innovation isn't limited to new products, of course; the application of new technologies to the internal workings of a company can yield savings so great as to give it a huge edge—and transform its industry in a different way.

Some of the myths about the innovation practice turned up by the Evergreen study were especially interesting. They showed that there was no correlation between Winners and any single source of ideas. Neither internal R&D labs nor external labs, neither frontline employees nor management, neither customers nor suppliers were necessarily where winning companies found their key innovations. Any one of the Winners might have relied successfully on one or more of those sources, but none proved to be essential to the Winners as a group.

Winners that showed special expertise in the innovation practice did, however, as a group, tend to fulfill the following mandates: they introduced disruptive technologies and business models; they did not hesitate to cannibalize existing products; they applied technology to enhance all their processes, not just those dedicated to designing products and services.

Now, let's consider these mandates one by one.

10.1 Innovation: Winners *versus* Losers

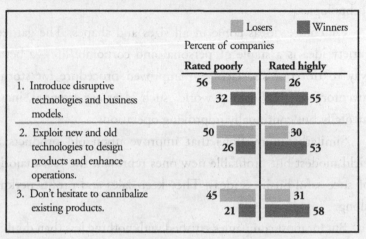

| | Losers █ Winners █ |
| | Percent of companies |

	Rated poorly	Rated highly
1. Introduce disruptive technologies and business models.	56 / 32	26 / 55
2. Exploit new and old technologies to design products and enhance operations.	50 / 26	30 / 53
3. Don't hesitate to cannibalize existing products.	45 / 21	31 / 58

This chart shows how winning and losing companies differed in their performance on the mandates of the innovation management practice. Fifty-eight percent of Winners, for example, received high ratings on their willingness to cannibalize existing products, while 45 percent of Losers rated poorly.

Note: A poor rating equals 1 or 2 and a high rating equals 4 or 5 on a 5-point scale with a score of 3 being average. Some mandates and their scores are the composite of several survey items. The percentages do not add up to 100% because companies with average scores are not included. Losers include the scores of all companies in losing periods and Winners, the scores of all companies in winning periods. The differences between Losers and Winners are statistically significant at the 95% confidence level.

Source: Evergreen team analysis.

Introduce disruptive technologies and business models.

Good ideas help. Great ideas move mountains. Evergreen research showed that among winning companies that excelled in the innovation practice, one of the main common denominators was a tendency to create market discontinuities with disruptive technologies.

Of course, ideas come in all sizes and shapes. The garden-variety idea is a staple of personal and corporate life—a better way to tie your shoelaces, an improved procedure for storing inventory. In the business world, such ideas are essential, incrementally but continually improving operations.

Similarly, innovations that improve upon old products or yield modest but profitable new ones represent the vast majority of successful business ideas. They keep sales and profits perking along.

But for most companies satisfied with nothing less than double-digit increases in growth and earnings—for the Winners and Climbers—modest improvements do not suffice. Their focus is more on the blockbuster innovation, the idea that will set competitors back on their heels.

Avery Dennison: *Pushing R&D authority downward*

Avery Dennison, a global leader in adhesive labels and dozens of other office products, is such company. Based in Pasadena, California, the company boasts more than 17,000 employees in 200 manufacturing sites and sales offices in 39 countries.

But it was not always thus. The company is a Climber.

Founded in 1935 as a maker of Kum-Kleen price-tag labels, Avery went on to produce pressure-sensitive paper that had dozens of uses, including bottle labels and tax-form peel-off labels. In the middle 1980s, Charles D. Miller, the chief executive, decided to challenge 3M and bring out its own version of Post-it Notes and Scotch tape.

The project was a disaster, and Avery Notes and Avery Tape were abandoned within a few years. The experience did, however, teach Miller a valuable lesson. He restructured the company in 3M's image, transforming it into an innovation machine with a close eye on customers' needs and dreams.

Miller trimmed the headquarters staff and pushed authority for imagining and creating new products down to lower-level managers. They came through. One of their first new moves was to adapt Avery's labels for use with computer-linked laser and ink-jet printers. Then Stephanie Streeter, an assistant product manager, sold Microsoft, Lotus, and other software companies on adopting the Avery label dimensions and stock codes as the industry standard.

In 1990, Avery acquired a competitor, Dennison Manufacturing, a maker of stationery, labels, ink markers, and other office products based in Framingham, Massachusetts. Avery became Avery Dennison, and the new organization soon had a commanding 85 percent share of the office-label market as 3M dropped out of the business—reversing Avery's previous experience with the giant tape-maker.

Miller's innovation mandate was now applied to Dennison's product area. The company's philosophy was well stated by Donald Thompson, vice president of the office products group: "The best way to control a market is to invent it."

His team followed that prescription with a drumbeat of breakthrough products, including: self-laminating security badges that can be laser printed when a visitor reports to a reception desk; invisible ink and ink that changes color; markers that use ink that glows in the dark; markers that smell of chocolate or lemon; and self-adhesive postage stamps.

Avery Dennison's innovation practice has been stellar over the years because it is based upon a demanding business model. This is a company that insists upon products that will create discontinuities in its markets.

Polaroid: *Research yields to marketing*

Polaroid, of course, was built upon a disruptive technology, the instant camera. Its first decades, under the leadership of its founder, Edwin Land, were dedicated to finding more such breakthroughs. Virtually every aspect of the organization was designed to make that happen, from the huge investments in R&D to the programs that sought to keep the company's skilled employees in place.

But Land's successors were ruled by different considerations. The company's huge debt, first assumed to fight off a hostile takeover, limited its ability to invest in R&D. As sales and profits lagged, pressure from shareholders pushed management to pursue lesser innovations that would cost less and, in theory at least, yield more immediate profits.

CEO Mac Booth was committed to "a fundamental change in our strategic orientation—to a greater customer focus, balancing a market-driven approach with our pioneering technology-driven heritage." In other words, under Booth, marketing became the coequal of invention; a far cry from the company's original value proposition. And Polaroid's R&D lab shifted away from consumer-based products toward industrial items.

The problem was, neither end of the equation was working very well. Sales of instant-camera products were slowly declining, and the new inventions coming out of the famous Polaroid labs were underwhelming. "We're not going for the home run so much as going for good singles and doubles," Mac Booth acknowledged. Yet most of the company's new products were not even getting on base, and some of them were costing hundreds of millions of dollars to develop.

In 1987, Polaroid became the target of a hostile takeover attempt by Roy Disney, Walt's nephew, who characterized the company as complacent and unable to commercialize its discoveries. Polaroid management fought off the raid, but the battle left the traditionally cash-rich company $1 billion in debt, a burden that weighed it down throughout the next decade. To compensate, Booth slashed spending on R&D and advertising and cut the workforce by 15 percent, giving the company its highest profits ever, although sales continued to lag.

One new product after another failed to attract a customer base. Helios, a medical imaging system and the company's first major effort in electronics, was a $200 million flop. Sales of the Captiva, a small point-and-shoot instant camera, never lived up to predictions. Joshua, a pocket-sized instant that produced a wallet-sized picture, had cost $300 million to develop, but it had to be tossed.

Meanwhile, the world of consumer photography was being

transformed by one-hour photo processing and disposable cameras. Polaroid's instant-camera patents were running out. Competitors were racing to bring out the first digital camera, and Polaroid was running behind. Shareholder returns had fallen dramatically.

In 1995, Booth was replaced by Gary Dicamillo, Polaroid's first outsider CEO. He called for a refocusing on the "neglected" instant photo business and proceeded to sell off unprofitable commercial businesses. "We have not talked to the last generation, maybe the last two generations, of consumer users," he said. It took a while, but in 1999 Dicamillo presided over the introduction of the I-Zone instant camera, which, at $25, was an instant hit with teenagers, who decorated their clothes with the stamp-size sticker prints.

But I-Zone was not enough. Digital cameras were taking over the market, and Polaroid was still struggling to get a foothold. By the spring of 2001, the share price had plummeted to $3 from the $45 level it had occupied when Dicamillo took over; debt was back up close to $1 billion. The renewed focus on instant cameras was now abandoned in favor of a new digital-printing system. But nothing worked, and in October of that year the company filed for Chapter 11 bankruptcy protection.

Slowly, slowly, Polaroid had been fading away for more than a decade, a once great company that had lost its ability to create breakthrough, innovative products

L.A. Gear: *The innovations ran out*

There could be no argument with L.A. Gear's president, Mark Goldston, when he observed: "You survive in any business by adapting to the evolution of the market, or you change the market via innovation. We think we can do both."

As it turned out, however, he and his company could do neither. L.A. Gear's failure to adapt to market changes during the period covered by the Evergreen study has been described in earlier chapters. Its record as a creator of market-changing technology has been hardly brighter, though it wasn't for lack of trying. With a single exception, its innovative products made little impact—on the industry or the consumer.

Innovation played little role in the enterprise's beginnings: it was only after Reebok made a hit with its fashionable aerobics shoes that Robert Greenberg thought of creating his Valley Girl sneakers. It was on Greenberg's watch, though, that the basic idea for L.A. Gear's industry-changing innovation emerged in the form of children's shoes and walking shoes with small lights in the heels. Goldston's technical team added an important wrinkle: the lights would now blink on when the walker's soles hit the ground.

L.A. Lights flew off the shelves and played a major role in keeping the company alive.

The company then ran changes on the product, including a running shoe called Light Speed. It had a fiber optic sheet in the top of the shoe's tongue, so the whole tongue would light up, a signal to oncoming traffic. Another Lights spinoff was a basketball shoe that lit up when the player rose off the floor for a jump shot or a dunk. It was called Leap Gear.

Spinoffs, however, were not what had brought L.A. Gear its initial success. More breakthrough products were needed, but they were not forthcoming. In the final analysis, the bulk of L.A.

Gear's innovations failed to move the industry, or keep the company afloat.

The results of an in-depth analysis of innovations in all the industries in the Evergreen Project are presented below in Exhibit 10.2. It suggests that a company that decides to focus on innovation as one of its management practices must be prepared to lead the pace of innovation in its industry, as Sony and Avery Dennison have. Laggards in the innovation race quickly become Losers.

This exhibit shows the disparity between Winners and Losers in their relationship to discontinuities in their individual markets.

10.2 Market Discontinuities: Winners *versus* Losers

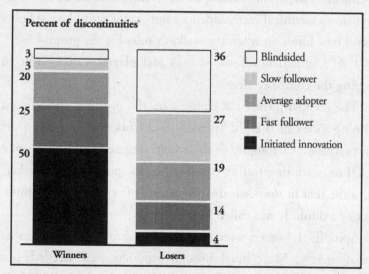

Source: Evergreen team analysis.

Winners either initiated the innovation or, in 25 percent of the cases, were fast followers in adapting to it. Rarely were they blindsided or slow followers. Losers were initiators or fast followers in just 18 percent of the cases.

Exploit new and old technologies to design products and enhance operations.

There is a natural tendency to emphasize the innovations and technologies that directly affect the products and services that companies rely on for their sales and profits. Particularly in a management era when customer focus is all the rage, that kind of reaction is to be expected. But in fact the impact of innovation on the internal operations of a business can be more important to the bottom line. As the Evergreen research made clear, winning companies that shone in the innovation practice found ways to use technical breakthroughs to advance both internal and external goals.

Walgreen: *Tracking 300,000 prescriptions daily*
Walgreen, the giant retail drug chain, epitomized that approach. On the customer side, the company became the first major chain in the industry to replace cash registers entirely with scanners. That sped customers through checkout lines much faster, since clerks no longer had to check prices, and allowed for automatic discounts. Walgreen also broke new ground in the industry with an electronic satellite communications network that sped information about products and customers to computers in all of their hundreds of stores. That allowed customers to get prescriptions

filled (and refilled) at any Walgreen's, the one down the block or one on the other side of the country.

Customers other than the consumer—third-party payers such as insurance companies and health-maintenance organizations—also benefited from Walgreen's powerful computer network, which, as far back as 1990, was coping with 300,000 prescriptions a day. The computer system and the chain's huge volume enabled Walgreen to offer the third-party payers a discount on all prescriptions filled. It was also able to let these customers know, through computer searches of prescription records, the names of doctors who never prescribed less-expensive generic drugs.

Walgreen's ability to apply technology to its internal operations led to major cost savings as well as marketing opportunities. The computer screening of prescriptions by zip codes, for instance, also aids the company in siting its stores. One example: in Evanston, Illinois, the computer turned up the fact that three existing Walgreen outlets had failed to tap a densely populated neighborhood a mile or so away. The company proceeded to locate a miniature store, called an RxPress, in the middle of that neighborhood, and it has done very well.

The RxPresses are innovations in their own right, 1,200-square-foot, free-standing stores with drive-through pharmacies selling prescriptions, OTCs, and some toiletries. Walgreen often uses the small-format stores in markets like Los Angeles where real-estate prices are too high to warrant a full-size operation. It is a leading-edge tool for blanketing the nation with Walgreen outlets. "The whole country's on the list," Charles R. Walgreen III, chairman and CEO, allowed in 1997. "We're looking at everything."

Computers operated the company's distribution centers, where they directed machines to place particular bottles of cold remedies and tubes of toothpaste on a conveyor belt and drop them into a box that had a bar-coded label on its side, indicating its contents and its destination. The computer actually arranged matters so that all the items in a given box were displayed on the same particular aisle in the destination store.

The computers and satellite connection also enabled any Walgreen employee to track an item from the time it was ordered from a supplier to the moment of customer purchase. And that, in turn, made it possible to closely monitor trends in customer purchases and to drastically reduce inventory.

Flowers: *Innovate to lift productivity*

At Flowers, the Georgia-based baking company, an all-out acquisition strategy was matched by a determination to harness the latest technical innovations to improve efficiency, pare costs, and raise quality.

"One of the things we recognized," one company executive told *Milling and Baking News* in 1996, "was that in order to be a survivor in this business we had to be in a position to take advantage of new technology." It didn't make any sense to hook computer chip–driven technology to an outmoded production line, he added. The dollars had to be invested to make plants and equipment state-of-the-art in order "to take advantage of new systems as they were developed, to be on the cutting edge of the baking technology."

The company had spent $350 million over the previous six years on expansions and improvements, Wood said, and would spend another $75 million in fiscal 1996. In 1995, Flowers's projects included a distribution center for its frozen goods that boasted laser-guided cranes and a computer-controlled bakery.

Amos R. McMullian, the chairman and CEO, described the role of innovation in his organization in these terms: "Good management must be able to break away from the habit of doing things the way they were done a long time ago. Habit is the enemy of innovation. Innovation is the mother of increased productivity. It is increased productivity that allows us to accomplish our company's mission and to enhance the standard of living for our employees."

Don't hesitate to cannibalize existing products.

It is one of the oldest truisms in the corporate canon: companies don't eat their young. They don't bring out new products that compete with existing products until the existing products are long past their prime earning days. It only makes sense, the conventional wisdom holds, to wring the last cent from your current items before releasing another item to take its place.

But as the Evergreen research demonstrated, winning companies that excelled in the innovation practice had a very different view. They believed in cannibalization and practiced it regularly.

The world moves too fast these days to hesitate for long with a new product. The competition is too likely to be close on your heels, and hesitation may allow your rivals to get to market first. Given the ever shorter shelf life of so many products, a head start is essential to get the most from an innovation before it is ripped off and commoditized.

Particularly for those companies that rely upon disruptive technologies and business models, the reluctance to sacrifice sales of previous products is self-defeating. Such breakthroughs are too rare to be allowed to wither on the vine.

Schering-Plough: *Consumed by OTCs*

As the industry pioneer and leader in shifting prescription items to over-the-counter products, Schering-Plough, the New Jersey–based drug company, is a confirmed cannibal.

The OTCs, which of course sell for less than the prescription versions, automatically displace those earlier items—but sales of the shifted drug typically double or triple quickly.

Home Depot: *Sales stolen by a sister store*

At Home Depot, as we mentioned in an earlier chapter, cannibalization is a routine strategy. It is applied when a store becomes so popular that its associates can no longer maintain a customer-friendly atmosphere. There are just so many customers a store, even the giants operated by Home Depot, can handle without its associates having to spend more time keeping up with new inventory and filling shelves than helping customers. When that happens, the company opens another outlet nearby.

The new store inevitably drains customers away from the overcrowded one, returning it to an appropriate level of business.

What Comes Next

The subject of the next chapter is the fourth of the secondary practices in the 4+2 formula: "Make growth happen with mergers and partnerships." Whereas the emphasis in the previous practices, like innovation, has primarily been on the internal strategies and performance of the organization, the companies cited in the following pages put a premium on their ability to get along with and get the most out of other companies. For many such organizations, acquisitions have been a major means of increasing sales and profitability. During the years covered by the Evergreen Project, for example, Valspar and Avery Dennison were prime examples of the corporate urge to merge.

11

Make Growth Happen
with Mergers and Partnerships

Diversification is good—sometimes. For most of the last century, mergers in the United States were mainly driven by the desire to broaden a company's portfolio of offerings as a hedge against the downside of its industry's economic cycle.

The idea had substantial intellectual support, and not just for companies. James Tobin, longtime Yale professor and a onetime member of the Council of Economic Advisors, won a Nobel Prize, in part, on the basis of his portfolio theory, holding that investors in search of security are best served by diversifying their holdings rather than simply looking for the highest rates of return.

In the 1960s and 1970s, many corporations went on a diversification spree, sold on the concept of "synergy"—the additional value to be realized by a company as the result of its purchase of another. Sadly, the buying binge turned out to be largely a disaster of synergies that never materialized; the acquisitions simply weighed down acquirers with new debt.

Diversification as the raison d'être for a buyout is still alive in the United States today, and, as the Evergreen Project demonstrated, still for the most part yielding negative results. We found that on average it cost shareholders 35 percent of the total return they might otherwise have received. SG&A costs were 50 percent higher. And those results were particularly compelling because the Evergreen sample companies were relatively narrowly focused operations.

Among Winners that excelled in the merger management practice, diversification was not a mandated goal. Yes, they pursued acquisitions as a route to growth, but only, as the survey results in Exhibit 11.1 show, when the move leveraged the buyer's or seller's existing customer relationships or the two companies complemented each other's existing strengths.

To a degree, that was not an unexpected outcome, since companies that sought diversification were generally weak in their primary practices and relying on acquisitions to make up for their own losses. In the deals analyzed by the Evergreen Project, 93 percent of the Winners created value while only 9 percent of the Losers did so.

Since it is difficult for any company to find enough internal sources of growth to keep up with the need for expansion, growth by mergers is a secondary practice that many Winners pursue. The Evergreen mandates for this practice also call upon companies moving into a new business with a partner to choose a field that is suited to the unique combination of talents the two organizations can muster. Companies are urged to develop expertise in recognizing and closing advantageous deals.

11.1 Mergers and Partnerships: Winners *versus* Losers

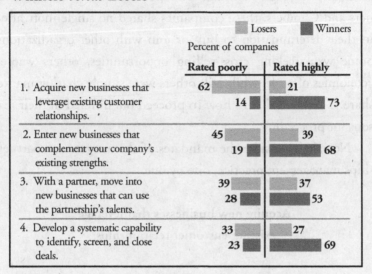

	Rated poorly	Rated highly
1. Acquire new businesses that leverage existing customer relationships.	62 / 14	21 / 73
2. Enter new businesses that complement your company's existing strengths.	45 / 19	39 / 68
3. With a partner, move into new businesses that can use the partnership's talents.	39 / 28	37 / 53
4. Develop a systematic capability to identify, screen, and close deals.	33 / 23	27 / 69

Legend: ▢ Losers ▪ Winners — Percent of companies

This chart shows the degree to which Winners and Losers carried out the mandates of the merger management practice. On a mandate concerned with leveraging customer relationships, for example, 73 percent of winning companies rated highly, while 62 percent of losing companies rated poorly. The discrepancy between the two groups was smaller on a mandate about joining a partner in a new venture. Thirty-seven percent of Losers had high ratings as compared to 53 percent of Winners.

Note: A poor rating equals 1 or 2 and a high rating equals 4 or 5 on a 5-point scale with a score of 3 being average. Some mandates and their scores are the composite of several survey items. The percentages do not add up to 100% because companies with average scores are not included. Losers include the scores of all companies in losing periods and Winners, the scores of all companies in winning periods. The differences between Losers and Winners are statistically significant at the 95% confidence level.

Source: Evergreen team analysis.

One of the findings of the Evergreen study was something of a surprise. Though the mandates above were followed by Winners and Climbers, these companies shared no single motivation in their determination to buy or join with other organizations. Some were seeking cross-selling opportunities, others wanted economies of scale, while still others were simply chasing market share. They agreed as to how to proceed but differed in their reasons for proceeding.

Now, let's consider the mandates of the mergers and partnerships management practice, one by one.

Acquire new businesses that leverage existing customer relationships.

If growth is the target, as it is for virtually every company, then the immediate goal is to build the customer base. That can be achieved by doing a better job of marketing your existing products and by developing new or improved products to corral additional customers. But that tends to be a slow and expensive process, and an uncertain one as well. Do you really have marketers who can ratchet up their efforts? Are your product-development people really good enough to drastically improve your customer offerings?

There is another way. You can simply buy a bigger customer base by acquiring companies whose customers will purchase your goods and whose goods will be attractive to your customers. That route is not, of course, so simple. It is expensive, certainly in the short-term, and it demands substantial skill on your part in select-ing the right businesses to buy and managing them efficiently after they are bought.

But as the Evergreen research showed, many Winners and Climbers did just that: they pursued acquisitions that delivered growth by making the most of customer relationships, both their own and those of the company acquired.

Avery Dennison: *Corralling new customers*

As noted in the previous chapter, Avery Dennison, the office-supply company, achieved notable success during the Evergreen decade, in part because of its development of breakthrough prod-ucts. But it also owed much to its aggressive policy of acquisitions and alliances. One of the most important of those acquisitions took place in 1990, when Avery bought Dennison.

This union of two major players in the stationery and office-products business, which led to the renaming of the company as Avery Dennison, was described by Charles D. Miller, Avery's chairman and chief executive, as "an old-fashioned strategic merger." Avery's 1989 sales of $1.7 billion were twice those of Dennison, which was just coming out of a far-reaching, five-year reorganization. One Boston analyst remarked of the merger: "We had thought Dennison had some glorious times ahead. Clearly, Avery agrees."

Dennison had a quarter of the office-labels market, and was on track to compete with Avery in computer-printer labels. "I wanted to knock them out," Miller said later. He also wanted to corral Dennison's customers for those products where the two companies did not compete, and see to it that his customers were properly exposed to Dennison's non-competing products.

By adding Dennison's customer base to its own, Avery was able to leverage the existing customer relationship each company had developed, creating a critical mass that would help take it close to the top of its industry.

Cardinal: *A regional goes national*

Another acquisition that lifted a company into the upper ranks of its industry occurred in 1994 when Cardinal Health, the Ohio drug wholesaler discussed in the chapter on the talent practice, took over Whitmire Distribution, based in California. It was Cardinal's twelfth acquisition in a decade, and it effectively doubled its sales.

Beyond that, the Whitmire deal lifted Cardinal from its regional status into the ranks of national wholesalers, able to serve customers in many parts of the country.

But for Robert D. Walter, Cardinal's CEO, one of the chief advantages of this acquisition was the quality of Whitmire's customer base. "You can buy the rest of it," he said. "We're not trying to be a price leader; we're trying to be a value leader."

To support its value strategy, Cardinal had become one of the industry's leaders in quality service, providing its retail customers with a variety of support functions through its finance and management-information systems. Its account teams had established close and ongoing relationships with customers, determining their problems and aggressively addressing them.

These were some of the advantages Cardinal could bring to Whitmire's customers, expanding upon the relationships it had with its own customers, tailoring them to the needs of the acquired organization's customer base. It was an approach that worked well for Cardinal during the Evergreen decade.

Enter new businesses that complement your company's existing strengths.

As mentioned above, diversification for the sake of diversification is generally a losing proposition. For an acquisition to work to your benefit, you need to make sure it will match up well with your own company's profile. The Evergreen research showed that this concern was shared by those Winners and Climbers, who excelled in the merger management practice.

If Company A manufactures top-of-the-line widgets, it should beware acquiring an organization that produces widgets for the discount market. The whole *gestalt* of the two companies could be incompatible, and it could require monumental, and perhaps futile, efforts to reconcile them. By the same token, if Company B has a performance-oriented corporate culture long on frontline empowerment and team loyalty, it should think twice about buying a company with a traditional command-and-control organization. The attitudes of the two workplaces and managements might be so divergent that they would mix about as well as oil and water.

The goal is to find potential acquisitions that complement your enterprise's strengths, that extend or complete its value proposition. That was precisely what the acquisition of Conner Peripherals did for Seagate Technology in 1996—and it also did a lot for the ego of Seagate's offbeat CEO, computer pioneer Alan F. Shugart.

Seagate: *Becoming a one-stop shop*

The day after Shugart graduated from college in 1951, he went to work at IBM, where he led the development of the technology that preceded today's hard drives. In 1969, he signed on with Memorex, and a few years later started Shugart Associates to develop the floppy disk. His associates included one Finis F. Conner, a former colleague at IBM.

When the company encountered delays in its development work in 1974, Shugart was abandoned by his backers, after which he spent four years running a bar and salmon fishing. Then Conner suggested they go into business developing hard drives for the PCs that were just starting to appear in stores. For years, Shugart, Conner, and their company called Seagate prospered mightily, racking up revenues of $344 million by 1984; but then they were overtaken by price wars and philosophical differences.

Shugart wanted Seagate to continue manufacturing the drives from the ground up; Conner insisted that the company should be taking the less risky route of outsourcing major parts. Eventually, Conner convinced Compaq Computer to support him in a new company called Conner Peripherals. It took off like a rabbit, achieving sales of $113 million in its first twelve months.

But the silver lining had a cloud: the PC demand reached

such heights that it caused a dire shortage of some essential components. In 1993, Conner Peripherals, and every other drive manufacturer—with the exception of vertically integrated Seagate—lost money.

That was why, three years later, Al Shugart was in a position to present his old friend with an offer Conner couldn't refuse. "Of course I have some seller's remorse," Conner commented, "but this should make Seagate the premier storage company in the world."

The acquisition was, in fact, a great match for Seagate, substantially enlarging its customer base in all the right places. For one, Seagate immediately became, by far, the largest maker of disk drives, with about a third of the $25 billion market. Already the leader in workstation and mainframe drives, Shugart's company was now king of the mountain in the huge PC market as well.

The purchase represented a giant step for Shugart in his plan to turn Seagate into a diversified "data technology company." Conner's tape-drive operations, for example, strengthened Seagate's appeal to large customers as a one-stop shop.

Avery Dennison: *An entree into barcodes*

Avery Dennison, too, has been busy acquiring companies that complement its core business, making it possible for Avery to move into new areas. In 1999, for example, it bought Stimsonite, of Niles, Illinois, a maker of highway safety products, such as the reflective coatings on highway signs. The purchase gave Avery a powerful entree into an allied field.

Stimsonite operated a proprietary microreplication technology platform that was a neat fit with Avery Dennison's technological capabilities in pressure-sensitive adhesives. The combination, said Avery's chief executive at the time, Philip M. Neal, would enable the company "to create and develop a variety of innovative new products and applications."

A similar scenario was played out a year earlier after Avery's purchase of Bear Rock Technologies, whose headquarters can be found on Mother Lode Drive in Shingle Springs, California. Bear Rock was a developer of barcode design and printing software, which dovetailed nicely with some elements of Avery's product line and gave Avery a major stake in the barcode market.

With a partner, move into new businesses that can use the partnership's talents.

Partnerships have some of the same advantages that attach to mergers, but they lack many of the disadvantages. In fact, one might say that partnerships are to mergers as dating is to marriage, which is to say, companies and individuals that merge must, willy-nilly, adjust to (or suffer with) each other's strengths and weaknesses. The arrangement is permanent, and a satisfactory conclusion is in no way guaranteed. As Ralph Waldo Emerson asked in a somewhat different context: "Is not marriage an open question, when it is alleged, from the beginning of the world, that such as are in the institution wish to get out, and such as are out wish to get in?"

That, of course, is one advantage of the partnership or

alliance: you can usually get out of it. Another: partners are not expected to change to accommodate all of each other's idiosyncrasies. They are separate entities, united in the expectation that their individual talents can be combined in a new business venture that will benefit both beyond what either might have gained alone.

As the Evergreen research concluded, winning companies that shone in the merger management practice tended to seek out and enter into partnerships of that nature.

Smithfield: *Toward vertical integration*

Back in 1969, when Joseph Luter sold the company his father and grandfather had founded, the Virginia-based Smithfield Foods was a regional pork wholesaler. The company subsequently suffered a series of reverses, caused, in part, by diversification into unrelated businesses, and in 1975 Luter bought it back at a bargain price. It soon became clear that he was now committed to a new plan: Smithfield was going to become much bigger, and vertically integrated. Luter was determined to free the company from its dependence upon midwest hog farmers.

Over the next decade, Luter acquired a number of pork processors, but the raw-materials end of integration eluded him. Then, in 1987, he tried the partnership route. He entered into a joint venture with Carroll's Foods, a pork producer, to obtain rights to raise the ultra-lean NPD hogs; as mentioned in an earlier chapter, they became the stars of a new brand, Smithfield Lean Generation Pork.

In 1994, Luter once again organized a partnership to, if you will, beef up the hog-production side of his business. This time, in addition to Carroll's Foods, there were two other producers. Together, they created Circle Four Farms, a huge pig farm in Utah. Luter's master plan was succeeding so well, and so profitably, that he was able to buy out his partners two years later.

The farmer partners had brought their hog-raising skills to the party; Smithfield had brought its financial clout, its role as an assured market for the product, and its management expertise. Together, they had created a new business that they would have had trouble establishing on their own, and they all benefited from the experience.

This is what Luter had to say about the partnership route in a 1994 interview in *National Provisioner:* "When you're a visionary looking way out, there is a hard way and an easy way to reach your goals. Strategic alliances can help you get there quicker than trying to do it all yourself."

Nucor: *One steel mill, two parents*

Ken Iverson, leader of steelmaker Nucor, had some similar thoughts as he gradually moved his company beyond its low-end mini-mill products to begin producing steel bolts and even, by the start of the Evergreen decade, machined steel parts and metal buildings and components. But there were built-in size limitations on how far he could take Nucor, and a joint venture seemed the answer.

In 1988, Nucor and the Japanese steelmaker Yamato-Kogyo built a mill in Blytheville, Arkansas, that used state-of-the-art technology to produce high-quality, low-cost steel beams for the construction industry. In this partnership, Yamato-Kogyo had the technological expertise in structural beam blank casting; Nucor had the management and construction talent. The result: one of the top structural steel mills in the United States.

Avery Dennison: *Of stamps and grapes*

Avery Dennison has also relied on alliances to carry it into new business areas. In 1998, for example, the company partnered with E-Stamp and Stamps.com, which had been licensed to peddle postage over the Internet. The deal called for Avery to provide special mailing labels so that Internet customers could print out the postage.

Meanwhile, Avery was invading the wine industry, working with paper companies and directly with wineries to produce labels that provide special effects or greater endurance. Avery partnered with the E&J Gallo winery, for example, to come up with a heat-transfer labeling process; it appeared on a new line of wines called Wild Vines and gave the bottle a frosted look.

Another Avery alliance was with Neenah Paper, which provided uncoated paper for wine labels, while Avery provided the adhesive technology. Their joint product gave designers many more graphic options—this at a time when the package design of all kinds of consumer products, wine included, was becoming an ever more crucial part of the marketing effort. Avery's pressure-sensitive, adhesive-coated film also allowed for labels that would stay on wine bottles no matter how wet they became.

By picking its partners with care, Avery was able to leverage their combined forces to successfully enter one new business after another.

Develop a systematic capability to identify, screen, and close deals.

As the Evergreen research revealed, Winners and Climbers excelling in the merger management practice did not treat acquisitions and partnerships as an unimportant sideline. Instead, they devoted substantial resources, human and financial, to developing an efficient, ongoing process that covered the various aspects of deal-making. Their rationale: mergers and partnerships are too important to be left to decisions made on an *ad hoc* basis.

The skills required for the task are many and varied. It takes people with sensitive antennae and a widespread network of business contacts to spot the opportunities for an advantageous deal. They must also have a clear sense of their own company's goals and resources.

The decision as to which of the merger candidates to pursue must rest with the top executives of the company and the board, but the chances of reaching the right decision are improved if they have the best and most up-to-date information about the candidates. Companies need to create a team of people who have the requisite investigative, financial, and business skills and experience.

The closing of the deal calls for yet another set of skills. Top executives should participate, of course, but if they don't have the gene for dealing, they should make use of those who have it.

Valspar: *A genius for mergers*

That was not an issue at Valspar, the paint and coating company. Its longtime CEO Angus Wurtele had a genius for all three aspects of the merger trade.

Wurtele started out on his dozens of buyouts because technological changes and growing marketing costs in his industry had put a premium on achieving economies of scale, and he saw acquisitions as the most cost-effective response. He soon developed a system for finding the best deals and making them happen. He began by establishing and maintaining relationships with the leaders of companies that might possibly, at some distant time, be candidates for mergers. Aside from giving him a better feel for the organizations themselves, it enabled him to know very early on when management might be interested in a deal. And at that point, Wurtele would be able to negotiate with that company from a position of trust.

In 1989, Peter Gillette, a longtime friend of Wurtele's, suggested to *Corporate Report Minnesota* that the CEO's bargaining skills might have something to do with his savvy at cards. The style he has adopted in the business world, Gillette said, "is a little like a poker player. He knows when to fold, and he knows when to go for it. He's willing to take risks, but they're always measured risks, with a high probability they'll pay off."

In the course of his acquisitions, Wurtele learned some hard lessons. "Not every acquisition has been equally successful," is the way he put it. For example, he preferred public companies to privately held family concerns. "You're never sure about the accounting" in the private businesses, he said. "There are always a lot more family members on the payroll than meets the eye. The work rules and traditions are sacrosanct. By the time you get done cleaning the company up, there's not much left."

On the financial side, Wurtele wanted to be sure he could eventually bring any potential acquisition up to Valspar's own 20 percent profit level. Short-term, it would not pass muster if there were any chance it could negatively affect Valspar's earnings in a major way. In other words, Wurtele went shopping for underperforming companies that could be fairly quickly absorbed into Valspar and brought up to snuff with its weakest operations sold off or ditched.

Valspar early on developed the know-how needed to uncover and successfully bring off acquisitions. So did the Ohio-based drug wholesaler Cardinal Health.

Cardinal: *Mergers are a line of business*

"Acquisitions are a line of business at Cardinal," CEO Robert Walter told the *Columbus Dispatch* in 1996. "It's not like a deal just popped up. We work on our ability to do acquisitions."

Like Valspar's chief executive, Walter is a patient pursuer. In one case, he spent more than nine years talking to the owner of an enterprise about a merger before it actually took place.

"He built the business into what I thought the business ought to be," Walter said, "and I paid more for it. In theory, it cost me money, but he delivered something of more value. By the time I got it, it was mostly fixed."

That is the way Walter liked it. He was only interested in companies that were well run and whose managers would remain with the organization.

Cardinal's acquisitions were not done at random, the CEO told *Chain Drug Review* in 1994. "They've been done in contiguous markets, enabling us to grow in a logical way, much as our chain customers have grown."

When Winners like Valspar and Cardinal acquire a company, it is not a spur-of-the-moment, seat-of-the-pants adventure. The ground has been carefully studied and prepared, the buyout plan worked out in detail, and the negotiations conducted with skill and a certain amount of panache. They know what they are doing, and that shows up in their outstanding results.

What Comes Next

With the end of this chapter, the detailed discussion of each of the eight management practices is complete. As you will have noted, most of the corporate examples we have used in the book are Winners and Climbers, on the theory that a description of a company doing the right thing in the right way is more likely to help the reader understand the practices and mandates that emerged from the Evergreen Project.

The next and final chapter of the book takes the opposite tack. It describes many of the challenges companies face in seeking to follow the 4+2 formula, excelling in four primary and two secondary practices. And the case study isn't a Winner or Climber, but a Tumbler—Nike. As the story of Nike unfolds in the pages ahead, you will see in detail how that company's failure to follow the Evergreen practices contributed to its decline.

Excel at Six Management
Practices at Once

For managers, the 4+2 formula is a road map to success. But they must learn to use it with patience, discipline, and consistency. And as the cautionary tale of Nike shows all too clearly, there are bullets to be dodged along the way.

If ever a company epitomized success, it was Nike in the spring of 1997. Sales of its sneakers and sports-clothing lines had jumped by 140 percent since 1994 to $9.2 billion; net profits were rising by 30 to 40 percent annually. In the space of just two years, the stock price had soared 320 percent, to $76 a share.

But trouble was in the offing, and it arrived full force toward the end of the decade of the Evergreen Project. On the face of it, the problems had less to do with the company's internal management practices than with outside forces. The economy of Asia, a major Nike market, was collapsing. Teenagers, always a volatile group, were switching away from athletic shoes. A number of retail chains—Nike customers all—were closing stores; some were going out of business altogether. Public protests over working conditions in the plants of the company's overseas suppliers were affecting Nike's sales.

Nevertheless, as we have argued throughout this book, business problems are seldom caused by external events. Because they have reliable warning systems in place, Winners are able to recognize outside storm signals at the earliest possible moment and trim their sails accordingly. The more difficult challenge is internal: to maintain the performance of their primary and secondary management practices. And that is a devilishly difficult task. Less than 5 percent of all publicly traded companies, our research found, are able to maintain a total return to shareholders greater than their industry peers for more than ten years.

It requires maximum discipline and alertness. The intent to focus on the 4+2 practices must not be allowed to waver. Should circumstances require a company to invest more in some practices—to meet a competitive threat, for example—the organization must not start to stint on the others. It is too easy for an enterprise, particularly one with a long track record of success, to let down its guard. Emphasizing growth, for example, might lead the organization to pay less attention to flawless execution. As Exhibit 12.1 shows, Tumblers don't differ all that much from Winners; slippage on one or two of the six management practices can lead to disaster. Like six plates being spun by a juggler at the same time, if one falls, the others are likely to fall as well.

The chart on the next page compares the ratings of Winners and Losers, Climbers and Tumblers on their efforts to fulfill the primary and secondary management practices during the two

12.1 Winning Is Difficult to Achieve and Sustain

	Primary Practices		Secondary Practices	
	Negative ratings	Positive ratings	Negative ratings	Positive ratings
Winners	0.3	3.1	0.3	1.5
	0.1	3.3	0.1	1.9
Losers	2.3	0.5	1.4	0.1
	2.3	0.5	1.6	0.3
Climbers	1.1	1.3	0.6	0.5
	0.2	2.8	0.4	0.9
Tumblers	0.6	2.2	0.6	0.8
	1.2	1.6	1	0.5

■ Period 1   ■ Period 2

Source: Evergreen team analysis.

consecutive five-year periods studied by the Evergreen Project. The results suggest how quickly companies can miss their way, once their ratings on the practices drop, and how far they can rise with a ratings improvement. Tumblers, for example, had a very positive rating on primary practices in the first five years, but the gap widened considerably in the second five years.

After years as a high-flyer, growing at a fevered pace, Nike's management lost its focus on the practices required to sustain success, and during the Evergreen decade this Winner became a Tumbler. The company tried to return to its earlier form by improving and, in some cases, reinventing those very practices. Among other things, this traditionally macho organization began hiring high-level women executives and catering, as it never did before, to the women's market. Unfortunately, it is much harder to climb back than it is to stumble.

Before Nike fell, it was a legendary Winner, envied by every retailer. Founded by Bill Bowerman, the University of Oregon's track coach, and Philip H. Knight, one of his runners, Nike began in 1962 as Blue Ribbon Sports, an importer and distributor of Japanese running shoes. Bowerman was the innovative designer whose expertise was running and runners; Knight was the businessman who has been the company's chief executive for most of its history.

In a speech before the National Press Club in 1998, Knight described the company's inception: "Everything was done either on a commission basis or [by] a relative. We had no money, no sales force, no employees, and no clout. Our first-year sales were $8,000, and we made a $254 profit. The outgoing freight company was the trunk of my 1963 Plymouth Valiant."

In 1980, having increased annual sales to $2 million and renamed itself Nike after the Greek goddess of victory, the company was cut loose by its Japanese supplier. Rather than simply fold their tent, Knight and Bowerman entered the sports shoe business on their own, designing a new product and lining up their own Japanese suppliers.

When Knight thinks back to that pivotal decision, he recalls John F. Kennedy's response when asked how he became a war hero: "It was easy. They sank my boat."

The reinvented company was brash and innovative, constantly creating new products, opening new markets, and spreading its brand and "swoosh" logo around the globe. The chief target was the male wannabe (or might-have-been) athlete. Nike fought off strong challenges from Reebok and others by linking its products with a succession of sports giants. It used Michael Jordan to peddle basketball goods; Bo Jackson to push cross-training items; and Andre Agassi, Lance Armstrong, and Tiger Woods, respectively, to sell tennis, biking, and golfing products. When athletic shoes became the fashionable choice in footwear in cities across the United States Nike recognized the opportunity and seized a commanding lead in its industry. At one point, it owned almost 50 percent of the $15.6 billion U.S. market for athletic shoes while, at the same time, Nike-brand clothing and accessories were penetrating other markets.

Then sales sank in Asia and stalled in the United States. What happened? A 4+2 analysis shows that the company lost its commitment to its primary and secondary management practices.

PRIMARY PRACTICE 1:

MAKE YOUR STRATEGY CLEAR AND NARROWLY FOCUSED

Started and staffed by jocks, Nike prospered with a strategy narrowly focused on athletes as its major market. It targeted anyone who dreamed of flying fifteen feet to the basket, like Michael Jordan, or sinking impossible putts under maximum pressure, like Tiger Woods—in other words, virtually every American male. For these customers, what counted most was not how a product looked, but how it helped them realize their dreams. Performance, not fashion, was the goal.

Though the strategy worked superbly for a long time, stress fractures began to appear in the corporate façade. In the middle 1990s, teenagers switched to casual leather shoes or hiking boots as their preferred footwear, tossing out their sneakers. Nike was blindsided.

The company's sensitive external antennae (long a component of its high-performance strategy) had gone dead, and their failure to recognize the new trend early exposed the company to an embarrassing and costly setback.

But even after the trend was obvious, Nike persisted in its old strategy, continuing to produce those white shoes while competitors, such as New Balance, jumped in with lines tailored to the new fashion. Around the country, former Nike customers were buying the lively-looking, less-expensive sneaker models offered by Reebok and Skechers.

The result was that Nike's market share of medium- and low-priced shoes in the U.S. fell dramatically. The company had learned a painful lesson: even the most successful strategy will fail unless it is continuously monitored and refreshed to meet changing market conditions.

Pushing energetically and insistently into every conceivable market, Nike's expansion came primarily through brand extension. By the mid-1990s, it was producing close to 500 footwear products, and even more accessory products: sunglasses, watches, backpacks, headsets, shirts, pants, sweaters, hats, and more.

Two years later, Phil Knight acknowledged that his brand

strategy had lost focus. Nike had entered tangential markets ruled by heavyweights such as The Gap, Nautica, and Ralph Lauren, and it had failed to offer goods with unique customer appeal. "We didn't make the products special enough," Knight said, and there were "too many Nike stripes and swooshes, too much general product, such as T-shirts."

As Nike's experience illustrates, Winners pursue very clear and narrowly focused growth strategies. When they move away from their core businesses to plunge into diversification, their performance is going to lag. Nike's brand extension turned into a chaotic rush in all directions and was a major cause of its descent from Winner to Tumbler.

PRIMARY PRACTICE 2:

EXECUTE FLAWLESSLY

Execution got shortchanged during Nike's wild growth spurt of the early nineties. The company dedicated itself so totally to unlimited expansion that it neglected to ride herd on such factors as efficiency and cost controls. In 2000, Phil Knight told *Business Week:* "We grew really fast from 1994 to 1997, but I don't think anybody would suggest we were efficient. We couldn't be. We were just chasing the growth."

Nike had forgotten that Winners can't afford to choose between growth and efficiency—they must achieve both. As Sumantra Ghoshal, of the London Business School, aptly puts it, "Winners, like great chefs, must learn how to cook sweet and sour."

Another operational failure came in two areas that had always been among the company's strong points, product quality and marketing. It was, after all, the superior quality of Nike's high-performance athletic shoes and its gung-ho marketing that had won the company its enormous customer base. Every time it introduced a new shoe, in a new sports area, something it did with some frequency, that shoe could be relied upon to be the best on the ground.

However, when Nike entered the nontraditional sports market—skateboarding and snowboarding, for example—it came a cropper.

At the time, the popularity of these sports was just beginning to take off. The participants were individualists with little interest in team sports, but they were already much admired—and their style emulated—by their teen peers.

The shoes Nike offered skateboarders and snowboarders failed to achieve any substantial market penetration. They were widely disparaged as mediocre—uncomfortable and easily worn down. When a group of skateboarders was asked in 2000 for their impression of the Nike skateboard shoe, many were unaware that one existed. It was an execution disaster. Both the legendary Nike marketing team and the proud product-design people had dropped the ball.

Another of Nike's longtime operational strengths had been its skill in getting merchandise to retailers where and when it was needed. But later in the decade, the sheer volume of its offerings overwhelmed its replenishment systems. Retailers were furious about losing sales because orders arrived too late.

In one typical example, some stores reported that they were running out of Nike tops and shorts for women, a matter of consequence to retailers, since many customers bought these more-expensive fashion items while shopping for Nike footwear.

It was not until 1999 that Nike announced plans to overhaul its supply chain to create a system "well ahead of anything our competition was doing." Two years after spending $400 million on i2 supply-chain management software, Nike explained a $50 million cut in its profit outlook for a quarter as the result of problems with that very software. (According to the software manufacturer, it was Nike's flawed use of the system that caused the problems.)

Nike's loss of customer focus and its weakness in execution were signs that the company was no longer committed to operational excellence. Looking back at the decade in his 2001 letter to shareholders, Phil Knight wrote, "It was as if we got bored with doing the simple things right."

PRIMARY PRACTICE 3:

BUILD A PERFORMANCE-BASED CULTURE

From the very beginning, as Nike's managers and employees were scratching their way toward industry domination, the company's culture demanded a lot from its people—and got it. In every nook and cranny of the organization, employees accepted the company's quest for greatness as their own. They were aggressive and entrepreneurial in Nike's behalf. The company's values—to serve customers with high-quality, high-performance products and blow away the competition—drove the culture; the culture drove the employees.

But Nike's culture had some unique characteristics that, over time, proved troublesome, and contributed to its fall in status from Winner to Tumbler.

Nike people weren't just confident—they tended to be over-confident, even brash, routinely flouting industry customs and conventions. On any given topic, they thought they knew better; and the corporate culture smiled on their go-it-alone independence.

The company's initial refusal to take seriously the protests against working conditions in its overseas suppliers' factories was a prime example of its confrontational culture. The complaints first surfaced in the early 1990s. A headline on an Internet site carried the message: "JUST DO IT: BOYCOTT NIKE." The text included the following: "Nike promotes sports and healthy living, but the lives of workers who make Nike's shoes and clothes in Asia and Latin America are anything but healthy. They live in extreme poverty and suffer stress and exhaustion from over-work."

For many months, Nike ignored or disputed the protests or insisted that it wasn't responsible for the working conditions of suppliers, which were, after all, separate organizations outside of Nike's control. Instead of vigorously meeting criticisms and correcting unsatisfactory conditions, Nike put the blame on campus radicals and the media. As late as 1999, Knight's letter to shareholders was confrontational: "Our friends in the media are slowly becoming more knowledgeable. This is good. It means that consumers are actually getting informed rather than just alarmed."

Nike's attitude simply increased public anger about the overseas sweatshops. The boycott—beginning on college campuses, then expanding into cities and finally to Nike markets abroad—seriously eroded sales. Even as this book went to press, the issue was still alive in the courts and on the Internet.

The insularity of the Nike culture was expressed in ways large and small. A grass-covered earthen wall surrounds the company's 175-acre campus in Beaverton, Oregon, and staffers actually talk about events "outside the berm," the way federal government insiders talk about life "outside the Beltway." Nike people prided themselves on finding their own way and solving their own problems. That attitude did promote entrepreneurial behavior, but it also worked to the company's detriment. Among other things, it tended to hold the company back from joint ventures and even from making acquisitions, depriving Nike of a relatively low-cost and reliable path to growth.

As the company prospered through the 1980s and early 1990s, its overly aggressive, insular culture proved to be a handicap. Later events show clearly that the company's performance-based culture had become too much of a good thing. An adjustment was needed if this corporate giant was to accommodate to its new position in the industry and the marketplace.

PRIMARY PRACTICE 4:

MAKE YOUR ORGANIZATION FAST AND FLAT

The structure management practice encompasses the systems that speed the flow of information within the organization and between the organization and the outside world. Winning companies are organized to recognize market changes before their competitors do and to adapt to them quicker. The means to that end is a flat and bureaucracy-free organizational structure.

As Nike rose in the sports-shoe and accessories industry, its single-minded focus on growth, along with its culture's emphasis on independence, dictated what the organization looked like. In the company's rush to develop new products and enter new markets, individual units were given a loose rein. Management controls were minimal as long as units increased their market share regularly. The company was simply too busy and too dedicated to speed to develop much of a bureaucracy; the organization was flat, and organizational structures were simple and lean. This one-for-all-and-all-for-one culture encouraged cooperation among departments.

But Nike's transformation from pipsqueak to titan put enormous pressure on every facet of the operation. Individual departments became unwieldy, and cooperation among them diminished. The structural controls that ordinarily contain costs were weak or nonexistent; budgets were made to be broken. And when Nike's growth began to lag, these financial shortcomings came back to haunt the company.

Because it was devoted to invading new markets, Nike had systems in place to monitor what was going on in its industry, allowing it to recognize opportunities and adjust to changes in existing markets. But when the growth strategy succeeded beyond expectations, these systems were overwhelmed.

As we discussed earlier, Nike was nonplussed when urban teenagers' taste turned from sneakers to casual wear. Its antennae had failed to see the change coming. That it took Nike eighteen months to design and manufacture a shoe is just one example of how ill-equipped it was to turn on a dime to meet new customer demand. Nike's organizational practices prepared it to invade, not defend; to initiate, not react. Nike's slowness allowed its competitors to pick up market share, and as a result its earnings suffered.

SECONDARY PRACTICE 1:

MAKE TALENT STICK AROUND AND DEVELOP MORE

Though talent management isn't a primary practice, it performs a key role in virtually every facet of an enterprise. In its drive to success, Nike had the talent it most needed to grow big fast. That happened because such a vibrant, risk-taking company was a magnet for vibrant, risk-taking people. Nike's managers knew how to attract, develop, and hold on to these go-getters.

Stock options helped. As the share price soared, the options took on a golden hue, to such an extent that Phil Knight worried: "We have lost experienced people for whom the stock option program has created lifetime financial security." Of greater moment to its talent base, however, was the company's willingness to let people run their own shops with minimal interference.

As the years passed and Nike achieved its early goals, many high-level veterans underwent a sea change. Once their company had metamorphosed from upstart to establishment, they began assuming the trappings of old-line managers. The company increased its rewards and incentives, but it had little effect, since they weren't closely tied to performance.

Knight at one point explained his company's difficulties this way: "We are a very well managed $5 billion company. Right now, though, we are a $10 billion company trying to get to $15 billion. Management has been stretched too thin."

Many critics agreed, but they also insisted that what Nike needed was new blood in its management ranks. The company made some efforts in that direction, but the newcomers often left abruptly when they found they could not penetrate the barriers to change set up by old-time executives in the name of "the Nike way." In 1996, twenty-six of the twenty-seven vice presidents were veterans.

SECONDARY PRACTICE 2:

MAKE YOUR LEADERS COMMITTED TO
YOUR BUSINESS

The measure of the importance of the leadership management practice can be seen in this: more than half of the Winners in the

Evergreen research sample excelled in this practice, while two-thirds of the Losers had trouble with it.

Phil Knight's direction through Nike's years of struggle and growth was essential to the company's success. Envisioning the direction that Nike should take, he pursued it aggressively and ingeniously. He was a serious presence who was totally involved in the operation of the company. Knight's decision to pursue endorsements from Michael Jordan helped to define the company as the one the superstars chose, and it proved to be a brilliant marketing strategy.

Knight had a brash, in-your-face personality and supreme confidence in his destiny. To this day, he likes to quote from *Into Thin Air*, by Jon Krakauer: "There are men for whom the unattainable has a special attraction. Their ambitions are strong enough to brush aside the doubts which more cautious men might have." Knight said he thought the author "was talking about our first twenty-six years."

Knight and Bowerman cared deeply about sports and its beneficial role in society. They were able to convey their enthusiasm to Nike's employees, who felt that it informed their attitudes toward their work. "I love the fact that Nike is about sports," Knight said on his company's website. "Sports is natural, instinctive, competitive, and, in the end, rewarding." In sharing these feelings with their employees, Knight and Bowerman imbued them with a sense of mission that yielded a high performance level.

Knight's unconventional leadership style energized his employees, but, in later years, it frequently annoyed shareholders, the public, and the media. He didn't take criticism well, as shown by his initial refusal to deal with the complaints against his suppliers. At times, he simply disappeared, dropping direct contact with his company's daily operations for weeks at a time.

When trouble hit, Knight acknowledged that he was to blame. According to *Business Week,* Knight eventually apologized to his headquarters staff for "taking his eye off the ball" and leaving the organization unprepared to cope with difficult times.

What Knight had not seen—or, having seen, ignored—was the degree to which the other leadership elements of the company had declined. As he admitted in his report to shareholders that same year, Nike would have to "upgrade management" and "bring in talented newcomers." As the Nike saga shows, even talented and dedicated leaders like Phil Knight can lose their focus over time. Maintaining the high level of management practices required to achieve sustainable success is hard duty; losing it is all too easy.

SECONDARY PRACTICE 3:

MAKE INDUSTRY-TRANSFORMING INNOVATIONS

Needless to say, successful companies know how to introduce new, improved products and services with some regularity. The Evergreen research showed that enterprises that choose innovation as one of their secondary practices must know how to be disruptive, with new products or business models that can transform their industry.

In that regard, Nike was the champion for decades. Year after year, it brought out athletic shoes and equipment calculated to redefine the parameters of one sport after another. Once Nike invaded a sport, be it basketball or tennis or golf, the other players had to scramble just to stay in the game.

That tradition began early in Nike's history when Bill Bowerman invented the waffle soles that would dramatically affect athletes' performance in nearly every sport. He shaped sample rubber soles in a waffle iron in his kitchen until he found the right design. A series of pioneering innovations followed, including wedged heels, cushioned midsoles, and nylon uppers. As the company matured, such breakthroughs came less frequently. Nike's entry into nontraditional sports not only failed to take over the market, it barely made an impression.

Why was Nike no longer creating industry-transforming products? One could argue that the mature state of the sports-shoe industry had left few opportunities for transformation. It is also true that today's athletic shoes are far more complex than they used to be. Nike now spends two years designing a shoe, and the company's advance product engineers, as they are known, work on forty to fifty projects at any given time, half of which will never make it to market.

Yet it seems clear that neither of those considerations would have stopped the old Nike from developing revolutionary products. What happened is that the company's capacity for innovation has lessened. In the language of the 4+2 formula, its innovation practice has weakened, and until it returns to full strength Nike is likely to remain a Tumbler.

SECONDARY PRACTICE 4:

MAKE GROWTH HAPPEN WITH MERGERS AND PARTNERSHIPS

Over the last decade, the urge to merge has swept through virtually every industry as companies struggled to adjust to globalization, increased competition, and the computer and Internet revolutions. Businesses looked for partners that could bolster their weaknesses while providing economies of scale and a fresh infusion of ideas and talent. It was evident that growth by acquisition tended to be more economical than internally generated growth.

But Nike wasn't much interested. By ignoring the opportunity to buy Converse when it went into bankruptcy, for example, Nike gave up a chance to move into down-market department stores with an already established brand. It also passed up a chance to purchase North Face, a manufacturer of outdoor clothing and related products.

The North Face incident is particularly instructive. The acquisition had been urged by Nike's president of outdoor products, Gordon O. McFadden, at a time when Nike had only a bit role in the outdoor clothing market. The purchase, McFadden said, "would have doubled the business overnight and made Nike the dominant player."

According to McFadden, "The decision not to act stemmed from an insecurity of moving outside the Nike domain." Another fact might also have played a role: the company had no serious system in place—as exists in most companies of comparable size—to smooth the way for integrating a newly bought addition.

In the Evergreen study, the Winners that excelled at acquisitions specialized in large numbers of relatively small, high-value deals. And they made them only when they were certain that the candidates would fit well with their own existing lines and would benefit from the Winners' existing skills. Nike had a number of opportunities to make such arrangements. That it was generally unwilling to take advantage of them demonstrated a serious weakness in its growth management practice.

Final Words

With this chapter, we conclude our book. It is our hope and expectation that the ideas set forth here will aid you and your company to achieve sustainable business success. But we also believe that the 4+2 formula has important applications beyond the borders of the corporation. It can be of substantial value, for example, to individual investors who must judge the future worth of their investments on the basis of past and present performance. In analyzing companies, the investor should pay closest attention to their level of achievement on the primary management practices listed here. That is where vital clues to a company's prospects can be found.

In fact, we hold that any organization, corporate or civic, public or private, profit-making or eleemosynary, can benefit from the insights yielded by the Evergreen Project. These insights can identify those areas of management practice that are crucial to long-term success—whether that success is measured in dollars or by some less commercial standard.

The 4+2 formula points to the practices that are essential to success, but it does not tell how to go about excelling in them. The mandates that accompany each practice provide only limited guidance. What we offer in this book, as we noted in the beginning, is not so much a recipe as a road map. The details of the journey—the route, the personnel, the means of payment—will vary with each organization. Our mission has been to identify the destinations you need to focus on, and, by extension, those that require less attention. The rest is up to you.

SOURCES AND SUGGESTED READING

Part One: Chapter 1

CORE READINGS—FOCUSED STRATEGY: Kenneth Andrews, *The Concept of Strategy* (Boston: Harvard Business School Press, 1962); Richard A. D'Aveni, *Hypercompetition: Managing the Dynamics of Strategic Maneuvering* (New York: The Free Press, 1994); Richard A. D'Aveni, *Strategic Supremacy: How Industry Leaders Create Growth, Wealth, and Power Through Spheres of Influence* (New York: The Free Press, 2001); Gary Hamel and C. K. Prahalad, *Competing for the Future* (Boston: Harvard Business School Press, 1994); W. Chan Kim and Renee Mauborgne, "Value Innovation: The Strategic Logic of High Growth," *Harvard Business Review*, January–February 1997; Henry Mintzberg, Bruce Ahlstrand, and Joseph Lampel, *Strategy Safari: A Guided Tour Through the Wilds of Strategic Management* (New York: Simon & Schuster, 1998); Michael E. Porter, *Competitive Advantage* (New York: The Free Press, 1996); Michael E. Porter, "What Is Strategy?" *Harvard Business Review*, November–December 1996; James Brian Quinn, *Strategies for Change: Logical Incrementalism* (Homewood, IL: R.D. Irwin, 1980); James Brian Quinn, *Intelligent Enterprise* (New York: The Free Press, 1994).

CORE READINGS—EXECUTION: Ronald Ashkenas, Steve Kerr, and David Ulrich, *The GE Work-Out* (Boston: Harvard University Press, 2002); Larry Bossidy, Ram Charan, and Charles Burck (contributor), *Execution: The Discipline of Getting Things Done* (New York: Crown Publishing, 2002); Subir Chowdhury, *The Power of Six Sigma: An Inspiring Tale of How Six Sigma Is Transforming the Way We Work* (Chicago: Dearborn Trade, 2001); Peter S. Pande, Robert P. Neuman, and Roland R. Cavanagh, *The Six Sigma Way: How GE, Motorola, and Other Top Companies Are Honing Their Performance* (New York: McGraw-Hill, 2000); Michael Treacy and Fred Wiersema, *The Discipline of Market Leaders: Choose Your Customers, Narrow Your Focus, Dominate Your Market* (Reading, MA: Addison-Wesley, 1995).

CORE READINGS—ORGANIZATION CULTURE: Franklin C. Ashby, *Revitalize Your Corporate Culture: Powerful Ways to Transform Your Company into a High-Performance Organization* (Houston: Cashman Dudley, 1999); Marlene Caroselli, *Creating a High Performance Culture* (Amherst, MA: Human Resource Development Press, Inc., 1997); James C. Collins and Jerry I. Porras, *Built to Last: Successful Habits of Visionary Companies* (New York: HarperCollins Publishers, 1997); Terrence E. Deal and Allan A. Kennedy, *The New Corporate Cultures: Revitalizing the Workplace After Downsizing, Mergers, and Reengineering* (Reading, MA: Perseus Books, 1999); William Joyce, *MegaChange* (New York: The Free Press, 1999); John P. Kotter and James L. Heskett (contributor), *Corporate Culture and Performance* (New York: Maxwell Macmillan International, 1992); Edgar H. Schein, *The Corporate Culture Survival Guide: Sense and Nonsense About Culture Change* (San Francisco: Jossey-Bass Publishers, 1999); Edgar H. Schein, *Organizational Culture and Leadership* (San Francisco: Jossey-Bass Publishers, 1991).

CORE READINGS—ORGANIZATION STRUCTURE: Jay Galbraith, *Designing Organizations: An Executive Briefing on Strategy, Struc-*

ture, and Process (San Francisco: Jossey-Bass Publishers, 1995); Michael Hammer and James Champy, *Reengineering the Corporation: A Manifesto for Business Revolution* (New York: HarperBusiness, 2001); Lawrence Hrebiniak and William Joyce, *Implementing Strategy* (London: Macmillan, 1984); Paul Lawrence and Jay Lorsch, *Organization and Environment* (Boston: Harvard Business School Press, 1968); Ray Miles and Charles Snow, *Strategy, Structure and Performance* (New York: McGraw-Hill, 1978); Henry Mintzberg, *Structure in Fives: Designing Effective Organizations* (Englewood Cliffs, NJ: Prentice-Hall, 1993); David Nadler, Michael L. Tushman (contributor), and Mark B. Nadler, *Competing by Design: The Power of Organizational Architecture* (New York: Oxford University Press, 1997); Nitin Nohria, Davis Dyer, and Frederick Dalzell, *Changing Fortunes: Remaking the Industrial Corporation* (New York: John Wiley & Sons, 2002).

CORE READINGS—TALENT: Brian E. Becker, Mark A. Huselid, and Dave Ulrich, *The HR Scorecard: Linking People, Strategy, and Performance* (Boston: Harvard Business School Press, 2001); Jim Collins, *Good to Great: Why Some Companies Make the Leap . . . and Others Don't* (New York: HarperBusiness, 2001); Jac Fitz-Enz, *The ROI of Human Capital: Measuring the Economic Value of Employee Performance* (New York: Amacom, 2000); Ed Michaels, Helen Handfield-Jones, and Beth Axelrod, *The War for Talent* (Boston: Harvard Business School Press, 2001); Charles A. O'Reilly and Jeffrey Pfeffer, *Hidden Value: How Great Companies Achieve Extraordinary Results with Ordinary People* (Boston: Harvard Business School Press, 2000); Jeffrey Pfeffer, *Competitive Advantage Through People: Unleashing the Power of the Work Force* (Boston: Harvard Business School Press, 1994); Jeffrey Pfeffer, *The Human Equation: Building Profits by Putting People First* (Boston: Harvard Business School Press, 1998); Bradford D. Smart, *Topgrading: How Leading Companies Win by Hiring, Coaching and Keeping the Best People* (Englewood Cliffs, NJ: Prentice Hall Press, 1999); Noel M.

Tichy and Eli B. Cohen, *The Leadership Engine* (New York: Harper-Business, 1997); David Ulrich, *Competing from the Inside Out* (New York: The Free Press, 1990); David Ulrich, *Human Resource Champions* (Boston: Harvard Business School Press, 1997).

CORE READINGS—LEADERSHIP: Warren G. Bennis and Robert J. Thomas, *Geeks and Geezers* (Boston: Harvard Business School Press, 2002); Warren G. Bennis, *On Becoming a Leader* (Reading, MA: Addison-Wesley, 1989); Jim Collins, *Good to Great: Why Some Companies Make the Leap . . . and Others Don't* (New York: HarperBusiness, 2001); Sydney Finkelstein, *Leadership Lessons from Failing Organizations* (New York: The Free Press, forthcoming); Daniel Goleman, Annie McKee, and Richard E. Boyatzis, *Primal Leadership: Realizing the Power of Emotional Intelligence* (Boston: Harvard Business School Press, 2002); Donald C. Hambrick and E. M. Jackson, "Outside Directors with a Stake: The Linchpin in Improving Governance," *California Management Review,* May 2000; Rakesh Khurana, *Searching for a Corporate Savior: The Irrational Quest for Charismatic CEOs* (Princeton, NJ: Princeton University Press, 2002); John P. Kotter, *A Force for Change: How Leadership Differs from Management* (New York: The Free Press, 1990); James M. Kouzes and Barry Z. Posner, *The Leadership Challenge: How to Keep Getting Extraordinary Things Done in Organizations* (San Francisco: Jossey-Bass Publishers, 1995); Jay W. Lorsch and Elizabeth MacIver (contributor), *Pawns or Potentates: The Reality of America's Corporate Boards* (Boston: Harvard Business School Press, 1989); Ralph Stogdill, *Handbook of Organizational Leadership* (New York: Wiley Interscience, 1974); Noel M. Tichy and Nancy Cardwell, *The Cycle of Leadership: How Great Leaders Teach Their Companies to Win* (New York: HarperBusiness, 2002); Noam Wasserman, Nitin Nohria, and Bharat Anand, *When Does Leadership Matter? The Contingent Opportunities View of CEO Leadership* (Boston: Harvard Business School Working Paper, 2001).

CORE READINGS—INNOVATION: John Seely Brown and Paul Duguid, *The Social Life of Information* (Boston: Harvard Business School Press, 2002); Shona L. Brown and Kathleen M. Eisenhardt, *Competing on the Edge: Strategy as Structured Chaos* (Boston: Harvard Business School Press, 1998); Clayton M. Christensen, *The Innovator's Dilemma: When New Technologies Cause Great Firms to Fail* (Boston: Harvard Business School Press, 1997); Richard Foster, *Innovation: The Attacker's Advantage* (London: Macmillan, 1986); Richard Foster and Sarah Kaplan, *Creative Destruction: Why Companies That Are Built to Last Underperform the Market—And How to Successfully Transform Them* (New York: Currency, 2001); Gary Hamel, *Leading the Revolution: How to Thrive in Turbulent Times by Making Innovation a Way of Life* (Boston: Harvard Business School Press, 2000); Geoffrey A. Moore, *Inside the Tornado: Marketing Strategies from Silicon Valley's Cutting Edge* (New York: HarperBusiness, 1995); Charles A. O'Reilly III and Michael L. Tushman, *Winning Through Innovation: A Practical Guide to Leading Organizational Change and Renewal* (Boston: Harvard Business School Press, 1997); James Brian Quinn, *Intelligent Enterprise* (New York: The Free Press, 1994); James M. Utterback, *Mastering the Dynamics of Innovation* (Boston: Harvard Business School Press, 1994).

CORE READINGS—MERGERS AND ACQUISITIONS: Dennis C. Carey, Robert J. Aiello, and Robert G. Eccles, *Harvard Business Review on Mergers & Acquisitions* (Boston: Harvard Business School Pub. Corp., 2001); Mark L. Feldman and Michael Frederick Spratt, *Five Frogs on a Log: A CEO's Field Guide to Accelerating the Transition in Mergers, Acquisitions and Gut-Wrenching Change* (New York: Harper-Business, 1999); Patrick A. Gaughan, *Mergers, Acquisitions, and Corporate Restructurings* (New York: Wiley, 2002); Philippe C. Haspeslagh and David B. Jemison, *Managing Acquisitions: Creating Value Through Corporate Renewal* (New York: Maxwell Macmillan International, 1991); James Brian Quinn, *Strategies for Change: Logical Incrementalism*

(Homewood, IL: R.D. Irwin, 1980); Stanley Foster Reed and Alexandra Reed Lajoux, *The Art of M&A: A Merger Acquisition Buyout Guide* (New York: McGraw-Hill, 1999); David M. Schweiger, *M&A Integration: A Framework for Executives and Managers* (New York: McGraw-Hill, 2002); Bruce Wasserstein, *Big Deal: Mergers and Acquisitions in the Digital Age* (New York: Warner Books, 2001).

Chapter 2

SOURCES FOR THE MATERIAL ON DOLLAR GENERAL CORPORATION INCLUDE: Linda Burnett, "Dollar Wise: The Interiors of Dollar General's Nashville Headquarters, Created by Design Collective, Bring Employees Together at Last," *Business and Management Practices,* Vol. 43, No. 7, July 2001; Dollar General Corporation 1999 *Annual Report,* www.dollargeneral.com; "Dollar General Investigates Irregularities," *Mass Market Retailers,* Vol. 18, No. 7, May 14, 2001; "Dollar General Is in Expansion Mode," *MMR,* Vol. 18, No. 15, October 29, 2001; "Dollar General Woes: Analysts Question Company Disclosures," *Nashville Business Journal,* Vol. 18, No. 3, January 18, 2002; Peter Eavis, "'Shrinkage' and Dollar General's Cash Concerns," TheStreet.com, April 30, 2001; "Extend of DG Accounting Problems Still Unknown," *Nashville Business Journal,* Vol. 17, No. 19, May 4, 2001; Martha McNeil Hamilton, "Dollar General Lowers Three Years' Earnings," *Washington Post,* January 15, 2002; Martha McNeil Hamilton, "Dollar General Wrestling with Doubts About Its Accounting," *Washington Post,* October 25, 2001; Mary Hance, "The Price Always Is the Point: Dollar General Stores Succeed on Simplicity," *San Antonio Express-News,* March 10, 1999; Stacey Hartmann, "Dollar General out of Laboratory with Fresh Look: Prototype Is Model for 2,700 Stores," *Cincinnati Enquirer,* April 10, 1997; Stacey Hartmann, "Dollar General: Testing 'Sacred Cals' Board Challenges Past, Future Ideas," *The Tennessean*, October 27, 1996; Stacey Hartmann, " 'Family' Together at New Dollar General Campus; Turner Underscores Employees as Key to Company's Future," *The Tennessean*, September 4, 1999; Laura Heller, "The Power Merchants: Leigh Stelmach, Dollar General: A Singular Sense of Mission," *Discount Store News*, December 8, 1997; Debbie Howell, "Dollar General's C. A. Turner, Sr., Dead at 85," *DSN Retailing Today*, December 11, 2000; Debbie Howell, "Dollar General Eyes Growth," *Discount Store News*, June 21, 1999; Debbie Howell, "Dollar General's Growth Justifies Expenditures," *DSN Retailing Today*, June 19, 2000; Debbie Howell, "Dollar General Hits Milestone: Opens 5,000[th] Store," *DSN Retailing Today*, February 19, 2001; Debbie Howell, "Dollar General Re-releases Finances," *DSN Retailing Today*, February 11, 2002; Debbie Howell, "The Right Reverend of EDLP," *Discount Store News*, May 24, 1999; Greg Jacobson, "Lawyer to Dollar General CEO," *MMR*, March 20, 2000; Candy McCampbell, "Dollar General Back to Basics," *The Tennessean*, February 27, 2001; Candy McCampbell, "Perks with Purpose: Dollar General Design Strives for Efficiency," *The Tennessean*, September 7, 1998; Dan Scheraga, "A Fresh Start, Generally Speaking," *Chain Store Age Executive*, September 2000; Valerie Seckler, "Dollar General Bets on $10 Apparel in Back-to-Basics Program," *Daily News Record*, September 23, 1998; Randy Southerland, "Protected Against the Enemy Within," *Access Control & Security Systems Integration*, June 2000; Jeff Taylor, "Dollar General's Cal Turner Jr.," *Investor's Business Daily*, August 28, 1997; "Tough Times at Dollar General," *MMR*, Vol. 19, No. 3, February 11, 2002; Cal Turner, interview by Sydnie Kohara, CNBC/Dow Jones Business Video, May 12, 1999; Cal Turner, interview by Jack Cafferty, "Dollar General CEO," *Before Hours*, Cable News Network Financial, November 9, 1999; Cal Turner, interview by Bill Griffeth, "Dollar General Chairman—Interview," CNBC/Dow Jones Business Video, February 27, 2001; "Turner Recounts His Retail Ministry," *The*

Tennessean, April 15, 2001; Arthur Zaczkiewicz, "Dollar General Bucks the Acquisition Trend," *HFN,* September 18, 2000; www.dollargeneral.com; www.hoovers.com.

Chapter 3

SOURCES FOR THE MATERIAL ON KMART CORPORATION INCLUDE: Linda Benson, "Showdown at the Strip," *Corporate Detroit,* 1991; Frederic M. Comins, Jr., "Renewal at Kmart" (Letters to the Editor), *Harvard Business Review,* 1992; Ken Cottrill, "Kmart Targets Logistics," *Traffic World,* February 19, 2001; Alice Z. Cuneo, "Retailing Stardom: Spritely Marketing Makes It Chic to Buy Cheap," *Advertising Age,* December 11, 2000; Andrew Dietderich, "Unplugged—Years of Neglecting Technology Cost Kmart on Its Road to Bankruptcy," *Crain's Detroit Business,* January 28, 2002; Judith H. Dobrzynski, "A Likely Next Company for a Board Room Coup," *New York Times,* March 15, 1995; Mike Duff, "Turning up the Intensity on a Storied Turnaround," *DSN Retailing Today,* May 21, 2001; Evergreen Study Report on Kmart Corporation; Greg Farrell, "Kmart CEO's Plan for Turnaround Struggles," *USA Today,* January 11, 2002; Lorrie Grant, "CEO Rings Up Plan to Restore Kmart," *USA Today,* September 12, 2001; Constance L. Hays, "Is Kmart out of Stock in Answers?" *New York Times,* March 17, 2002; Debra Hazel, "Kmart—Is the Rebound Real?" *Chain Store Age,* May 1, 1997; Debbie Howell, "Kmart Vows to Pursue Fast-Track Recovery," *DSN Retailing Today,* February 11, 2002; "Kmart Must Shop for More Honest, Strategic PR Plans," *PR Week,* February 4, 2002; Laura Liebeck, "Antonini and Kmart Move On," *Discount Store News,* April 4, 1995; Laura Liebeck, "Kmart at the Crossroads," *Discount Store News,* February 21, 1994;

Laura Liebeck, "Kmart Under Pressure," *Discount Store News,* March 21, 1994; Laura Liebeck, "Power Retailer—Kmart," *Discount Store News,* March 9, 1998; Andrea Lillo, "Conaway Implements Kmart Culture Shock," *Home Textiles Today,* June 11, 2001; Tony Lisanti, "Antonini Ushers in a New Era of Risk-Taking, Trendsetting," *Discount Store News,* December 17, 1990; Tony Lisanti, "Kmart Is Making History Again," *Discount Store News,* March 5, 2001; Tony Lisanti, "Okay, Now It's Time for Results," *Discount Store News,* December 9, 1996; Don Longo, "Kmart Puts on a Fresh New Face for the 90s," *Discount Store News,* December 17, 1990; Alexandra R. Moses, "New Executives Are Best Team to Save Kmart, Experts Think," *Associated Press,* March 12, 2002; Joann Muller, "A Kmart Special: Better Service," *Business Week,* September 4, 2000; Joann Muller, "Kmart's Last Chance," *Business Week,* March 11, 2002; Matt Nannery, "Picking Up the Pieces," *Chain Store Age,* March 1, 2002; Bob Ortega, *In Sam We Trust* (New York: Times Books, 1999); Jean E. Palmieri, "Kmart Gets More Focused, but Picture Isn't All That Clear," *Daily News Record,* May 6, 1998; David Pinto, "The Course Conway Charted," *Mass Market Retailers,* February 11, 2002; Bill Saporito, "Kmart—The High Cost of Second Best," *Fortune,* July 26, 1993; Charles R. Schoenberger, "How Kmart Blew It," *Forbes,* January 18, 2002; Gus G. Sentementes, "Kmart Will Close 7 Stores in Maryland," *Baltimore Sun,* March 9, 2002; "Shopping Experience Sets Agenda for Customer Service Initiatives," *DSN Retailing Today,* March 5, 2001; Brent Snavely, "Kmart's Name Game," *Crain's Detroit Business,* February 4, 2002; George Stalk, "Competing on Capabilities," *Harvard Business Review,* 1992; "Vendors: Kmart Has Lots of Room for Improvement," *Home Front News;* Bill Vlasic and Keith Naughton, "Kmart—Who's in Charge Here?" *Business Week,* December 4, 1995; Lorene Yue, "New Team Takes Full Command at Kmart," *Detroit Free Press,* March 12, 2002; www.kmart.com.

Part Two: Chapter 4

SOURCES FOR THE MATERIAL ON TARGET CORPORATION INCLUDE: Alice Z. Cuneo, "Retailing Stardom: Spritely Marketing Makes It Chic to Buy Cheap," *Advertising Age,* December 11, 2000; Miguel Helft, "Target Sings Joy to the Web," *Industry Standard,* October 16, 2000; Laura Heller, "Target Shows Off Visa Card and Pines for All Credit," *DSN Retailing Today,* November 19, 2001; Pete Hisey, "Target's Getting Smart," *Retail Merchandiser,* 2001; Katherine Hutchison, "Target Exec Says Multichannel Strategy Can Triple Revenue," *DSN Retailing Today,* July 9, 2001; Janet Moore, "Raising Its Sights, Target Goes Upscale," *Star Tribune,* July 23, 2000; Shawn Neidorf, "Target Is Taking Aim at Younger Shoppers," *San Jose Mercury News,* March 6, 2001; "Retail Competition in the Current Economy," *Retail Merchandiser,* 2001; "Right on Target," *Greater Baton Rouge Business Report,* October 9, 2001; Debby Garbato Stankevich, "Target Now Segments Apparel Lines," *Retail Merchandiser,* 2001; "Target Founder Originated Upscale Discount Concept," *Retail Merchandiser,* 2001; "Target Leverages Brand in Expansion Strategy," *Home Textiles Today,* June 11, 2001; Bob Ulrich, "Letter to Shareholders," Target Corporation 2000 *Annual Report;* www.target.com; www.hoovers.com.

SOURCES FOR THE MATERIAL ON L.A. GEAR, INC., INCLUDE: Deborah Adamson, "L.A. Gear Trying to Walk Back Uphill," *The Ledger,* May 7, 1995; Susan Chandler, "Designers Finding Their Target," *Chicago Tribune,* August 19, 2001; Vivian Chu, "Caught in the Bull's Eye," *Pittsburgh Post-Gazette,* February 10, 2002; Benjamin Mark Cole, "Is L.A. Gear on Its Mark for New Dash to Profits?" *Los Angeles Business Journal,* 1993; Alice A. Cuneo, "Retailing Stardom: Spritely Marketing Makes It Chic to Buy Cheap," *Advertising Age,* December 11, 2000; Damon Darlin, "Getting Beyond a Market Niche," *Forbes,* November 22, 1993; Evergreen Study Report on L.A. Gear, Inc.; Vanessa L. Facenda, "Making the Most out of the Mundane," *Retail Merchandiser,* 2001; Denise Gellene, "Sole of a Woman," *Los Angeles Times,* April 29, 1995; Matthew Grimm, "Gearing Up for the Long Run," *Brandweek,* February 3, 1992; www.hoovers.com; David J. Jefferson, "Don't Walk a Mile in His Shoes," *Los Angeles Magazine,* December 1991; Kathleen Kerwin, "L.A. Gear Calls in a Cobbler," *Business Week,* September 16, 1991; "L.A. Gear," *Sporting Goods Business,* 1993; Laurie MacDonald, "L.A. Gear Moves Hit Retail Nerve," *Footwear News,* June 20, 1994; Robert McAllister, "The Goldston Prescription," *Footwear News,* January 27, 1992; James F. Peltz, "L.A. Gear's Gold Put It Back in the Race?" *Los Angeles Business Journal,* 1993; James F. Peltz, "L.A. Gear Runs Hard," *Los Angeles Times,* February 2, 1993; James F. Peltz, "L.A. Gear Seeks Chapter 11 Bankruptcy Reorganization," *Los Angeles Times,* January 14, 1998; Stuart Silverstein, "It's Been a Bumpy Ride for L.A. Gear," *Los Angeles Times,* January 31, 1991; Linda Williams, "On the Right Foot," *Los Angeles Times,* July 31, 1989.

SOURCE FOR THE MATERIAL ON FLOWERS FOODS, INC., INCLUDES: Eric Palmer, "Working Over the 'Long Pull,'" *Milling & Baking News,* January 23, 1996.

SOURCES FOR THE MATERIAL ON LIMITED BRANDS, INC., INCLUDE: Susan Caminiti, "Can the Limited Fix Itself?" *Fortune,* October 17, 1994; Jennifer Steinhauer and Edward Wyatt, "The Merlin of the Mall Tries Out New Magic," *New York Times,* December 8, 1996.

SOURCE FOR THE MATERIAL ON TERADYNE, INC., INCLUDES: Larry Marion, "Changing the Culture at Teradyne," *Electronic Business,* January 1993.

Chapter 5

SOURCES FOR THE MATERIAL ON DUKE ENERGY INCLUDE: Michael T. Burr, "Three for the New Millennium," *Electric Light & Power,* April 2000; Michael T. Burr, "Utility of the Year," *Electric Light & Power,* December 1998; Bill Coley, speech, American Association of Blacks in Energy National Conference, March 3, 2000; Jim Donnell, speech, Financial Times Energy Powermart Conference, Houston, Texas, October 18, 2000; Evergreen Study Report on Duke Energy; Richard B. Priory, "Letter to Shareholders," Duke Energy *2000 Annual Report;* Richard B. Priory, speech, *Business Today Forum,* New York, New York, December 2000; Richard B. Priory, speech, Duke Energy Annual Meeting, April 26, 2001; Richard B. Priory, speech, Houston Forum, Houston, Texas, May 24, 2000; Nelson D. Schwartz, "The Un-Enron," *Fortune,* April 15, 2002; www.hoovers.com.

SOURCES FOR THE MATERIAL ON SMITHFIELD FOODS, INC., INCLUDE: Jim DiLorenzo, "Man with a Mission," *National Provisioner,* August 1995; Peter F. Drucker, "Management's New Paradigm," *Forbes,* October 5, 1998; Evergreen Study Report on Smithfield Foods; Sari Horwitz, "Smithfield Fattens Its Bottom Line," *Washington Post,* September 30, 1985; Rita Koselka, "$Oink, $Oink," *Forbes,* February 3, 1992; Carole Sugarman, "This Little Piggy Comes to Market a Lot Leaner," *Chicago Sun-Times,* November 1, 1995; Barbara Young-Huguenin, "Making Waves," *National Provisioner,* December 1994; www.hoovers.com.

SOURCES FOR THE MATERIAL ON HOME DEPOT INCLUDE:
J. P. Donlon, "Beyond the Bar Code," *Chief Executive,* November
1991; JoAnne Donner, "Bernard Marcus Talks about Corporate Cul-
ture," *Georgia Trend,* July 1994; Evergreen Study Report on Home
Depot; Rodney K. Sutton, "Growth at Home Depot Shows No Limit,"
Building Home Supply Centers, February 1995.

SOURCES FOR THE MATERIAL ON WALGREEN CO., INCLUDE:
Daniel M. Bergin, "Walgreen—Pharmacy Chain of the Year," *Drug
Topics,* April 23, 1999; "Cork Walgreen Shapes Industry's Top Chain,"
Chain Drug Review, December 15, 1997; Evergreen Project Report on
Walgreens; Lisa M. Keefe, "Walgreens, Wonder Druggist," *Crain's
Chicago Business,* October 26, 1992; Rick Reiff, "Convenience with a
Difference," *Forbes,* June 11, 1990; Nancy Ryan, "Simplicity Is Wal-
greens' Cure for the 90s," *Chicago Tribune,* January 21, 1991; Eben
Shapiro, "A Drugstore Industry Leader Raises the Level of Its Game,"
New York Times, August 26, 1990.

SOURCES FOR THE MATERIAL ON CAMPBELL SOUP COM-
PANY INCLUDE: "A Sample Set of Guidelines," *New Jersey Law Jour-
nal,* May 23, 1994; Reed Abelson, "Turning to the Former Chief for
Help in Troubled Times," *New York Times,* October 29, 2000; Reed
Abelson, "The First Family of Soup, Feeling the Squeeze," *New York
Times,* July 30, 2000; Amy Barrett, "Souping Up Campbell's," *Business
Week,* November 3, 1997; Steve Berne, "Self-Directed Teams Soup Up
Operations," *Prepared Foods,* September 1997; John M. Coleman,
"Good Governance Is Good Business," *Directors & Boards,* March 22,
1994; Glenn Collins, "Moves by Campbell Soup Send Shares Surging
to Reach a High," *New York Times,* September 6, 1996; Glenn Collins,
"Updating an Icon, Carefully," *New York Times,* November 17, 1995;
David Diamond, "Campbell's New Kid," *Business Journal of New Jersey,*
April 1991; J. P. Donlon, "Top Spoon Stirs It Up," *Chief Executive,*

November 1996; Steve Dwyer, "Red Alert: The Soup's Back On," *Prepared Foods,* September 1997; Evergreen Project Report on Campbell Soup Company; Linda Grant, "Stirring It Up at Campbell," *Fortune,* May 13, 1996; Paul Leone, "M'm! M'm! Souper!" *Food & Beverage Marketing,* April 1990; Claudia Dziuk O'Donnell, "Campbell's R&D Cozies Up to the Consumer," *Prepared Foods,* September 1997; Mike Pehanich, "Campbell R&D Leads Soup Renaissance," *Food Processing,* February 1, 2000; Bill Saporito, "Campbell Gets Piping Hot," *Fortune,* September 9, 1991; Brenda Paik Sunoo, "Campbell's Global Growth," *Workforce,* April 1998; Jim Wagner, "Campbell R&D Means Business," *Food Processing,* April 1992; Joseph Weber, "Campbell Is Bubbling, but for How Long?" *Business Week,* June 17, 1991; Joseph Weber, "Campbell: Now It's M-M Global," *Business Week,* March 15, 1993; David Wellman, "Campbell: The Next Generation," *Food & Beverage Marketing,* August 1990; www.hoovers.com.

SOURCES FOR THE MATERIAL ON TARGET CORPORATION INCLUDE: Miguel Helft, "Target Sings Joy to the Web," *Industry Standard,* October 16, 2000; Pete Hisey, "Target's Getting Smart," *Retail Merchandiser,* August 2001; "Target Leverages Brand in Expansion Strategy," *Home Textiles Today,* June 11, 2001; www.target.com.

Chapter 6

SOURCES FOR THE MATERIAL ON HOME DEPOT, INC., INCLUDE: J. P. Donlon, "Beyond the Bar Code," *Chief Executive,* November 1991; JoAnne Donner, "Bernard Marcus Talks about Corporate Culture," *Georgia Trend,* July 1994; Evergreen Study Report on Home Depot; Rodney K. Sutton, "Growth at Home Depot Shows No Limit," *Building Home Supply Centers,* February 1995.

SOURCES FOR THE MATERIAL ON CAMPBELL SOUP COMPANY INCLUDE: "A Sample Set of Guidelines," *New Jersey Law Journal*, May 23, 1994; John M. Coleman, "Good Governance Is Good Business," *Directors & Boards*, March 22, 1994; David Diamond, "Campbell's New Kid," *Business Journal of New Jersey*, April 1991; J. P. Donlon, "Top Spoon Stirs It Up," *Chief Executive*, November 1996; Jo Anne Donner, "Bernard Marcus Talks about Corporate Culture," *Georgia Trend*, July 1994; Evergreen Study Report on Home Depot; Linda Grant, "Stirring It Up at Campbell," *Fortune*, May 13, 1996; David Wellman, "Campbell: The Next Generation," *Food & Beverage Marketing*, August 1990.

SOURCES FOR THE MATERIAL ON POLAROID CORPORATION INCLUDE: Steve Bailey and Steven Syre, "New Polaroid Chief," *Boston Globe*, March 22, 1996; Ruth G. Newman, "Polaroid Develops a Communications System—But Not Instantly," *Management Review*, January 1990; Phil Patton, "Style Team Reinvents Polaroid as a Toy," *New York Times*, May 18, 2000; David Whitford, "Polaroid, R.I.P.," *Fortune*, November 12, 2001.

ACADEMIC SOURCES INCLUDE: www.transcendentalists.com; Henry King, *Twelve o'Clock High*, produced by Twentieth Century Fox, 1949.

Chapter 7

SOURCES FOR THE MATERIAL ON NUCOR CORPORATION INCLUDE: Martin Dickson, "How Nucor Is Stealing a March on the Big Mill," *Financial Times*, May 29, 1991; Evergreen Study Report on Nucor Corporation; Ken Iverson, "Changing the Rules of the Game," *Planning Review*, September 1993; Ted Kuster, "How Nucor Crawfordsville Works," *Iron Age New Steel,* December 1995; Jo Isenberg O'Loughlin, "Hot Steel and Common Sense," *Management Review,* August 1992; Stephanie Overman, "No-Frills HR at Nucor," *RMagazine,* July 1994; Thomas M. Rohan, "Maverick Remakes Old-Line Steel," *Industry Week,* January 21, 1991; Michael Schroeder and Walecia Konrad, "Nucor: Rolling Right into Steel's Big Time," *Business Week,* November 19, 1990; www.hoovers.com.

SOURCES FOR THE MATERIAL ON CAMPBELL SOUP COMPANY INCLUDE: Bill Saporito, "Campbell Gets Piping Hot," *Fortune,* September 9, 1991; David Wellman, "Campbell: The Next Generation," *Food & Beverage Marketing,* August 1990.

SOURCES FOR THE MATERIAL ON LIMITED BRANDS, INC., INCLUDE: Susan Caminiti, "Can the Limited Fix Itself?" *Fortune,* October 17, 1994; Jennifer Steinhauer and Edward Wyatt, "The Merlin of the Mall Tries Out New Magic," *New York Times,* December 8, 1996.

SOURCE FOR THE MATERIAL ON HOME DEPOT, INC.: Rodney K. Sutton, "Growth at Home Depot Shows No Limit," *Building Home Supply Centers,* February 1995.

SOURCE FOR THE MATERIAL ON TERADYNE, INC.: Larry Marion, "Changing the Culture at Teradyne," *Electronic Business,* January 1993.

Chapter 8

SOURCES FOR THE MATERIAL ON CARDINAL DISTRIBUTION INCLUDE: Reed Abelson, "It's My Money," *Forbes,* March 29, 1993;

Ron Carter, "Shopping Spree," *The Columbus Dispatch*, August 5, 1996; Jonathan Gaw, "Growing by Gobbling," *Cleveland Plain Dealer*, June 23, 1995; "The Emergence of Cardinal," *Chain Drug Review*, June 20, 1994.

SOURCE FOR THE MATERIAL ON FLOWERS FOODS, INC.: Eric Palmer, "Working over the 'Long Pull,' " *Milling & Baking News*, January 23, 1996.

SOURCE FOR THE MATERIAL ON NUCOR CORPORATION: Ken Iverson, "Changing the Rules of the Game," *Planning Review*, September 1993.

SOURCES FOR THE MATERIAL ON SEAGATE TECHNOLOGY HOLDINGS INCLUDE: Peter Burrows, "The Man in the Disk Driver's Seat," *Business Week*, November 27, 1996; James Eckardt, "One Big Happy Family," *Manager*, April 1996; Brian O'Reilly, "How Tom Mitchell Lays Out the Competition," *Fortune*, March 30, 1987; Walter Parker, "The Secret of Seagate's Success," *Saint Paul Pioneer Press*, May 1, 1995; Evelyn Richards, "Why an American High-Tech Firm Recruits in Asian Rice Fields," *Los Angeles Times*, June 25, 1990; Sean Silverthorne, "The Spin Doctor," *PC Week*, January 24, 1994.

SOURCES FOR THE MATERIAL ON VALSPAR CORPORATION INCLUDE: Richard Broderick, "Old Paint Takes the Lead," *Corporate Report Minnesota*, April 1989; Dick Youngblood, "CEOs Wurtele, Koch," *Star Tribune*, January 29, 1996.

SOURCES FOR THE MATERIAL ON SCHERING-PLOUGH CORPORATION INCLUDE: "Growing Together Through Profitable Partnerships," *Chain Drug Review*, December 9, 1991; Diana T. Kurylko, "Robert Luciano," *Business Journal of New Jersey*, June 1987; Michael

Roberts, "Schering," *Chemical Week,* March 19, 1992; "Schering-Plough Growth in Sun Care Preparations," *Cosmetics International,* May 25, 1990; www.sch-plough.com.

Chapter 9

SOURCES FOR MATERIAL ON CAMPBELL SOUP COMPANY INCLUDE: John M. Coleman, "Good Governance Is Good Business," *Directors & Boards,* March 22, 1994; J. P. Donlon, "Top Spoon Stirs It Up," *Chief Executive,* November 1996; Linda Grant, "Stirring It Up at Campbell," *Fortune,* May 13, 1996; Mike Pehanich, "Campbell R&D Leads Soup Renaissance," *Food Processing,* February 1, 2000; Bill Saporito, "Campbell Gets Piping Hot," *Fortune,* September 9, 1991; Joseph Weber, "Campbell Is Bubbling, but for How Long?" *Business Week,* June 17, 1991; David Wellman, "Campbell: The Next Generation," *Food & Beverage Marketing,* August 1990; www.hoovers.com.

SOURCES FOR THE MATERIAL ON NUCOR CORPORATON INCLUDE: Ken Iverson, "Changing the Rules of the Game," *Planning Review,* September 1993; Ted Kuster, "How Nucor Crawfordsville Works," *Iron Age New Steel,* December 1995; Thomas Rohan, "Maverick Remakes Old-Line Steel," *Industry Week,* January 21, 1991.

SOURCE FOR THE MATERIAL ON SEAGATE TECHNOLOGY HOLDING: James Eckardt, "One Big Happy Family," *Manager,* April 1996.

SOURCE FOR THE MATERIAL ON SCHERING-PLOUGH CORPORATION: "Growing Together Through Profitable Partnerships," *Chain Drug Review,* December 9, 1991.

SOURCES FOR MATERIAL ON VALSPAR CORPORATION INCLUDE: Richard Broderick, "Old Paint Takes the Lead," *Corporate Report Minnesota*, April 1989; Dick Youngblood, "CEOs Wurtele, Koch," *Star Tribune*, January 29, 1996.

Chapter 10

SOURCES FOR THE MATERIAL ON AVERY DENNISON CORPORATION INCLUDE: "Avery Dennison and Steinbeis Plan European Venture," *New York Times*, October 27, 1998; Jane Applegate, "U.S. Approves Merger of Office Supply Giants," *Los Angeles Times*, October 17, 1990; Damon Darlin, "Thank You, 3M," *Forbes*, September 25, 1995.

SOURCES FOR THE MATERIAL ON POLAROID CORPORATION INCLUDE: Norm Alster, "Polaroid's Mac Booth Ducked a Takeover Bid," *Forbes*, September 4, 1992; Steve Bailey and Steven Syre, "In Hindsight, Perhaps Polaroid Should Have Sold," *Boston Globe*, December 17, 1998; Steve Bailey and Steven Syre, "New Polaroid Chief," *Boston Globe*, March 22, 1996; Lynnley Browning, "Polaroid Makes a Digital Leap, But Is It Enough?" *New York Times*, August 13, 2001; Christopher Byron, "The Rape of Polaroid," *New York Post*, July 22, 2002; Claudia H. Deutsch, "Through a Lens, Digitally," *New York Times*, March 27, 2000; Claudia H. Deutsch, "Two Images of Polaroid, but Which Is Sharper?" *New York Times*, March 21, 1999; Brian Eckstrom, "Developing Picture at Polaroid Is Not Pretty," *Daily Deal*, January 5, 2000; Tom Ehrenfeld, "No Land in Sight," *Boston Business*, August 1990; Greg Gatlin, "The Big Picture," *Boston Herald*, August 13, 2001; Bob Greene, "The Polaroid Camera and the Heavy Briefcase," *Chicago Tribune*, April 29, 2002; Wendy Hower, "Polaroid in Search of

Another Instant Success," *Boston Business Journal,* August 20, 1990; Jeffrey Krasner, "Bank One Complete Polaroid Purchase," *Boston Globe,* August 1, 2002; Jeffrey Krasner, "DiCamillo Quits," *Boston Globe,* July 22, 2002; Jeffrey Krasner, "Paying the Price for Polaroid's Risk," *Boston Globe,* October 24, 2001; Tim McLaughlin, "Land Developed a Company That Had Instant Success," *Houston Chronicle,* October 14, 2001; Gary McWilliams, "Larry, We Hardly Knew Ye," *Business Week,* January 3, 1994; Ruth G. Newman, "Polaroid Develops a Communications System—But Not Instantly," *Management Review,* January 1990; Phil Patton, "Style Team Reinvents Polaroid as a Toy," *New York Times,* May 18, 2000; "Polaroid, Sharper Focus," *Economist,* April 24, 1993; Jane Poss, "Edwin Land Dead at 81," *Boston Globe,* March 2, 1991; Jane Poss, "Edwin H. Land, the Soul of an Inventor," *Boston Globe,* March 3, 1991; Ronald Rosenberg, "A Photo Finish—Struggling Polaroid Shoots for Turnaround with Instant Digital Printing Technology," *Boston Globe,* May 31, 2001; Ronald Rosenberg, "Polaroid to Fire 700, Top Executive Quits," *Boston Globe,* December 17, 1998; Ronald Rosenberg, "Snapping Back," *Boston Globe,* April 4, 1999; Rochelle Sharpe, "Hazy Picture at Polaroid," *Business Week,* December 4, 2000; Jane Fitz Simon, "Polaroid: One Year After Shamrock, Same Managers, Same Problems," *Boston Globe,* March 11, 1990; Geoffrey Smith, "Polaroid: A Sweet Deal," *Business Week,* August 5, 2002; Steve Syre, "Polaroid Slowly Fades Away, but, at One Time, Edwin Land and His Audacious Firm Could Do No Wrong," *Boston Globe,* October 14, 2001; Amy Tsao, "Polaroid Awaits a Positive Development," *Business Week,* June 26, 2001; David Whitford, "Polaroid, R.I.P.," *Fortune,* November 12, 2001; Noel Young, "How Polaroid Lost Sight of the Bigger Picture," *Scotland on Sunday,* October 28, 2001.

SOURCES FOR THE MATERIAL ON L.A. GEAR INCLUDE: Benjamin Mark Cole, "Is L.A. Gear on Its Mark for New Dash to Profits?" *Los Angeles Business Journal,* July 26, 1993; Matthew Grimm, "Gearing Up for the Long Run," *Brandweek,* February 3, 1992; Kathleen Kerwin, "L.A. Gear Calls In a Cobbler," *Business Week,* September 16, 1991; "L.A. Gear," *Sporting Goods Business,* August 1993; Laurie MacDonald, "L.A. Gear Moves Hit Retail Nerve," *Footwear News,* June 20, 1994; James F. Peltz, "Can L.A. Gear's Gold Put It Back in the Race?" *Los Angeles Times,* February 15, 1993; Linda Williams, "On the Right Foot," *Los Angeles Times,* July 31, 1989; www.hoovers.com.

SOURCES FOR THE MATERIAL ON WALGREENS COMPANY INCLUDE: "Cork Walgreen Shapes Industry's Top Chain," *Chain Drug Review,* December 15, 1997; Evergreen Study Report on Walgreens Company; Rick Reiff, "Convenience with a Difference," *Forbes,* June 11, 1990.

SOURCE FOR THE MATERIAL ON FLOWERS FOODS, INC.: Eric Palmer, "Working Over the 'Long Pull'," *Milling & Baking News,* January 23, 1996.

SOURCE FOR MATERIAL ON SCHERING-PLOUGH CORPORATION: "Growing Together Through Profitable Partnerships," *Chain Drug Review,* December 9, 1991.

Chapter 11

SOURCES FOR THE MATERIAL ON AVERY DENNISON CORPORATION INCLUDE: "Avery Dennison to Buy Stimsonite," *Adhesives Age,* July 1, 1999; Damon Darlin, "Thank You, 3M," *Forbes,* September 25, 1995; Edvard Pettersson, "Wall Street Labels Avery a Good Buy, as Earnings Rise," *Los Angeles Business Journal,* November 8,

1999; Jody Schwartz, "Labeled for Growth," *Adhesives Age,* November 1, 1999; Jane Fitz Simon, "Dennison to Merge with Competitor," *Boston Globe,* May 26, 1990.

SOURCES FOR THE MATERIAL ON CARDINAL DISTRIBUTION INCLUDE: Reed Abelson, "It's My Money," *Forbes,* March 29, 1993; Ron Carter, "Shopping Spree," *The Columbus Dispatch,* August 5, 1996; Jonathan Gaw, "Growing by Gobbling," *Cleveland Plain Dealer,* June 23, 1995; "The Emergence of Cardinal," *Chain Drug Review,* June 20, 1994.

SOURCES FOR THE MATERIAL ON SEAGATE TECHNOLOGY HOLDINGS INCLUDE: Peter Burrows, "The Man in the Disk Driver's Seat," *Business Week,* November 27, 1996; Brian O'Reilly, "How Tom Mitchell Lays Out the Competition," *Fortune,* March 30, 1987.

SOURCES FOR THE MATERIAL ON SMITHFIELD FOODS, INC., INCLUDE: Sari Horwitz, "Smithfield Fattens Its Bottom Line," *Washington Post,* September 30, 1985; Rita Koselka, "$Oink, $Oink," *Forbes,* February 3, 1992; Carole Sugarman, "This Little Piggy Comes to Market a Lot Leaner," *Chicago Sun-Times,* November 1, 1995; Barbara Young-Huguenin, "Making Waves," *National Provisioner,* December 1994; www.hoovers.com.

SOURCES FOR THE MATERIAL ON NUCOR CORPORATION INCLUDE: Thomas M. Rohan, "Maverick Remakes Old-Line Steel," *Industry Week,* January 21, 1991; www.hoovers.com.

SOURCE FOR MATERIAL ON VALSPAR CORPORATION: Richard Broderick, "Old Paint Takes the Lead," *Corporate Report Minnesota,* April 1989.

Chapter 12

SOURCES FOR THE MATERIAL ON NIKE, INC., INCLUDE: Philip H. Knight, "Letter to Shareholders," Nike, Inc., *2001 Annual Report;* Philip H. Knight, "Letter to Shareholders," Nike, Inc., *2000 Annual Report;* Philip H. Knight, "Letter to Shareholders," Nike, Inc., *1999 Annual Report;* Philip H. Knight, "Letter to Shareholders," Nike, Inc., *1998 Annual Report;* Philip H. Knight, speech, Annual Shareholders Meeting, Portland, Oregon, September 22, 1997; Philip H. Knight, speech, National Press Club, Washington, D.C., May 12, 1998; Louise Lee, "Can Nike Still Do It?" *Business Week,* February 21, 2000; "Philip Knight of Nike," *Institutional Investor,* January 2000; Douglas Robson, "Just Do . . . Something," *Business Week,* July 2, 2001.

INDEX

IBM, 4–5, 242
Imprimis Technology, 197
information technology, 7
innovation management practice, 14,
　　20–21, *21,* 219–34, *220*
　of Avery Dennison, 222–24
　cannibalization of products and, 221,
　　221, 232–34
　disruptive technologies and, 221–29,
　　221
　at Dollar General, 38–39
　exploitation of technology and, 221,
　　221, 229–32
　of Flowers Industries, 231–32
　of Home Depot, 233–34
　at Kmart, 62–63
　of L.A. Gear, 226–28
　market discontinuities and, 228–29,
　　228
　of Nike, 268–69
　of Polaroid, 224–26
　of Schering-Plough, 233
　of Sony, 219–20, 228
　technology and, 221, *221,* 229–32
　of Walgreen, 229–31
In Search of Excellence, 10–11
Intel, 98
Internet, 87, 94, 247, 262, 263, 270
　Target's approach to, 94, 129
Into Thin Air (Krakauer), 267
Intranet, 205
Ireland, Kathy, 44
Iron Age New Steel, 169
Iverson, F. Kenneth, 159–60, 163,
　　169–70, 173, 174–75, 182, 206–7,
　　217, 246
　on talent management, 194–95
I-Zone camera, 150, 226

Jackson, Bo, 257
Jackson, Michael, 90–91
J.L. Turner & Son, 26
Johnson, David, 126–27, 141, 144–45,
　　165, 167–68, 170, 205–6, 210, 215
　on leadership practice, 205–6
Jordan, Michael, 257, 267
Joshua instant camera, 225
Joyce, Bill, 13
Justice Department, U.S., 134

Kayser-Roth, 89–90
Kennedy, John F., 256
Kmart, 38, 41, 42–66
　Antonini's tenure at, 54–55, 57, 60
　bankruptcy of, 43, 54, 58, 61
　Blue Light Specials of, 46–47
　corporate culture of, 51–54
　corporate structure of, 54–56
　customer base of, 44, 47
　distribution network of, 50–51
　employees of, 52–54
　in Evergreen Study, 43, 48
　execution practice of, 48–51
　innovations in, 62–63
　inventory problems of, 49–50
　leadership in, 59–61
　market share of, 43–44
　mergers and partnership practice of,
　　63–65
　"mystery shoppers" in, 52–53
　product development program of, 44–45
　product selection of, 49–50
　promotion policy of, 57–58, 60
　specialty retailing by, 45, 63–64
　strategy practice of, 43–48
　Super K stores of, 63, 99
　supply network of, 56
　talent practice of, 57–69
　technology adopted by, 50–51, 62–63
　top-down management in, 54–56, 59
　upscale remodeling project of, 44–46
　Wal-Mart's rivalry with, 45–48, 58, 61,
　　65
Knight, Philip H., 256, 258–59, 261,
　　262–63, 265–68
Kombat Gear, 91
Krakauer, Jon, 267
Kresge's, 42, 54
Kroger, 189
Kum-Kleen, 222

La Brea, 100
L.A. Flak, 96
L.A. Gear, 69
　bankruptcy of, 78, 95
　and failure to communicate strategy,
　　94–96
　growth strategy of, 102–3, 105
　innovation practice of, 226–28